D0065425

Ravishing Tradition

Also by Daniel Cottom—

The Civilized Imagination: A Study of Ann Radcliffe, Jane Austen, and Sir Walter Scott (1985)

Social Figures: George Eliot, Social History, and Literary Representation (1987)

Text and Culture: The Politics of Interpretation (1989)

Abyss of Reason: Cultural Movements, Revelations, and Betrayals (1991)

RAVISHING
TRADITION

❦ *Cultural Forces*

and Literary History

DANIEL COTTOM

Cornell University Press

ITHACA AND LONDON

Copyright © 1996 by Cornell University

First published 1996 by Cornell University Press.

Printed in the United States of America

⊚ The paper in this book meets the minimum requirements
of the American National Standard for Information Sciences—
Permanence of Paper for Printed Library Materials, ANSI Z39.48-1984.

Library of Congress Cataloging-in-Publication Data

Cottom, Daniel.
    Ravishing tradition : cultural forces and literary history / Daniel Cottom.
        p. cm.
    Includes bibliographical references (p.   ) and index.
    ISBN 0-8014-3245-6 (cl. : alk. paper). —ISBN 0-8014-8324-7 (pb. : alk. paper)
    1. English literature—History and criticism—Theory, etc. 2. American poetry—
History and criticism—Theory, etc. 3. Borges, Jorge Luis, 1899- —Authorship.
4. Influence (Literary, artistic, etc.).5.Literature and history. 6. Civilization, Modern.
I. Title.
PR25.C68   1996   96-4199
820.9—dc20

for Donald Cottom and Zoya Cottom
in gratitude for what they've taught me
of love and work

Contents

Preface

IN THIS BOOK I STUDY tradition as an issue of cultural forces with which we are bound to be preoccupied in every aspect of our being. My examples are drawn primarily from post-Renaissance Western drama, poetry, fiction, and criticism, but my reach (if not my grasp) extends to broader periods of time and also touches on matters of popular culture, social history, and contemporary politics. In my concern to emphasize some of the most important ways in which the past must be of compelling interest to us, I examine literary history in the context of forces such as war and slavery; technology and sexuality; repetition, imitation, stereotypy, and travesty; censorship, abduction, appropriation, and rape; and grief, protest, and ecstasy. In thus approaching tradition in terms of protean forces that must move, divide, inflame, and shatter us, this book also comprises a critique of more common ways of conceptualizing this term (such as those that define tradition in opposition to reason, progress, modernity, or postmodernism). In this regard I have been led to think through certain theoretical writings that are especially relevant to my topic, including works by Sigmund Freud, Walter Benjamin, Jacques Derrida, and Adrienne Rich.

The project derives in part from my last book (*Abyss of Reason: Cultural Movements, Revelations, and Betrayals*), in which I sought "to see interpretation in terms of urgencies, pulsions, gestures, historical desires, struggling oppositions, and impromptu deviations." It derives as well from my frustration with the stultifying way tradition has so often been invoked in recent "culture wars." Especially deplorable is how tradition is commonly reduced to a rhetoric of idealization and demonization, as in cheerleading for Western or native or authentic traditions or as in condemnation of the same. In contrast to this kind of rhetoric, which would halt thoughtful critical labors before they have a chance to get started, I have tried to show that we cannot even reach after the necessities of judgment if we fail to confront the complexities of ravishing tradition.

For the encouragement they have given me through their nagging, niggling, embarrassing, tendentious, and baffling criticisms of various pieces of this book at various stages of its composition, I am grateful to Stephanie Smith, John Murchek, Caryl Flinn, Brandy Kershner, David Leverenz, Chris Coates, Al Shoaf, John Leavey, Jeff Franklin, Michelle Lekas, Elizabeth Langland, and Ira Clark. Deserving of special note is my great good fortune in having had Elizabeth Langland next door and Stephanie Smith across the hall while I was engaged in this endeavor. I also express my appreciation to Barry Weller, for his extraordinarily generous and thoughtful reading of the manuscript, and to Bernhard Kendler, executive editor of Cornell University Press, for his patience and care in dealing with the anxious author. Furthermore, I continue to be grateful to Nancy Armstrong for various sorts of help, including the grace she shows in being at the other end of the phone line when I need her to be there. Mary Childers, as always, proved an invaluable friend in the responses she offered to parts of this book at crucial stages of their composition—and in other respects. And Deborah Brackenbury, as always, supported me throughout in ways without which I could not have done anything.

I also express my appreciation to the editors and publishers of *SubStance*, in which a shorter and somewhat altered version of Chapter 6 was first published under the title " 'Getting It': Ashbery and the Avant-Garde of Everyday Language." And I thank the following copyright holders for permission to quote from their works:

DANIEL COTTOM

Norman, Oklahoma

RAVISHING TRADITION

CHAPTER ONE

Conspiring with Tradition

Jorge Luis Borges and the Question of the Miracle

As BORGES TELLS THE STORY, tradition has never been illumination. Despite its storied origin as a sacred fire blazing out from a past of animalic darkness, it is nothing of the kind. And yet tradition ought not to be thought of in the opposite terms, as the enemy of enlightenment, an irrational power of darkness implacably arraying its forces against all bright modern things. According to Borges, the apparent opposition between these two accounts is a labyrinth of false turnings, as are the supposed conflicts and the telling details that give each account its persuasive form. Some traditional images certainly do suggest these configurations of thought, but tradition has no quarrels with animality or reason. It may fail even to distinguish between the two.

As Borges tells the story, the opposite of tradition is something else, somewhere else. The opposite of tradition is the miracle.

Yet there is no duality without a duel—in its denials any figure must still admit itself—and so tradition is also a miracle.

From such humble premises, as of the straw and muck of a legendary stable floor, terrific effects.

According to David Hume, a miracle is a "violation" or "transgression" of the laws of nature by *"the Deity, or by the interposition of some invisible agent."*[1] As one might say: a rapture in which the sense of one's own will is devastated, as when Friedrich Nietzsche invited his readers to "imagine a man seized and carried away by a violent passion for a woman or a powerful idea."[2]

In Hume's words, "The passion of *surprise* and *wonder*, arising from

1

miracles, being an agreeable emotion, gives a sensible tendency towards the belief of those events, from which it is derived." Therefore, even though the miracle must be dismissed from reason and rational communication—as the miracle not only "destroys the credit of testimony, but the testimony destroys itself"—we find that "the mind observes not always the same rule."

Similarly, describing the man carried away by a miraculous passion, Nietzsche would continue: "What a transformation of his world! ... He asks himself why he has so long been the dupe of strange expressions, strange beliefs. ... His is the most unjust condition in the world. ... And yet this condition—unhistorical, antihistorical through and through—is the womb not only of an unjust act, but of every just act as well."

Of course, unlike Nietzsche, the English philosopher must conclude that belief in miracles is a corruption of reason spread only by vulgar, ignorant, and barbarous people.

He does note, however, that some "dangerous friends or disguised enemies" might lead Christians, who are presumptively rational, to ally themselves with these despised others. The temptation toward this alliance would arise from the fact that any Christian must be "conscious of a continued miracle in his own person, which subverts all the principles of his understanding, and gives him a determination to believe what is most contrary to custom and experience."

Curiously, then, Hume must conclude that "experience" is of a kind with "custom"—hence his pairing of these terms. The problem is that even within his own reasoning the argument from experience finally rests on a customary faith in causality that is impervious to rational understanding, like the continuous miracle of the Christianity which he handles with the most civil, and politic, of kid gloves. In other words, the custom of which Hume wrote turns out to be such custom as Nietzsche called (not without considerable approbation) "stubbornness and unreason." And therefore, in the end, Hume and Nietzsche might well appear to be in a disguised, dangerous, and even conspiratorial agreement with each other despite all the oppositions and differences of detail between them.

This appearance ought not to be surprising. In the debate on miracles that developed in the seventeenth century, and to which Hume was a late contributor, belief in these events was by no means categorically opposed to a commitment to science and progress. In fact, with believers such as Robert Boyle, Isaac Newton, and John Wilkes (the founder of the Royal Society), the situation was arguably the reverse. Only a world that has submitted history to an overwhelming process of ideological pacification and conversion, like that portrayed by Borges in "Tlön, Uqbar, Orbis Tertius," could make tradition in this era seem either blindly opposed to rationality, on the one hand, or unquestionably allied with miracles, on the other.[3] No wonder Hume freely admitted that modern reason is a traditional ritual, a form of thaumaturgy, and not a particularly impressive one at that: "The most perfect philosophy of the natural kind only staves off our ignorance a little longer: As perhaps the most perfect philosophy of the moral or metaphysical kind serves only to discover larger portions of it. Thus the observation of human blindness and weakness is the result of all philosophy, and meets us, at every turn, in spite of our endeavours to elude or avoid it."[4]

And so it turns out to be a most passionate story—in cold, sober, philosophical prose—this tale of how "we" moderns confront the ancients, along with barbarians and plebeians who figure as the living past, and not forgetting their counterparts even among the most respectable and genteel elements of advanced society. The story features characters in disguise—some knowingly, some unwittingly—together with others who are half disguised (as if winking to the freethinking audience) and still others who are little more than cat's-paws invented to forward a plot. And though there are many plots, there are few, perhaps only one; for they all tell of alliances that may twist themselves into no end of despairing betrayals. In this respect, too, Hume's writings might make us think of the world of Tlön, in which "works of fiction are based on a single plot, which runs through every imaginable permutation" ("Tlön, Uqbar, Orbis Tertius," 28).[5] Miracles face off against miraculous denials of miracles, tradition divides against itself, until it becomes virtually impossible to tell friends from foes, traitors from heroes, and disguises from the disguised—as in another story by Borges, "Theme of the Traitor and the Hero," in which the bloody history of the struggle for the independence of Ireland provides the nominal subject.

By way of Hume's argument, we may even come to the conclusion of the narrator in "The Other Death," who suggests that the most reasonable account of things in our world may turn out to be a kind of miracle. From beginning to end and from top to bottom, reason then would be treason. Alluding to Virgil's fourth eclogue, Borges's narrator writes, "I have divined [adivinado] and set down a process inaccessible to men [no accesible a los hombres], a kind of scandal [escandalo] of reason.

... A few years from now, I shall believe I made up a fantastic tale, and I will actually have recorded an event that was real, just as some two thousand years ago in all innocence Virgil believed he was setting down the birth of a man and foretold the birth of Christ" (110–11).

Traditionally speaking, the miracle is reality and nothing but reality, as pure and simple as it comes. As such, it is reality at its most rude, refusing to allow one to turn away, to voice a *no*, or to look after other pressing concerns for even just a minute. Utterly intemperate, the miracle is deaf to all questions. "The miracle has a right to impose conditions" is Borges's wry comment ("Ulrike," 23–24). That is why civilized moderns, committed as they are to science and rationality, must categorically reject miracles as hallucinations: as the impossible appearance of desire in civil reality.

Presumably, this usurpation of the public sphere by private impulses is now officially unthinkable, intolerable. Yet we are possessed by innumerable signs of the persuasive power of miracles not only throughout history but on into the everyday life of our own time. They appear in the stigmata of tortillas in New Mexico, in prayers that turn away hurricanes and hemorrhoids as they are bounced off satellite dishes by Pat Robertson's *700 Club*, in the apparition of the Virgin Mary to those assembled at Medjugorje in the maddened land that used to be Yugoslavia, in the UFOs with which aliens fascinated by human genitals carry off their victims, in the crystals of Hollywood actresses, in the fiction of Gabriel García Márquez, and in Quentin Tarantino's *Pulp Fiction* (1994), among innumerable other places. If miracles may be made unimaginable in spite of all such evidences, which move some persons to adoration, nakedness, murder, and scholarly writing, then must it not be true that there is a tradition of *reason* that certain civilized persons are unable to avoid? And that this tradition, in its opposition to miracles, must be regarded as a form of supplication: as the civil appearance of desire in impossible reality?[6] As an eruption of fantasy *as* the public sphere?

If such may be the case, then we might consider the miracle to be that which sustains us with transporting routines, as John Ashbery has suggested; that which holds out hope by making it impossible for us ever to be angry in truth, as Virginia Woolf suggested; that which makes the commonest stereotypes burn with unsettling originality, as Charles Dickens suggested; that which violently seizes us in our very own names and images, as Phillis Wheatley suggested; that which makes us desire the terrible losses that we grieve, as William Shakespeare suggested; or that which draws us into profound conspiracies with those very same others whom we hate, despise, and fear, as Borges suggested.

In which case the miracle must still be the reality on which we moderns stake our claims even as we officially avert our eyes from it. This was a point noted by J. G. Lockhart when he observed the "hallucination" of Scottish tradition that was treated as reality in the civic ceremonies welcoming George IV to Edinburgh in 1822,[7] but the conclusion here must be that we live by way of such cultural hallucinations in every aspect of our lives. However risible it may be, it seems we must regard behavior of the sort generated in the myth-machines of Hollywood as being real as real can be.

John Ford's film *The Man Who Shot Liberty Valance* (1962) tells us, "When the legend becomes fact, print the legend"; and thus it also conveys an epic suggestion that facts in general are legendary.[8] In the films of John Ford, as in all public ceremonies, Borges's stories, and other sorts of formally sanctioned realities, facts are such only from the perspective of an assumed, and hence ultimately legendary, community. That is why even so sober a sociologist as Edward Shils was brought to comment, "Insofar as the transmission of tradition has an element of the 'unconscious,' it is also present in science and reason themselves."[9] The hallucinatory implications of Shils's admission may be pointed out through the theater of the considerably less sober but in some ways more astute Antonin Artaud, who took the time to note that "the question of progress does not arise in the presence of any authentic tradition."[10]

Among newspaper columnists, as among prominent philosophers and theorists of cultural forms, it has become popular to observe that we are now in a post-Enlightenment age, disabused of the redemptive promises of reason. People who take their identities to be rooted in gender, race, class, sexuality, and material culture rout the humanist self from its modern representational technologies to show it for the very bad wizard that it is, quite white and notably male and fully as contingent as any tornado that might chance to whirl on by. Meanwhile, the return of repressed ethnicities, as in Bosnia and Rwanda, mocks the transcendence that is supposed to justify nationalism at the same time that religious fundamentalisms, as in the United States and the Middle East, belie the definitively modern and supposedly universal appeal of secularism. The death of state socialism in all but the most isolated and attenuated instances suggests the triumph of international capital over

liberal as well as socialist and communist ideals. A media age, the age
of the simulacrum, scoffs at both the letter and the spirit of rational
discourse. Art virtually surrenders any pretense of radically differentiating itself from commerce and commodification. The hypersublimity
of digital technology gives birth to the cyberpunks of the Internet, who
wave bye-bye to the last of the metahistorians as they plunge into their
brave new asynchronic, asymptotic, labyrinthine non-space. Such is the
popular image of this age of popular images, certainly a caricature, but
perfectly appropriate to the age in being so.

The abysmal irony here is that in believing we have disabused ourselves of the Enlightenment faith in reason, we may show ourselves to
be captivated by just such a faith.[11] Our denials are then our confessions. Breathing out a sigh of relief at our postmodernity, figuring that
we are enlightened in not being so, we may celebrate our differences
from the past with a confidence precisely as unbounded as is our ignorance of all that might be called, of all that has been called, tradition.
That is why, for example, we currently must suffer so many hymns to
the nonlinearity or multilinearity of hypertext, as if (for example) Borges had never written in and of labyrinths—or as if Sir Thomas Browne,
one of the figures of tradition favored by Borges, had not found cause
over three hundred years ago to identify his *Pseudodoxia Epidemica* as a
labyrinth.[12]

To make this point is not to call for some sort of return to tradition.
Tradition is not waiting out there for anyone to return to or recover,
even if it were one's desire to do so.

In thinking of Borges, it makes more sense to say this: *tradition is
dream, sword, memorial.* The only way to challenge or overcome it is
through the exploration of its power, its attractiveness, and even its
necessity, even in our fondest modern and postmodern visions. For just
as describing is also, always, prescribing, and prescribing proscribing,
so there is no getting away from reinscription—tradition—in any description. As an old quibble would have it, in our every sentence we
sentence ourselves: to a vital heritage of identities, alliances, references,
blindnesses, privileges, pains, and desires.

It is from this perspective that it makes sense to describe every con-
stative act as also being performative. Just as any act of representation
sets forth demands, if only by virtue of the cultural grounds it takes
for granted in its language, lexicon, syntax, logic, and presumed scope
of application, and just as these constitutive grounds can exist as such
only through the establishment of discursive hierarchies, margins, and
exclusions that are neither submitted nor susceptible to any purely log-

ical justification, so does any act of representation enshrine a past, even if only implicitly or unconsciously. No matter how the past may be imaged, and even if it is made out to be absolutely surpassed, tradition is inextricable from the act of representation. That is why we cannot stop learning how to do things with tradition—even, and especially, when what we are doing is denying it.

Ravishing is then an apt term to represent the complex interplay of forces in which we are bound to be concerned with the past. We ravish tradition, it ravishes us, and it is preoccupied with acts of ravishing. Through the staggering permutations of this term, which I take to be at issue throughout Borges's writings, hallucinatory reifications of subjectivity and objectivity can be rearticulated in the terms of historical conflict, movement, and desire—and so may be made available to criticism and change. For instance, by thinking through some of the more important anachronologies and anamorphologies that we sum up (always too hastily) in the name of tradition, we may find how certain key words—*miracle, grief, caption, fire, anger, it*—are living theaters that yank people into complex dramas even while they may believe themselves to be sitting in the most comfortable, secure, perfectly illuminated armchair in the world. (That is one way to describe the succession of chapters in this book.) By letting ourselves feel the uneven, unequal, and discordant challenges in this traditional word, *ravishing*, we may come across ourselves in alien letters, rituals, images, stereotypes, feelings, and discourses. (That is another way.) And then of course *ravishing*, as Borges might have suggested, must also be something of an accident here, no matter how traditional a term it may seem to be. Among other things, it is the meeting place of the diverse impulses that have informed my writing over the years before I gathered it into the traditional form of a book.

Tradition is dream, sword, memorial: it is to Borges's works, among others (including the works of Shakespeare, Emily Brontë, Artaud, Wheatley, Dickens, Woolf, and Ashbery) that I am indebted for this formulation. Another way of describing this book is then to call it an exercise in gratitude, by which I am moved to analyze the concept of tradition through some writings that have made more reality available to me.

Perhaps the miracle is the continuing embarrassment of tradition? To modern and postmodern minds alike—and, in point of fact, to all inquiring minds who want to know? For Hume argued that we live with miracles insofar as we must jump to conclusions, and surely we nominal subjects are always jumping to conclusions in all our everyday theories and theoretical lives, as through the varieties of syncopes studied by Catherine Clément.[13] Just as surely as we all find (to our never-ending astonishment) that we are something less than everything, we *jump*, we beg the question, no matter what the question may be. We even beg the question in its formulation as such, in which we are bound to misrecognize the diverse designs informing it and often transforming it into other things. That is, we fail to recognize that a question may also be a promise of betrayal, the proclamation of a tortuous destiny, a repudiation of one's assigned nationality, or the representation of a fantasy of self-generation, among other things. And so, whether we want to admit it or not, in the traditional way that we pose even the simplest of queries we show our trust in miracles: in that which is radically unpredictable. The inescapable conclusion is that the everlasting problem of tradition is to think of the question that would pose itself irresistibly, ravishingly, once and for all, and thus be a true question at last.

As with trials, so with questions: if they were ever to be posed truthfully, their beginnings would have to be entirely ignorant of their ends. Absent a miracle, we never meet with trials or inquiries in this absolute form. That is why, if we wish to inquire into the meaning of "justice," we do better to look at the traditional rituals of the courtroom than at the logic formally offered for the sentences arrived at through the proceedings that take place there. That is why, in considering questions, we are wise to concern ourselves in the first place with how a given example was posed: "But what did she *mean* by asking that?" And that is why, in Borges's fiction, the portentous metaphysical questions with which they are preoccupied are really of no interest whatsoever. Instead, all the really notable events take place in remarks, images, details, mannerisms, and stylistic turns presented offhandedly, in all their inessential and accidental assurance—for who would bother to lie about, who to suspect, such things?

The first paragraph of "Theme of the Traitor and the Hero" refers us to literary and philosophical tradition so as to point out that the power of tradition lies in the manner of its invocation—but in both senses of "lies." We are told that this story was created under the influence of G. K. Chesterton and Leibniz, while the epigraph of this piece further refers us to Plato (by way of William Butler Yeats). Shakespeare comes to figure in the plot, too, and Hegel, Spengler, and Vico, among others, as we are told an imaginary tale of a revolutionary in early nineteenth-century Ireland. This protagonist redeems his earlier betrayal of his insurrectionary brethren by arranging for his own assassination and, thus, his seeming martyrdom to the cause (as he will figure thenceforth in popular memory).

The real story, however, is elsewhere. It is located in the date mentioned at the end of the first paragraph: "the third of January of 1944" (123). This date goes without any further remark and yet remains as the only definite identification in the entire story.

The date is given to us as the time of the story's telling, the moment in which the author is imagining it, in relation to which all else is imaginative (and pedantic) design. In its intense triviality, this date then serves to make all the topics, plots, allusions, and themes of the story *almost* betray a sense of real horror; *almost* shatter the fantasy of literary order in history; *almost* turn the casual naming of dates ("Let us say, for the purposes of narration, that it was in Ireland, in 1924" [123]) into a rare, brave defiance of immiseration on the part of the nominal subjects of history, which is here understood as best exemplified by war, whether civil and long-standing or recent, worldwide, and unmentionable in its dimensions.

Thus, between the miracle and tradition, the "imminence of a revelation which does not occur is, perhaps, the aesthetic phenomenon" ("The Wall and the Books," 188).[14] Art departs from and yet still must recall baffling tradition, which is a miracle in disguise, forever threatening even as it still looks after us—faithfully observing the unspeakable difference between what we say and what we want. All these designs wrought from literary and philosophical and historical allusions—all this that gets called tradition—if only it could stop raising questions, stop being a past so *extremely* alive, then we might have a chance to enshrine it. As it is, even the naming of dates must appear a kind of superstitious ritual, the dates themselves legends no less terrifying than sacred, the names supposedly our own in fact an unpredictable jump from one subject to another, and thus one's very self even when in a posture of leisurely meditation a figure dangerous, disguised, riven by strife, and profoundly conspiratorial. This is why philosophical writings by figures such as Hume and Nietzsche have sometimes been viewed as malignantly allied with one another in their opposition to orders of governance that are supposed to transcend all time and place: because we are bound to betray our desire for miracles even in our most rational denials of them.

Of course, because of the way tradition is understood in popular legends, it must always be jarring when someone takes it up as a question. Since tradition is commonly considered to be a set of cultural structures, materials, and practices taken as unquestionable, blithely ignorant of justice, or simply set out there before us, it is virtually impossible to mention it, much less to study it, without giving offense. That is why "the family" is such a touchy subject in the teaching of history, science, civic values, and literature in American public schools; that is why the wearing of the *hijab* in public schools has provoked controversy among some citizens of France and Egypt; that is why the music of Richard Wagner remains a matter of such passionate controversy in public performances in the nation of Israel; that is why, as I write this, Radovan Karadzic and other leaders of the Bosnian Serbs have been able to use the term "ethnic cleansing" without showing the slightest consciousness that it is barbarous. And then of course the question of tradition is many questions: of tropes, artifacts, behaviors, bodies, events, institutions, and nations, all of which make the present out of the past in ways so diverse as often to become more difficult to resolve, not less, the more one looks into them. In writing of India, J. C. Heesterman has taken note of "the irritating flexibility and fluidity of tradition";[15] his scholarly impatience might lead us to recall the exasperated adage of the police chief in *Cape Fear* (1962): "It's a hell of a note, isn't it? Either we have too many laws or not enough."

But to write of the question of *tradition*, not of *traditions*, then may serve to emphasize the violence in the way we are bound to jump to conclusions: the wrenching necessity of this aesthetic experience in which we feel the enigmatic power of law, statement, genre, form, and idiosyncratic idiom grabbing at our very bones. This is the violence figured forth in such things as auguries, stigmata, signs, taboos, charms, incantations, ghosts, glossolalia, metamorphoses, doppelgängers, labyrinths, sacred books, and world-historical conspiracies: the way tradition will find its way through all the objects of the world, including our selves. Even if we deny or forget it, tradition forces us to recognize the occult identity of speech, blood, art, reflection, bewilderment, babbling, creativity, and subjection, among other things.

"You're getting carried away, don't get carried away," someone might say at this point, recoiling from the monstrous prospect of further lists of words that might go on indefinitely—for this is something we often say as a miracle is about to happen—it happens all the time that this is said.

"How can you say that, I can't believe you're talking that way," we may say as a metamorphosis takes place before our very eyes and the one with whom we are conversing suddenly appears as an unforeseen

query, a hideous proposition, an irruption of uncivil desire, or the barbarous animation of an alien tongue, skittering and squeaking there before us, detached from its proper body like Philomela's in Ovid's tale, right there in the impossible ravishing light of day. So Bosnian Muslims have testified to their astonishment when Serbian neighbors with whom they used to sip wine in their gardens suddenly turned upon them, seizing them, raping and murdering and exiling their kin; so Chinua Achebe has testified to his outrage that Conrad's "offensive and deplorable" *Heart of Darkness* should be widely taught and praised within the very academic communities to which he belongs;[16] so we turn around one day, see the familiar face, and find ourselves unable to remember what it looked like in the past—that now always legendary past—before love fled.

Tradition is a Judas, and "Judas in some way reflects Jesus" ("Three Versions of Judas," 153).

The Latin etymology of *tradition* includes the sense of betrayal along with the suggestion of transfer (as of property), transmission, and surrender. *Betrayal*: a revelation, a deception.

That is why voices in Borges's stories are so often nested within other voices, and those within still others, to such an extent that the notion of a single voice becomes absurd. In this he resembles one of his contemporaries, Mikhail Bakhtin—who did not live in a world apart from that of the Argentinian writer, not by any means, even though the latter does not appear to have known of his existence. In all his writings Borges emphasized the relative autonomy of words, informed as they are by diverse histories and conflicting contemporary motivations. Like swords they have a materiality distinct from that of individual human will along with the power to cleave human flesh so as to give bodies the mutilated form of the memorialized ideal.

"Let us not be unduly amazed," writes Borges's David Brodie, D.D., in a copy of Lane's *Arabian Nights' Entertainments*, while describing a strange people in the language of Jonathan Swift: "In our own tongue, the verb 'to cleave' means both to divide asunder and to adhere" ("Dr. Brodie's Report," 117).

In this retelling of *Gulliver's Travels*, *Heart of Darkness*, and all the other texts that appertain to the legends of Christianity and Western tradition, the horror of which Borges writes differs from that of Swift and Joseph Conrad. It differs most markedly in that for Borges, horror never comes as a surprise. Not for him the irascibility of Swift, who so prided himself on being condemned to disappointment; not for him the jejune Kurtz, who required a narrator as absurdly pompous as Charlie Marlow to make him seem worthy of note. For Borges, all things appear in the ineluctable modality of the traditional, within which horrors are as commonplace as miracles.

"They worship as well a god whose name is 'Dung,' and whom possibly they have conceived in the image and semblance of the king; he is a blind, mutilated, stunted being, and enjoys limitless powers" ("Dr. Brodie's Report," 116–17).

Surely the will of the skeptical English philosopher was to militate against the belief in miracles, and yet this will itself must appear to be something of a miracle. As Nietzsche would describe it (as he wrote in the tradition of Hume), the very notion of the will appears to be an aftereffect "of the most ancient religiosity": "the faith in the will as the cause of effects is the faith in magically effective forces."[17]

If he had composed a meditation titled "Borges and Nietzsche and I," Hume might have concluded, "Which of us is writing this page I don't know" ("Borges and I," 279). This "us" of which he might have written would also have been the "we" that wrote itself into such complex antagonisms in his *Enquiry*, in a stylish and seemingly inevitable choreography, as in the most heartbreaking war imaginable: the one in which what we must believe is that we do wholeheartedly believe.

As with the fate of Virgil's fourth eclogue, the issue is not one of explaining away particular accounts of miracles. Hume and many others have shown that there is nothing easier to do, insofar as explanations may serve us in such matters. The real problem is to explain a given course of action—including the course that may lead one to explain away miracles. In other words, the problem is to explain the miraculous conviction in the precipitate way we jump to conclusions. How do we come to demand certain answers of the world—even to demand that "incompatible things . . . only because they coexist" must be "called the world" ("There Are More Things," 52)? In considering this and all other questions, the problem is to explain why we are addressing things in *this* way and not in *this* or *this* among all the infinite number of imaginable poses we might assume.

In other words, the problem is in how to explain history without relying on unhistorical terms, terms at once miraculous and traditional, to do our explaining for us, as if by the power of a conspiracy ultimately beyond our ken. The figure of the miracle in and of tradition preoccupies, even as it extends far beyond, the writings of Hume and Nietzsche; and it is this figure that leads Borges on in his writings. The

relation between tradition and the miracle forms what Borges called, in
another context, a "necessary monster" ("Preface to the 1957 Edition,"
17), one that must and cannot be fought.

Unknowingly, it would seem, Virgil miraculously predicted the birth
of Christ; and for Borges the fate of Virgil's fourth eclogue is exemplary,
not extraordinary. Virgil jumped from *here* to *there*, as one must in any
act of communication. (The communication the *Aeneid* shares with *The
Man Who Shot Liberty Valance* is another such jump.) And with an
equally exemplary, uncanny prescience—such prescience as must always come before science—Hume's custom found its meaning in a determining *priority* of reason that could only have come *after* the so-called
"fact" of custom . . . miraculously.

Placing even more emphasis on this scandalous miracle than Hume
did, Borges was even less willing than Hume or his great critic, Kant,
to see tradition as the rational instauration of community. In this respect
his view is more akin to Nietzsche's: "The *origin* of the tradition makes
no difference, at least concerning good and evil, or an imminent cate-
gorical imperative; but is rather above all for the purpose of maintaining a *community*, a people."[18]

Since tradition as he conceived it had little concern with justice, the
community Borges was given to foreseeing is not one of redemption
through the glory of Caesar, Christ, or enlightened reason. For the same
reason, it is not the community of conservative custom overseen by a
superior social, cultural, and intellectual class of white men such as
Hume presumed. The sense of community in Borges's writing is more
in keeping with the prediction of Dr. Yu Tsun in "The Garden of Forking Paths": "I foresee that man will resign himself each day to more
abominations, that soon only soldiers and bandits will be left. To them
I offer this choice: *whosoever would undertake some atrocious enterprise
should act as if it were already accomplished*, should impose upon himself
a future as irrecoverable as the past" (92–93).

The future Borges miraculously divined for himself is that all his
learning, all these connections wrought among words and texts and a
multiplicity of voices, must have been foretold in violence. In this respect he resembles the narrator of Franz Kafka's "Report to an Academy," who describes his conversion from ape to man by concluding
that "if one achieves the impossible," promises then appear retrospec-
tively, "precisely where one had looked in vain for them before."[19] For
Borges, it is of such impossibilities that tradition is composed. He could
see no way past the miracle of tradition, which answers all questions
in advance, atrociously. As far as he was concerned, the questions we

ask are all cloven by their knife-like, instrumental, martial comprehensibility. (*Tradition is dream, sword, memorial . . .*) That is why the Yahoo and the librarian are equally bound to betray themselves: because both represent tradition, despite their differences and oppositions.

As if in the tradition of Borgesian scholarship, Terence Ranger has written: "The most far-reaching inventions of tradition in colonial Africa took place when the Europeans believed themselves to be respecting age-old African custom. What were called customary law, customary land-rights, customary political structure and so on, were in fact all invented by colonial codification."[20] In the perspectives offered by Borges's writing, this historical event is as exemplary as cinematic Western showdowns or Virgil's account of the sack of Troy and the founding of Rome. The agonizing ironies and paradoxes to which colonial experience has given rise may clarify the workings of tradition, but they do not misrepresent it. As Borges tells the story, tradition is of its nature brutal, hallucinatory, and unconscionably inequitable.

True, in most of his writings, and especially in the early works to which I am devoting most of my attention here, Borges mimes a popular image of traditional art as an object inaccessible to all but a small, erudite, leisured, spiritually and materially favored elite. Simply in their form—with their casual allusions to a wealth of cultural knowledge, much of which would have to be considered recondite even by persons who would consider themselves highly educated—works such as "Theme of the Traitor and the Hero" effectively demand that readers enter into them as into esoteric mysteries. This is the case even though there is a certain modesty about them, as if they were inflected by the tone of G. K. Chesterton's comment on classical tradition as "the popular thing, the common thing; even the vulgar thing."[21] One might say that each of his fictions is like a *Wunderkammer*, the Renaissance room of splendid exotica, but cut down to a scale appropriate to the reduced circumstances of art in its relation to the popular culture of the twentieth century—like a Joseph Cornell box. Nevertheless, in their conveyance of tradition, these things still invite readers to feel privileged, in possession of a superior culture, to the extent that they are able to appreciate the *knowingness* of the pleasures to be had in their hermetic circumstances, all of which are premised on a sense of having risen above popular understanding.

And just as in Conrad's *Lord Jim*, that tale of besieged cultural possessions, this sense of privilege is always shown to be a delusion and a trap. As measured through an assured familiarity with the art, literature, philosophy, and manners traditionally associated with the dominant classes of Argentina, Europe, India, and other areas of the world, a sense of superiority almost invariably is associated with ineffectual and absolutely pathetic characters in Borges's writings. In fact, he so fully appreciated the potentially destructive power of cultural symbols that he focused especially on the covert identity of books with battles and of libraries with inexorable and unfathomable laws. In this way he showed tradition as the mnemotechnics of war and civic madness. One cannot imagine that he would have had any argument with Stephen Orgel's comment that "imperial rapes, once they get into history, are a source not of shame but of national pride: the rape of the Sabines, wedding as it did the lands beyond the Tiber to the empire, remained an outrage only to the Sabines."[22] Every invocation of art in the works of Borges seems to come captioned with a label like that placed in the books transferred from the Palatine Library to the Vatican in 1623: "I am from the Library which, after the capture of Heidelberg, Maximilian, Duke of Bavaria . . . , took as spoil and sent as trophy to Pope Gregory XV."[23] The effect of all the toying with idealist metaphysics in Borges's work is to emphasize that no properties exist outside of an ongoing history of appropriations and expropriations. From this perspective Walter Benjamin's famous thesis, "There is no document of civilization which is not at the same time a document of barbarism,"[24] is less a critique of tradition than a rather bland statement of its self-professed modus operandi. One can imagine Borges reading Benjamin's statements about the violence caught up in art and saying, with Captain Louis Renault, the Vichy officer in *Casablanca* (1942), "I'm shocked! Shocked!"

And yet an occult identity links Borges, the conservative Argentine who regards cultural violence with such an air of detachment, to his German contemporary, Benjamin. Among other things, their bibliomania and their shared admiration of Franz Kafka and Gershom Scholem may be taken to suggest a strange correspondence between them; the suggestion is even stronger if one considers their mutual fondness for using theological rhetoric in modern discursive circumstances that might seem to forbid it.[25] And surely it was Borges, as much as Benjamin, who wrote, "In every era the attempt must be made anew to wrest tradition away from a conformism that is about to overpower it." Similarly, the relation between tradition and the miracle in the writings of Borges is nowhere explicated better than in one of Benjamin's letters to Scholem, in which the topic at hand is modern physics:

What is actually and in a very literal sense wildly incredible in Kafka is that this most recent world of experience was conveyed to him precisely by . . . mystical tradition. This, of course, could not have happened without devastating processes . . . within this tradition. The long and the short of it is that apparently an appeal had to be made to the forces of this tradition if an individual (by the name of Franz Kafka) was to be confronted with that reality of ours which realizes itself theoretically, for example, in modern physics, and practically in the technology of modern warfare. What I mean to say is that this reality can virtually no longer be experienced by an *individual*, and that Kafka's world, frequently of such playfulness and interlaced with angels, is the exact complement of his era which is preparing to do away with the inhabitants of this planet on a considerable scale. The experience which corresponds to that of Kafka, the private individual, will probably not become accessible to the masses until such time as they are being done away with.[26]

It would still be possible to argue that in his writings Borges is the virtual opposite of Benjamin and all that he has come to represent. It might be said that the Argentine deliberately ignored issues proper to industrial and postindustrial capitalism in favor of an impressionistic, effectively timeless realm of fantasy, and in such a way as to make it legitimate to characterize his writings as luxury commodities for the leisured aesthete. In fact, this criticism has attended Borges's work from the very beginning of his career, though rarely with the intelligence and eloquence that Achebe, for example, turned upon Conrad's work. His fellow Argentines accused Borges of an irrelevant cosmopolitanism and of an apparent lack of concern with the masses, among other sins.[27]

Although it often was crude enough, this sort of criticism need not be vulgarly realist, as that Borges ought to have written more of factories and strikes. It might make the more telling point that the *kind* of wonder to which Borges devoted his writings, despite all its pretensions, is itself a vulgar tool abjectly serving the pleasures of reactionary ideological positions. After all, taking "Tout comprendre, c'est tout pardonner" as one's most powerful ethical insight bespeaks a trivial mind glorying in the devastation of distinctions that we dare not allow to be completely confounded, as between bravery and cowardice; and Borges risked identifying himself with this vulgarity, even fell prey to it in his lesser works just as he did in some appalling public comments, such as the compliments he paid to the likes of Francisco Franco and Augusto Pinochet. "Qui s'excuse s'accuse," one might reply.

Yet it still seems to me that this type of criticism of his work must finally be misguided (just as I must finally find Achebe's reading of Conrad to be misguided). This kind of criticism cannot help but fall into the error that Wole Soyinka has called (in a neologism Borges might have appreciated) "neo-Tarzanism." As Soyinka puts it, "The error is really a simple one: the equation of the 'immediate' with 'commitment.' "[28] Through the pathetic, ineffectual nature of his hypererudite narrators, Borges anticipates the desire for what Soyinka calls "pseudo-tradition" and effectively disables it, emphasizing his art's desacralized, marginalized, trivialized status as this stands in contrast to the fantasies of hierophantic centrality with which it is preoccupied. As Raphaël Lellouche has written, "Borges has thus integrated into his writing the consciousness of an unsurpassable relation to tradition."[29] Tradition is always his concern, but he does not give in to the error of supposing that tradition possesses an immediacy to which one can simply commit oneself. He takes tradition always to be before us, in both senses of that shadowy word: behind and in front of us, already there and yet still waiting to be made out.

Or to put it another way, why should I allow my enemies to own Borges? Why should I allow *Heart of Darkness* to be exclusively the property of racists?

Tradition is in the very air we breathe: in the ontologies and theologies of its physical conception; in its poetry, as in our tropes of blue or stormy skies; in its humanity, as when it orients itself to our sense of gravity in being "light as air"; in its political and economic condition, as when it lends itself to the "environmental racism," as Benjamin Chavis has termed it, which generously offers Americans of color more than their fair share of pollution—in fact, in any aspect one might care to distinguish. And as with the air, so with every element of the world.

As Borges tells the story, repeatedly, there is no getting around the question of tradition: this situation *is* tradition.

"He wanted to dream a man" ("The Circular Ruins," 124).

Borges, Hume, and Nietzsche all tell of the rapture of men, which women nominally may serve to incite but more generally serve only to represent.

So imagine a story in which tradition is a child becoming human. We watch it so we may learn what it is to become human, to become ourselves. At the same time, we are trying to raise it up in our own image because we seek some reassurance that we are bound to be ourselves. Therefore, the questions asked of it will have been promised answers in advance by its doting parents, the very people who are doing the asking.

This is tradition: that which we cannot know—or cannot admit—is our own doing.

In a sense this tradition will be like every child, insofar as the concept of "every child" will suffer itself to come unto us with any coherence whatsoever. This tradition will be "one of us," or made in our own image, like Conrad's Lord Jim. In this respect it will be as fully our progenitor as our offspring. And yet at the same time, it will be unrecognizable as our creation, a subject of study that promises nothing in the way of reassurance. In other words, it will not be all children but disjunctively male or female, rich or poor, black or brown or white— again like the tormented and tormenting Jim, who at one point is offered a marvelous chance to be the mutilated god of an island of guano.

Tradition, this child that is father to the man, can assert itself only through the destruction of its own ancestry in body, memory, and culture. Rather than simply "passing on" or "handing down," tradition also carries back and away, shattering the present in the very act of suggesting that it is what it is.

"For what had happened many centuries before was repeating itself. The ruins of the sanctuary of the god of Fire was destroyed by fire" ("The Circular Ruins," 127).

Alluding to the well-known study by Eric Hobsbawm and Terence Ranger, Kwame Anthony Appiah remarks, "The phrase 'the invention of tradition' is a pleonasm."[30] Consider, then—as we are bound always to do, once upon a time and over and over again, in all our voices within voices—a story of tradition: "Lacking a sacred book to unify them as the scripture does Israel, lacking a common memory, lacking that other social memory which is language, scattered over the face of the earth, differing in color and features, only one thing—the Secret, unites them and will unite them until the end of time. Once upon a time, in addition to the Secret, there was a legend (and perhaps also a cosmogonic myth)" ("The Sect of the Phoenix," 164). As Borges tells the story, the bare minimum of tradition is a "rite" that is "sacred, but . . . also somewhat ridiculous. . . . There are no respectable words to describe it, but it is understood that all words refer to it, or better, that they inevitably allude to it." In other words, it is an act of "generation after generation": "One commentator has not hesitated to assert that it is already instinctive." In all respects it is like a comical version of sex

("The practice of the mystery is furtive and even clandestine"), but in this version focused not on the genitals but on some equally common and outwardly unprepossessing things: "The necessary materials are cork, wax, or gum arabic." One may remember that Borges's admired Schopenhauer wrote of the relation of the sexes as "really the invisible central point of all action and conduct" and thus as "the key to all allusions."[31]

In this most hilarious of his stories, Borges makes the invisible key open a universal story of tradition, which is characterized in terms of an ancient and obscure legend of men. Herodotus, Tacitus, Flavius Josephus, and the *Saturnalia* are among the sources cited at the outset, and Borges is careful to note that "usage does not favor mothers teaching [the secret] to their sons"; that some German poems "whose nominal theme is the sea, say, or the evening twilight" are really about this secret; that those who deliberately refrain from participating in the rite, like "John of the Rood," may be honored for their restraint; and that the sect's devotees at first "could not reconcile themselves to the fact that their ancestors had lowered themselves to such conduct." After noting how the men of the sect are like and yet unlike Gypsies and Jews, Borges further notes "the undeniable fact . . . that they resemble, like Hazlitt's infinite Shakespeare, all the men in the world" ("The Sect of the Phoenix," 163–66).

All of which leaves us with a question. For if tradition is the disguised reproduction of sexual relations, as they are seen from a viewpoint that is at once overwhelmingly learned and remarkably childish, then what are we to conclude about the author's humor? In this story, in which he rewrites Schopenhauer, Plato, William Hazlitt, and Sigmund Freud, among others, Borges mentions men on both sides of various battles and wars, men of various countries and creeds and classes and colors; and surely the result is a terrific joke on traditions of all sorts, from the pseudo-scholarship of the opening lines right on through to the end, which gives instinct the last word. If, however, the most fundamental element of tradition may be imaged as the phoenix, in whose supernatural regeneration there is neither male nor female, then the emphasis on masculinity throughout this story would seem to suggest that even as Borges is making his jokes about men of tradition, he still is fucking with us.

Perhaps this is the joke to which all the others secretly allude—the joke of one who cannot imagine a tradition in which he would not have to submit to the ravishing childishness of men, those Yahoos, who sometimes take (or are taken by) the disturbing form of women?

If there were such a one, might he not be inclined to regard metaphysics as a kind of fantastic literature, hallowed tradition in general as sublime nonsense?

Imagine a man writing of men fighting in slums, in wars, in the city and in the country—with women sometimes appearing as the effective, but never as the final, cause of battle.[32] And imagine that in writing of all this, this man always alludes to a secret, which, like any good joke, may secretly be unbearable, especially to the one who repeats it.

Or think of the ravaged Ancient Mariner of Coleridge's poem, and imagine him navigating (as of course he did, he does) a library of books written exclusively by men—and then imagine him *feeling* this library to be his fate.

No education without seduction and abduction: the demonic ravishment in the tale of Socrates suggests that this might be the disturbing motto of tradition. John Keats made a similar suggestion when he invited us into his "Ode on a Grecian Urn," in which the quietness of the still unravished bride of cultural tradition simultaneously figures as her ravishment, the poet's, and, the gods willing, ours.

The words *education, seduction,* and *abduction* bear more than an etymological relation to one another. They are historically conjoined in every corruption that forms tradition, such as that extremely powerful and unthinkably ancient legend, going back to and beyond Kabbalistic tales of the golem, by which men dream of creating children (or of having been made men) without women.

But still we should try not to throw out too much of a conclusion in advance of our question. For if the minimal tradition in "The Sect of the Phoenix" is the disguised reproduction of sexual relations, the minimal joke in this story is the suggestion that sex is not what we normally take it to be and does not take place where we imagine it does. In his writings Borges was more akin to Freud than he sometimes liked to admit, and this may be an important joke to remember when we consider a writer whose work, like Freud's, always assumes a kind of global community and an atmosphere of literary cosmopolitanism. In this respect it is important to remember also that Borges was writing in a culture in which the assertion of manliness was often bound up with nationalism. (Of course, this situation is not peculiar to modern Argentina: witness the assistant to Radovan Karadzic who stated in 1994 that the Serbian state "must be formed with a firm, man's hand," adding, "It should be based on Serb nationalism, with all Orthodox and national traditions.")[33] In this situation Borges's identification with a global, cosmopolitan community did not make for a very manly posture, to say the least. In fact, Borges typically portrayed himself in his writings as a timid, bookish, "unmanly" man, quite unlike his martial ancestors, and he was portrayed by various critics as a traitor to the Argentine nation and as a eunuch rather than a true man.[34]

In his youth Borges had contributed to that prideful form of nationalism known as *criollismo*, which was devoted to articulating a specifically Argentinian cultural tradition, which in turn was often defined especially through the heritage of virile rural and frontier life. Borges, however, never identified with this movement simplistically or exclusively—for instance, he contributed simultaneously to the modernist movement of *ultraísmo*—and he soon turned against most of the signs of this early enthusiasm, as in the cult of picturesque local color. This history is notable if one considers how nationalism was bound up with other issues in the Argentina of the early decades of the twentieth century, when a great increase in the immigrant population, among other factors, was taken by many writers as making the definition of national identity a most pressing matter. In this context Borges's cosmopolitanism conveyed a critical attitude not only toward a traditional image of manliness but also toward contemporary attempts to invent tradition around narrow conceptions of the state and of race.[35] In his xenophilia, as in his use of generically diverse allusions, Borges rejected the imagery of purity in ethnicity, race, nationality, and art, as well as in gender. Accordingly, although Borges was very much taken with Nietzsche when he was a young man, his writings certainly do not show him to be as one with the Nietzsche who opposed a sober, elevated, scientifically minded "manliness" to "all belief in inspiration and a seemingly miraculous communication of truths."[36] And as Edna Aizenberg points out, it is important to recognize that when Borges gave his 1951 lecture "The Argentine Writer and Tradition," in which he recommended a concept of tradition that was open to all literatures, he was speaking in the context of his opposition to Juan Perón's dictatorship, which he saw as being defined by its fascist, anti-Semitic, xenophobic, and martial features.

In point of fact, the miracle of Borges's stories, this blinding literary device, always marks the spot where manliness is carried away. Whether it appertains to the role of the scholar, fighter, worker, or lover, manliness is transported by a sexual experience to which these stories, with a repetitive desperation, seek to surrender themselves. And though women do not play much of a role in Borges's fiction and are virtually absent from the literary canon (both historical and imaginary) to which his works refer, the question that arises from this point does not surrender itself to a simple answer marked out in advance. After all, who is the teller, who the listener, and who the object of this joke about tradition as a disguised reproduction of reproductive sex? If women seem scarcely to figure in the desired sexual transport here, is it because Borges's writings are fodder for Luce Irigaray's analysis of "ho(m)mo-sexuality,"[37] or because she has been working in a tradition of criticism in which he also participated? After all, although Borges gave us few characters identified as women, few writers have given us more unmanly male characters than he did.

In this context it may be important to remember how Borges treats as emotions traditional literary elements such as eternity, repetition, disguise, fire, or the labyrinth. His characters are stricken with the infinite possibility of things such as fire the way characters in more conventional works of fiction are stricken with happiness or grief; and Borges knew very well, from Plato by way of Romantic literature, that "infinity" may be construed as the quintessential emotion of sexual longing, whether homosexual or heterosexual or otherwise. Whenever he wrote of this corrupting concept of infinity, in which the manhood of tradition is rapturously broken on the wheel of the world, he wrote of a longing like a child's, sweet as a knife.

"Things last longer than people; who knows whether these knives will meet again, who knows whether the story ends here" ("The Meeting," 184).

Typically, Borges wrote of tradition in the singular: "What is good no longer belongs to anyone—not even the other man—but rather to speech or tradition" ("Borges and I," 279).

He certainly did not imagine that there was but one tradition *quod ubique, quod semper, quod ab omnibus*. For instance, "The Circular Ruins" explicitly alludes to "Gnostic cosmogonies," *Through the Looking Glass*, "a thousand and one secret nights," "gods now burned and dead," an abandoned temple "where the Zend language has not been contaminated by Greek" (124–27)—and so on. These heterogeneous elements could have no coherence save through the assumption, communicated by the traditional style of the narrative, that the fictionality of tradition may sustain them.

Within the evocative context of mysterious temples, legends, wizards, and rites, the story tells of the making of a man. Deliberately undertaken and yet somehow assigned, this task finally frustrates all deliberations. As Borges tells the story, tradition is just this loss and failure of coherence. Tradition betrays, cleaves us. Through reference, quotation, allusion, image, stereotype, and various other devices—within which we are told the story of a father who dreams a son only to find that he himself is the dream of another—the dream symbolizes the corruption, or eternal breaking apart, of all the devices that lend a sense of singular coherence to tradition. (These devices, the elements of fiction, are miracles.) Hence the repetition in the story: for where there are two dreams, we must know there are infinite others.

Fools think of tradition as what binds us together. Borges knew that tradition is breakage, corruption, which demands nothing short of a miracle to bring its multiplying duplicities together, if it ever does or will.

True, an old formula that Borges repeated in various works, in slightly altered forms, runs as follows: "Words are symbols that assume a shared memory" ("The Congress," 48). But he emphasized the necessity of this assumption only to show in how many ways it is untenable. After all, to say that words demand a tradition is not to guarantee that they will receive it—not by any means. And then of course there are many ways of sharing, among which there is none more fantastic than the notion of sharing *totally, equally, happily*, or *justly*, unless it be the notion of sharing *knowingly*. David Brodie notes, "Memory is greatly defective among the Yahoos, or perhaps is altogether nonexistent" ("Dr. Brodie's Report," 115); and one can say the same of memory among those fantastic things, those alien beings, "words." Therefore, in "The God's Script," after the narrator comments that a god "ought to utter only a single word and in that word absolute fullness," Borges has this broken priest of a devastated religion conclude, "Shadows or simulacra of that single word equivalent to a language and to all a language can embrace are the poor and ambitious human words, *all, world, universe*" (171).[38]

This is the context in which to tell of tradition, not of the plural "traditions," may serve to focus attention on every word as an infinitely demanding, longingly corrupt question. Although no writer has been more aware of diverse traditions than Borges—who drew upon tales from the East and from the West, from Judaism and Islam and Hinduism and Christianity, from ancient Scandinavians and medieval Arabs and modern Argentines, from peasant and working-class and highbrow arts, from works both sacred and profane, and from oral, literate, and cinematic cultures—his stories show how important it is to consider the word of tradition in the singular if we are not to take for granted, unthinkingly, a certain sense of tradition. Heesterman's conclusion—"Modernity, then, would seem to find its predestined place within tradition's own, essentially broken, and contradictory framework"[39]—is very much in the spirit of Borges. By transferring the issue of multiple traditions into the many questions bound up in the singular word of tradition, Borges tried to catch us daydreaming, to wake us into another dream, as in his retelling of the tale of the butterfly and Chuang Tzu.

Hume was right thus far: there is nothing more banal than the miracle.

The miracle is so totally unprepossessing that in the face of it we lose our self-possession.

Tradition, which gives us some blessed time to think even as we are being moved by it, transported by it, must profess itself appalled at the mingling of love and cruelty in the miracle, which gives us no time at all—which takes us out of time.

In a lovely translation of Borges's poem "Matthew 25:30," Alastair Reid captured this relation between tradition and the miracle by rendering Borges's term "temporal" as "time-bound" (33). In this poem, as elsewhere in Borges's writings, one is bound at once *for* and *by* time; one is ravished by it, but in the form of a question; subject to it, one still is looking for it.

The first sign of a tradition: the creation of rules by which to judge the truth of miracles.

An example of a miracle: Yahoos producing literature.

Nothing short of a miracle could cause us to be so preoccupied with tradition.

After all, we know—do we not?—that traditions often serve opposing ends. The examples could be multiplied endlessly, as by the "one concept that corrupts and perplexes all others" ("Avatars of the Tortoise," 105), the concept of infinity: for every devoted follower, a heresiarch (who, of course, considers the other the traitor).

And this is not even to mention how far we would still be telling stories, in this tradition, about fathers as distinct from mothers, about broken men, and about men broken apart from women.

We are driven to evaluation, to cleaving, by the infinite banality of corrupt tradition. (This is the case even if we name our tradition, with heartbreaking hopefulness, "multiculturalism.") If Borges writes, "The heresies we should fear are those which can be confused with orthodoxy" ("The Theologians," 120), he also challenges us to find any that will not be thus confused, and repeatedly, as in "Theme of the Traitor and the Hero."

This is why realism in art was never anything but a formal question to Borges. As an ideological program realism would seem to deny repetition and thus must be condemned endlessly to repeat itself in this denial, betraying its assertion of originality as it produces nothing but fantastic displacements of identity in place of the solid truth to which it lays claim. Therefore, even at its best, such an art is bound to be of a kind with the man, "some twenty-four centuries ago," who "did not know, when he awoke, if he was a man who had dreamt he was a butterfly or a butterfly who now dreamt he was a man" ("A New Refutation of Time," 230).

Or "Homo homini lupus," man is a wolf to man, as the traditional saying has it. As Borges tells the story, as in his retelling of the dream of Chuang Tzu and the butterfly, realism cannot hope to improve on this fantastic image of our everyday state of affairs.

"Homo homini lupus"—or "As you read this," as Borges wrote and Hume might have written, "which one of us is writing this page I don't know."

Tradition is what we pose against the insufferable, infinitely corrupting banality of opposition. Hence its kinship to its own opposite, the miracle, which is never anything but the conquering of a banal figure of speech through the gift of life which makes this banality literal.

"He wanted to dream a man . . ."

Figuration is always banal. To find something literally alive, now that would be something.

So the banality of the question of tradition may drive us into literature, into thriving letters. As tradition has recognized, as in Nathaniel Hawthorne's scarlet A or as in the indistinct a of Jacques Derrida's différance, the miracle may have the form of letters.

If only we could know what letters are.

Imagine a man born not of woman but of letters . . .

Imagine a man of letters . . .

Defining a miracle in the traditional modern way, as a contravention of the laws of nature, obviously begs the question. In formulations of this sort, one takes for granted the tradition that confers legitimacy upon laws. On this point, as in his appreciation for Judaism and Islam, which the other despised, Borges diverged from "the passionate and clear-headed Schopenhauer" ("Tlön, Uqbar, Orbis Tertius," 28).

Schopenhauer argued that a "stupid person has no insight into the connection of rational phenomena, either when they follow their own course, or when they are intentionally combined, i.e. are applied to machinery. Such a man readily believes in magic and miracles."[40] Borges would have it that if one wishes to be scrupulous—keeping to the letter of the law—one must think of the miracle as a momentous collision of irreconcilable traditions. This is the recognition to which we are driven even when one of these traditions is in a nascent state and so articulable only in the form of an isolated individual's bitter confusion or self-loathing. According to Borges, to think otherwise must still be to admit one's disguised agreement with this conclusion. For in such opposition one still affirms nature's coherent spirit with a confidence that must be accounted nothing short of miraculous, considering what one is given to understand by even a quick perusal of a newspaper, say, or by a passing glance at one's own unlikely face in a mirror.

The intimacy between tradition and the miracle is betrayed by the supernatural character of tradition: by the assumption that it transcends difference, individuality, and mortality. Reassuringly, we could call this supernaturalism *culture*, but in doing so we would simply be substituting one fantastically wolfish term (now dressed up in the realist finery of social science) for another. There is no more coherence in such a use of *culture* than there is in the spirit of nature or in the pluralization of *tradition*. To stop at *culture* is to use this term as the ground of consciousness and the grave of unconsciousness—as the miraculous god of mutilated being that enables us to deny our apprehension of loss as all that really lasts—of loss as our only continuous, uncorrupted tradition.

Time and the break in time, tacit background and borderless foreground, continuity and discontinuity, knowledge and event, culture and otherness—these are the sorts of oppositions that are rejected in the way Borges portrays the monstrous relation between tradition and the miracle.

The supernatural, of course, is that through which we signify unacceptable loss. We cannot give it up: we must surrender to tradition on this point. It is the miracle of oblivion at any imaginable origin of consciousness. It is the artful way we account for the chattering strangers who cannot be kept from crowding into the room with us even in the moment of our most dire intimacies.

"Probably without realizing it," writes Borges of Pedro Damián, "he was preparing the way for the miracle" ("The Other Death," 103–11).

The narrator finds that his attraction to this tale extends beyond the story itself to "The Past," a poem by Ralph Waldo Emerson, and to a theological work, De Omnipotentia, by Pier Damiani, to whom Dante referred in Canto 21 of the Paradiso, as the narrator notes.[41] Emerson's work "centers around the irrevocability of the past," whereas Damiani's is said to maintain "that it is within God's power to make what once was into something that has never been." (One may remember Nils Runeberg in "Three Versions of Judas," who grudgingly admits that Jesus "could count on the considerable resources which Omnipotence offers" [153].) Through his reflections on these conflicting sources, our narrator comes to doubt his own story. "I suspect that in my story there are a few false memories," he says. "It is my suspicion that Pedro Damián (if he ever existed) was not called Pedro Damián and that I remember him by that name so as to believe someday that the whole story was suggested to me by Pier Damiani's thesis."

Although Schopenhauer is not mentioned as among its sources, this situation seems to recall, in a broken way, Schopenhauer's account of madmen. The malady of these men, he wrote,

> especially concerns the memory. . . . The thread of memory is broken, the continuity of its connection destroyed, and no uniformly connected recollection of the past is possible. Particular scenes of the past are known correctly, just like the particular present; but there are gaps in their recollection which they fill up with fictions. . . . Although the immediate present is correctly known, it becomes falsified through its fictitious connection with an imaginary past; they therefore regard themselves and others as identical with persons who exist only in their imaginary past.[42]

In his story Borges calls forth a conspiracy of oblivion and memory like that which Schopenhauer described as madness, but he makes it describe the relationship between the miracle and tradition. As its title indicates, then, "The Other Death" is a twice-told tale—and so a tale that can come to no proper end.

Initially this story appears as an account of Pedro Damián, a soldier in the 1904 revolution who may have miraculously made for himself an alternative history in which he died heroically in battle instead of acting in a cowardly way and living on to an ignominious death in 1946. (The difference is "infinite": "It involves the creation of two universal histories" [110].) This story of double histories then recurs in the narrator's own reflections on his telling of the story, in which he is led to conclude that his own life, insofar as it involves his knowledge of

this story, is as divided from itself in space, time, and consciousness as
(for instance) a medieval Italian theologian is from a nineteenth-century
American pantheist. As Sylvia Molloy has put this matter, in writing
of the way names appear in Borges's works, "The pause in which they
are fixed is a passing conceit, the necessary frivolity of an author of
fiction, or of history."[43]

This situation resembles that in "Pierre Menard, Author of Don Quixote," which opens with "Error" in the form of violence, crime, and
conspiracy besmirching "*visible* works" and, through them, "Memory"
(45). In other words, like Alexander Pope's "Rape of the Lock," it opens
with a mock-heroic struggle over the establishment and perpetuation
of a tradition, which in this case concerns not a ravishing and ravished
lock of hair but an authorial canon and its interpretation. This narrator's
story is the double of the project of Menard, which is the avowedly
impossible one of trying definitively to reconstruct an original text: to
bring the literal word to life.

Twice-told, the story is then told infinitely. (We may remember that
Cervantes's *Don Quixote* was already at least a twice-told tale, in that
Cervantes presented it as being translated from an Arabic manuscript
on which he had chanced to stumble.) In this way Borges insists that
tradition is always an *oblivious* pretext to whatever comes of it. Tradition is remembered not in spite of forgetfulness but through it, because
even though "reality is exact, memory is not" ("Preface," 9). In the
words of Sir Thomas Browne, "knowledge is made by oblivion."[44] So
one of Borges's narrators is brought to say, of a text no longer in his
possession, "But I will outline its plot, exactly as my forgetfulness now
impoverishes (exactly as it now purifies) it" ("An Examination of the
Work of Herbert Quain," 74). In ultimately proving to be unaccountable, memory's losses to itself are definitive of culture, in all its provisionally definitive aspects, including not only plots but also custom,
common sense, and sacred tradition.

Borges does allow what is due to the rationalist rejection of tradition
as prejudice. Yes, certainly, tradition is that, as the marvelously fussy
narrator of "Pierre Menard" is designed to indicate. Tradition, however, is also much more than that. For as Borges tells the story, if we
were to do away with prejudice, with pretexts of all sorts, we would
not then enter into the presence of enlightening truth. Instead we would
face the fiery miracle, by which we would be consumed, even as the
butterfly is "blinded and confused," according to Nietzsche, "by the
unknown light, the realm of freedom."[45]

This is the madness of tradition, here in this skittering, broken *jump* of identities: Damiani, Emerson, Schopenhauer, and Borges (or Hume, Nietzsche, and Freud . . . or Kafka, Borges, and Benjamin) in the same time and place, or in times and places that exist repeatedly. "All this is a miracle," says the narrator of "The Other" about his involvement with his alter ego, "and the miraculous is terrifying. Witnesses to the resurrection of Lazarus must have been horrified" ("The Other," 325).

It may be that all letters translate the shapes of butterflies and other fantastic animals. Many centuries after Chuang Tzu's dream, Nietzsche wrote:

> The degree of the historical sense of any age may be inferred from the manner in which this age makes *translations* and tries to absorb former ages and books. In the age of Corneille and even of the Revolution, the French took possession of Roman antiquity in a way for which we would no longer have courage enough—thanks to our more highly developed historical sense. And Roman antiquity itself: how forcibly and at the same time how naively it took hold of everything good and lofty of Greek antiquity, which was more ancient! How they translated things into the Roman present! How deliberately and recklessly they brushed the dust off the wings of the butterfly that is called moment![46]

The dreamer, the fiery phoenix ("This multiple god revealed to him that his earthly name was fire" ["The Circular Ruins," 126]), Chuang Tzu: throughout Borges's writings we see tradition as translation. His every version of the story is a story of perverse conversion. Here again he recalls Benjamin, or at least the Benjamin who wrote that "all translation is only a somewhat provisional way of coming to terms with the foreignness of languages," much as Hume had written of philosophy as a provisional warding off of our utter ignorance.[47]

Because tradition is a kind of spell, which spells out its rule over us without ever literally bringing rules to life, it is "a form of conquest,"[48] as Nietzsche said. We make use of it; but no matter how deliberate and reckless we may be, we cannot have done with it. (So Nietzsche would mockingly note that whether we stray from or remain in tradition, "Destruction follows in any case."[49]) Ravishing us as we ravish it, with sublime banality tradition is forever translating us—and thus, as the traditional saying must have it, betraying us.

In some of his writings Nietzsche portrayed tradition much as Voltaire had, as a kind of superstition. He made it out to be closely bound up with what he supposed to be the femininity of morality—"the greatest of all mistresses of seduction"—but nonetheless a power that might be overcome: "The free human being is immoral because in all things he is *determined* to depend upon himself and not upon a tradition: in all the original conditions of mankind, 'evil' signifies the same as 'individual,' 'free,' 'capricious,' 'unusual,' 'unforeseen,' 'incalculable.' . . . What is tradition? A higher authority which one obeys, not because it commands what is *useful* to us, but because it *commands*."[50] But just as he translated Hume's skepticism into a wonder at miracles and Schopenhauer's natural order into a traditional literary design, Borges translated Nietzsche's free spirit into a spirit bound eternally to repeat the same questioning movement. His way of translating these others is especially notable for its turning away from those moments in their writings where they privilege an idealized masculinity and show contempt for people characterized by their commonness.

To be sure, Borges was not particularly sentimental about people considered in this character. If anything, his fiction and the popular image of his political attitudes would suggest the contrary. Relatively early in his career he formulated for himself a lasting conservatism skeptical alike of government and of reform—a position that seems bound to end up favoring the established institutions of state. Nonetheless, this conclusion is overly simplistic, both in relation to his explicit political gestures and in relation to his writings, which translate the masterly position assumed by Hume, Schopenhauer, and Nietzsche into a viewpoint that shows their commonality with those they disdained.[51] This way of taking these predecessors is of a piece with the general statements about tradition that Borges was given to making: "Each language is a tradition, each word a shared symbol, and what an innovator can change amounts to a trifle" ("Preface to the First Edition," *Dr. Brodie's Report*, 11).

Certainly one may read a tale of fastidious conservative gentility in the writings of Borges. Demonstrably, such a tale is there to be read. This is simultaneously retold, however, as a tale of inevitable and even eager—even wistful—abduction and seduction by the traditions of common life. Moreover, as Borges retells the tales, these traditions of common life include a disregard for letters that may have much to teach the attentive reader. It is as if his early attraction to the movement of *criollismo* remained in Borges as a corrosive irony toward the erudite, eminently civilized cosmopolitanism of his own presumed maturity. After all, it is because his higher education makes him so naive about letters that Espinosa, in "The Gospel According to Mark," must find the infinity of the story of Christ lovingly foretold and repeated for him all the way to its logically killing extreme: "Bowing their knees to the stone pavement, they asked his blessing. Then they mocked at him, spat on him . . ." (21–22).

Tradition, which maintains the present, does not take us into the past. Tradition is the housebroken past, the past made tractable and polite, like a domesticated animal. That is why tradition always tells a story of perverse conversion. The past is something else again.

This is not to say that the opposite of tradition, in the direction of the past, is wildness. This is the conventional wisdom, just as it is conventional to imagine that the opposite of tradition in the direction of the future is progressive change, innovation, or modernization.[52] It is the willful dullness of tradition that tells the story in this way.

As Borges tells the story, the past is miraculous. For as long as it seems securely bounded by tradition, the past must participate in a story of conversion that tells us of before and after, better and worse, the one and the other, dream and reality, and so on. The past, however, is not itself a conversion, and tradition simply cannot contain it. Tradition, which cannot progress, finds also that it cannot contain the absolute pastness of its identity. Breaking out of the tradition it otherwise serves to maintain, the past then becomes a miracle: the absolute presence of an overwhelming identification. In bringing conversion, this miracle brings into question the supposed differences between past and present and, indeed, all the differences assumed within images of conversion. Such is the course of events traced, for instance, in the grotesque folk tale that Borges drew out of the Gospels through the story of Espinosa. Surely "Espinosa" is meant to recall Spinoza; and as that philosopher darkly said, from the miracle "we can gain no knowledge."[53]

Spinoza, Espinosa—so small a change in the lottery of letters may have such a big effect—so great is the ravishing, ravaging difference made by the change of a letter or two in a fiery name.

Having attributed reports of miracles to the poetic devices necessary to move the masses, Spinoza made his statement dismissively. Miracles are figures of speech, he argued, which must be considered banal by those few who are capable of reason, which is a matter of eternal and unchanging divine law. Despite what his life might seem to indicate, then, Spinoza's reason aspired to be the justification of tradition. In effect, he conceived of tradition as a power that will not recognize anything it cannot convert to itself—if not in its own name, then in the binding contrasts of wildness and reason. For Spinoza, tradition cannot recognize a past outside the production of knowledge; it cannot recognize a past that is simply stunning, powerful enough truly to disorder the present.

Such a past is imaginable only if one does not measure it by the scale of the present, or in the terms of tradition, which never hesitate in turning it into a matter of knowledge. In fact, such a past cannot be measured at all. Instead, one must simply meet with it, as Espinosa does. Then one suddenly finds oneself (in Nietzsche's words) "as it were clinging to a tiger's back in dreams."[54] Without warning, one is bestriding a figure (like William Blake's tiger) that cannot be converted to any other standard except that of the question that would be a true question at last.

"Homo homini lupus": it is not wildness that is in question in this motto. At question is the animal so fantastically divided that it does not fall under the reassuring standards of wildness as opposed to domestication, the past as opposed to the present, or the animal as opposed to humanity. "Error has turned animals into men," Nietzsche wrote, asking, "Might truth be capable of turning man into an animal again?"[55] In other words, he was asking what would be the *literally* animalic figure: "Even this costs him effort: to admit to himself that the insect or the bird perceives a completely different world than man does, and that the question which of the two world-perceptions is more right is a completely senseless one, since it could be decided only by the criterion of the *right perception*, i.e., by a standard *which does not exist.*"[56]

Following Borges and Nietzsche, we might argue that all our dreams are of animals, since all we know for sure in our dreams is that we are not assured of being human. Whatever measures there may be of man and, through man, of all things, we find that we cannot rely on them. The measure of woman comes into play here, deranging the fantastic "us" of *Lord Jim*'s "one of us," as do measures of racial, national, economic, historical, and cultural difference, all of them refusing to obey an overarching logic or a story unchanged by repetition. Therefore, to understand the grammar of waking consciousness, one must turn the question of tradition over to the signs and wonders of dream tigers and other marvelous animals.

Freud, famously, was also very interested in this question:

> In the course of the development of civilization man acquired a dominating position over his fellow-creatures in the animal kingdom. Not content with this supremacy, however, he began to place a gulf between his nature and theirs. He denied the posssession of reason to them, and

to himself he attributed an immortal soul, and made claims to a divine
descent which permitted him to break the bond of community between
him and the animal kingdom. Curiously enough, this piece of arrogance
is still foreign to children, just as it is to primitive and primaeval man.
. . . [The child] is not astonished at animals thinking and talking in fairy-
tales; he will transfer an emotion of fear which he feels for his human
father onto a dog or a horse, without intending any derogation of his
father by it. Not until he is grown up does he become so far estranged
from animals as to use their names in vilification of human beings.[57]

In Freud's analysis, what gets repeated in tradition is this ancient act
that is the making of humanity. This act is suggested and yet never
completely captured by terms such as *translation, conquest, conversion.*
This is the act that we cannot know to be our own doing; this is the
miracle that can only happen to us. For insofar as we recognize our
dominions, we are bound to misrecognize genealogies of domination.

Like Nietzsche, then, and like Michel Foucault after him, Freud points
out that there is not *first* a measure and *then* a difference; instead the
two arise together out of a fantastic "gulf" that is the effect of "denial,"
whence all knowing originates. As the stories of Borges suggest, to get
the measure of how impossible it is for any community to admit that
tradition is of its own making, one need only consider how brutally
innocent, grotesque, and amazingly persistent is the joke by which men
imagine that women have no more part in their making than in the
creation of culture and reason, in which their participation traditionally
has often been assumed to be negligible.

So we do not break with tradition if we see humanity as a distinguished kind of animal: the political animal, the rational animal, the
playful animal, and so on. Such terms simply repeat the just-so story
of tradition. Nor do we break with it in arguing that humans may still
be like animals in certain conditions, or may revert to animalic instincts
and behaviors, or even may be inferior to animals in some respects,
whether these be aesthetic, ethical, biological, or some combination of
all three. (Jerome Rorarius argued in the sixteenth century that beasts
are superior in rationality to man, but this is really quite a traditional
line of thought, as is the neo-Swiftian thinking of dolphin enthusiasts
in our own day who consider animals to be more humane than humans
themselves.) Arguments like these still assume that the animal is
known, and so they still remain comfortably within the bounds of tradition. The child is still the child, the grownup still the grownup, men
still men, and the animal still the animal.

After all, as no one argued better than Hume, there never has and never will be anything miraculous in simple doubt, uncertainty, and ambiguity. Even when Freud admitted, "I do not myself know what animals dream of,"[58] he as much as boasted that he did know the nature of animals and of dreams. (Otherwise, he could not have drawn distinctions between them, along with the distinction between animals and the humans whose dreams he was claiming to interpret.) Similarly, even as he told the story of reason as one of arrogant domination over one's fellow creatures, Freud characterized this as "the *biological* blow to human narcissism," thus identifying with a scientific tradition so as to keep himself from seeming like one who was credulous enough to believe in miracles. (His denials here become especially apparent if one considers the very different way his tale was retold by the surrealists in the 1920s and 1930s.[59]) Freud's story of civilization is not a simple one, and it does not remain unchanged from one work to another; but insofar as it keeps faith with conquering reason, it must deny its own striking insights into the animal dream, which might be called the dream of the conquering worm— even such a "fat worm of error" as Nietzsche found in Kant's aesthetics[60]—or perhaps such a worm as man is when on the verge of being transformed into a butterfly, that traditional figure of spiritual transcendence.

We do not break with tradition until we feel the fur on the letters slinking across the pages of our books. Then things *probatur ex scriptura* and *probatur ex traditione* are alike disproved by the animality of letters. When we finally understand that the pedant's nightmare—to look down at a piece of writing and be completely unable to make it out— must reveal to him that the script is an animal, as is every man of letters, it is then that we may enter into the fiction of Borges. The joke that Freud quoted from Georg Christoph Lichtenberg—"He wondered how it is that cats have two holes cut in their skin precisely at the place where their eyes are"[61]—this, too, points us to the animal as a miraculous apparition that tradition must always and yet cannot ever convert to itself.[62]

"Good liquor will make a cat speak," says an old proverb to which Shakespeare alluded in *The Tempest*.

The writings of Kafka provide an especially interesting comparison on this score, for in his works the story of conversion that constitutes tradition never quite takes place. Always getting under way or assumed or even absolutely necessary, it never actually happens. Instead, his works tell us in various stunning ways that we cannot know the animal that is language.

The overwhelming effect of his most famous story, for instance, is to convey the sense that a metamorphosis, despite all signs to the contrary, has not occurred. Although it seems that a radical change of some sort has taken place, Gregor Samsa is still recognizably Gregor, communication is no more difficult than it seems to have been in the past, and in fact everything is just as it was—and just as it will be in the healthy animality that marks the ending of the story. Events happen as they have not recently been happening, and that fact is something of a miracle in itself, but not one sufficient to disturb the arrogance of familial, civil, and spiritual traditions. As with Chuang Tzu's dream of being a butterfly, Gregor Samsa's awakening to find himself a dung beetle does not yield knowledge. Instead, this story is designed to dwell upon the comedy of tradition, which (like Gregor himself) is amazingly oblivious to the revelation of its animal letters:

> Gregor had a shock as he heard his own voice answering [his mother], unmistakably his own voice, it was true, and yet mixed, as if from underneath, with an irrepressible, painful squeaking, which actually allowed the words a momentary clearness only to destroy them in such a reverberation that one could not be sure one had heard them rightly.

> In die sich aber, wie von unten her, ein nicht zu unterdrückendes, schmerzliches Piepsen mischte, das die Worte förmlich nur im ersten Augenblick in ihrer Deutlichkeit beließ, um sie im Nachklang derart zu zerstören.[63]

The upsetting reverberation here is the sound of the unlikeliness of language. This squeaking is the sound of a man repeatedly being broken . . . the echo of a jump from Chuang-Tzu to Nietzsche to Benjamin to Borges . . . the most traditional sound imaginable.

This is the sound one hears when the assurance of tradition is disturbed, not by primitive wildness or progressive change but by a perception of the atrocity of conversion. (After all, *conversion* is not simply a figure of speech, and it is not simply a coincidence that Spinoza, Kafka, and Freud were Jews in an embattled relation to predominantly Christian cultures or that Borges felt called upon, in his fiction and essays, to identify himself with Jews.) This sound is the reverberation of a twice-told tale that will not allow us to linger on its telling even for a moment before it promises no end of repetitions. Among other things, one might hear in it the sound of the words of Borges's Kabbala becoming the words of Artaud's, thus unimaginably fulfilling this word, *Kabbala*, "tradition." Even though this shared interest in the Kabbala is, as we say, a mere matter of chance, Artaud wrote—in a Borgesian moment—"If we did not have faith in the possibility of a miracle, we would not enter upon this path full of hazards. But only a miracle is capable of rewarding our efforts and our patience. We are counting on a miracle."[64]

If a man of letters, hunched so long over his books that the letters began to swim before his eyes, tried to pronounce what he then saw, the sound he would make would be this sound from "The Metamorphosis." And perhaps he would recognize this sound as the animal voice of letters that cannot be kept in line by the zookeepers of tradition. He would know enough to fear that we would all have to produce this inhuman twittering if the letters in the books in our libraries no longer kept miraculously to their places when left unattended overnight—as Borges in his childhood thought might be the case, and thought justly.

The letters that compose our words are so many animals speaking to our oblivious senses: this is another way of making the point that Kafka suggests through his animal narrators. (One might think also of William Blake's *Four Zoas*, with its creatures struggling for apocalyptic recognition.) Whether the narrator is an ape that has "managed to reach the cultural level of an average European," a dog obsessed with the measure of its kind ("All knowledge, the totality of all questions and all answers, is contained in the dog"), or a kind of opera fan among mice, as in "Josephine the Singer," all of Kafka's animal narrators, like Gregor Samsa, prove to be as comically oblivious to their unlikely condition as they are excruciatingly self-conscious about the questions they think they are pursuing.[65] The ape knows he "cannot reach back to the truth of the old ape life" but is sure "that it lies somewhere in the direction" he has articulated; although he may not yet have the answer, the dog is sure of the "great question" of his life, and certain that it is a question for him alone; in "Josephine" the narrator's every sentence chases after an effect, a quiddity, unquestionably demanding recognition and yet, as far as the narrator is concerned, always left untouched by the responses it does in fact evoke from other mice.[66]

To feel the fur on the letters slinking across the pages of our books is to see all the designs that compose tradition as not even so much as a scribbling, but rather a scrabbling or squeaky scratching at the materiality of things, including our own bodies. The scrabbling is done for obscure reasons and is oriented to ends we can hardly begin to grasp.

It is imperceptible to us in this character, however, until we become bored enough—remember the detachment Hume momentarily allowed himself?—to appreciate the remoteness of these signs from any conceivable will of our own. (This scrabbling is the sound you are hearing now, that squeaking reverberation right here, in these letters shaped like dreaming lepidoptera.) In fact, the wonder on which Kafka's stories are based is the wonder that we are not more bored. Or to put it another way, Kafka's stories propose that the miracle of humanity is its profound irritability, which keeps it moving in the directions we call "answers" and "art" and "tradition."

Our letters are then so many marks of our irritability. If this were not the case, we would not have to read them: they could simply be eaten like bread. Obviously it is because he cannot swallow language that the hunger artist dies.

For Kafka the other side of art is not life, not reality, but the unthinkable animal, to which we aspire in our ecstatic images: for instance (as Borges would have it in his retellings), to be the animal that is knife, that is fire. What is crucial in this impression of the animal being also knife and fire (among other things) is the effect of literal *precision*, as in the exact coincidence between a cat's glowing eyes and the openings in its skin, or as in the letters that you are reading right now, in this sentence that you understand even as it is transformed from an insect to a beast that stalks off under your very eyes, stuck as they are there in holes in your face.

All our measures are implicated in this uncanny precision that we assume in language. No wonder Tristram Shandy concluded, "But with an ass, I can commune forever"; no wonder Mrs. Reed traced her hatred to the sight of that Caliban, Jane Eyre, furiously confronting her, in her words, "as if an animal that I had struck or pushed had looked up at me with human eyes and cursed me in a man's voice"; no wonder Mr. Palomar, listening to blackbirds whistling, was "gripped by anguish"; no wonder the horses of Achilles found it necessary at least once to speak their minds.[67] In describing various moods, these scenes all betray the fantastic beast that is tradition.

In a recent movie, *Dead Again* (1991), the detective hero Mike Church says to an amnesiac, and formerly aphasic, woman, "You know, I can't get used to the sound of your voice—you know, it's like, uh, one day you wake up and your cat talks to you."

Who would deny that if animals could speak, they would tell us things we would want to know? Yet it is not at all obvious that we are

justified in drawing such a conclusion. It rests on nothing more sub-
stantial than an analogy, which is another name for a failed conversion:
from the fact that other people speak and yet never tell us precisely
what we want to hear, we conclude that an animal might.

Traditionally, the speaking animals of children's toys, books, and car-
toons thus serve as our reassurance that language is not as terribly
unlikely as it must otherwise seem. If we admitted to children that
animals never speak, we would also have to admit that letters never
tell us what we need to know, that they might even be as repellent to
our understanding as tigers or conquering dictators—and that we will
never do.

Borges dwells on this point throughout his works, but perhaps most
centrally in "The God's Script" (169-73). In this story the point of literal
precision—the point of miraculous simplicity—is a formula of "forty
syllables, fourteen words," lettered in the spots of a tiger and deciphered by the narrator, Tzinacán, as he lies dying in prison. This formula is the answer to a question of tradition apprehended through
memory: "One night I felt I was approaching a precise memory [un
recuerdo preciso]; before he sights the sea, the traveller feels a quick-
ening in the blood. Hours later I began to perceive the outline of the
memory. It was a tradition of the god. The god, foreseeing that at the
end of time there would be devastation and ruin, wrote on the first day
of Creation a magical sentence with the power to ward off those evils."
Having deciphered the sentence in the spots of the tiger imprisoned
next to him, Tzinacán does not pronounce it, although he is sure that
doing so would renovate the empire conquered by the Spaniards and
restore him to his high place in it. Instead, he leaves everything as it is
because a miraculous ecstasy, in which he is joined with God, has left
him no longer himself: "I saw an exceedingly high Wheel, which was
not before my eyes, nor behind me, nor to the sides, but every place at
one time. That Wheel was made of water, but also of fire, and it was
(although the edge could be seen) infinite."

It is a very clever story, this story of tradition, founded on nothing
more than the oldest trick in the storyteller's book: the telling detail. To
convey the impression of reality, one casually mentions a detail that is
absolutely inessential to the pronounced purposes of one's story. (Bad
liars, like the Ray Milland character in Dial M for Murder [1954], try to
get every detail of their story down pat; those better schooled in literature, like Alfred Hitchcock, know that success in such matters depends
on the assurance conveyed by the random observation, the casual aside,
the unnecessary digression, the prosaic redundancy.) Never to be pro-

nounced, the "forty syllables, fourteen words" of this magic sentence are the apotheosis of this storytelling formula, which is thereby suggested to be the formula of identity, history, and divinity. The telling detail is the metonymy from which our desires in and for narrative hook us with a knowing grin. It is as much as to say that every letter, every word, is a tiger on which we are carried away in a dream; it is as much as to say that the words we do pronounce are destroyed in the moment of their utterance, so that all one can hear is a kind of scrabbling at walls of sullied sand, as by a burrowing animal. Thus, instead of the classic metaphysical relation between particulars and universals, Borges offers details in relation to labyrinths and so seeks to image a universality beyond imagining.

This is *precisely* the terrifying miracle that tradition must and cannot accept: the simple poetic device, the trick of narration. Because questions are raised only in relation to answers that are foretold, twice-told, and retold through potentially infinite repetitions—"I considered that we were now, as always, at the end of time and that my destiny as the last priest of the god would give me access to the privilege of intuiting the script"—the answer of answers can only be to leave everything as it is.

Thus it is that a story of conquest (of an indigenous by a Spanish civilization) turns into a story of translation (of an incantation by an imprisoned magician) and thence into a story of conversion (of the magician, through a miracle, into the universe and no one). Spelled out in beastly letters, tradition is bespelled. It is a story that betrays itself to the very end, finding cause even in its utmost revelation to conceal itself. Miraculous and ultimately unpronounceable, betrayal—of nation, language, and self—is its impossible essence.

Yet this end of the story is, in a sense, not the end of the story at all. Before the ecstasy in which he lost himself by identifying with his torturer (among infinite other things), the narrator fell into a dream in which he was being suffocated in sand while being told, "*You have not awakened to wakefulness, but to a previous dream. The dream is enclosed within another, and so on to infinity, which is the number of grains of sand. The path you must retrace is interminable, and you will die before you ever really awake.*" It is only in rejecting this pronouncement, in denying this image of dreams, that he comes to his ecstasy and thence to his understanding of the formula.

In other words, among other things—we must pay close attention to such magical rhetorical formulas—the writing of the god *is* pronounced. It is pronounced by this voice of the dream, which is forgotten in the story's ecstatic revelation. This is the betrayal, the gulf of denial, that is essential to the unspeakable truth of tradition: the betrayal of infinite repetition.

If we remember this betrayal, instead of forgetting it as he does, the capitulation of Tzinacán to his condition takes on a different appearance. Fatalistic, masochistic, and schizophrenic, this surrender then exemplifies the madness of tradition but in no way represents knowledge of tradition. For such knowledge one would have to return to the denial of dreams in this story. One would have to ask what is destroyed when the animal is converted to letters, letters to prescribed words, words to tales told twice and infinitely. In other words, one would have to return to the priest made prisoner and consider all that this situation suggests as to the power of cultural differences—as Borges does, in effect, throughout his writings.

This story of a tortured, maimed, dying prisoner is (among other things) a retelling of "A Hunger Artist." And in repeating Kafka as well as Freud and Nietzsche, among others, Borges gives us a good idea of what we might find in the time and place where dreams are denied: the body, precisely.

When Borges writes (as he does, in so many words) of the letter as being also fire, a labyrinth, a butterfly, a knife, and a beast (among other things), he maps the road between letters and eyes, words and emotions, stories and our most passionate movements. We meet the body on that road, and sometimes, in a miraculous moment, we may even recognize it as our own.

The way the things of our world look back at us: that is tradition.

As Borges tells the story, tradition dictates; the miracle demonstrates.

As opposed to the miracle, tradition is a matter of precedent. (Even if the tradition in question is one that allows for miracles, it is this allowance, this anticipation and foretelling, that is crucial.) The miracle is violent; tradition, without shock or animus. (Even if the tradition in question is one of hostility and warfare, it is not itself violent but rather that which prepares one for violence, which it calmly comprehends.) The miracle tests the belief that tradition takes for granted. It defies with terror and splendor tradition's insistence on the ordinary. (And it does so even though that which is ordinary may be a terrible and splendid dream, as of a father's creation of a son or a priest's union with God.) Where tradition tells of control, the miracle tells of powerlessness; and so where tradition tells of despair (of the despair of control, in which the dreamer is also a figure being dreamed, as in the grammar explicated by Chuang Tzu, Borges, and Freud), the miracle tells of hope.

For of course there is no hope if we cannot imagine the possibility of our powerlessness.

Tradition is a question that cannot appear undisguised, as gods in their frolics cannot appear in their full majesty, lest they destroy us.

Since it can answer all questions, tradition answers none. Because it is always in advance of the question, it is no answer at all.

Since it is an answer without a question, an answer in excess of any conceivable question, the miracle is no more of an answer.

So it is the question of the question that joins together tradition and the miracle. This is the question that cannot be formulated as such without suffering destruction, as in the ecstasy of an overwhelming passion.

Tradition and the miracle together pose this question, in which their shared passion betrays itself, and in which bravery and cowardice embrace: What would it be to exist without question, unquestioningly?

Imagine a scene of passion:

> Oh friends, the innocence of this friend
> Of Jesus, the candor that moved him
> From the ignominy of his end
> To ask for Heaven and receive it,
>
> Was the very same that so many times
> Had hurled him into sins and bloody crimes.
>
> ("Luke 23," 177)

It may be important to note this: I had already drafted three of the chapters that follow before I realized that the book to which they now belong was going to be on the subject of tradition. This realization was delayed over two years even though this word, *tradition*, appeared prominently in each chapter. It was as if my discovery of my subject was actually this subject, tradition, discovering itself to me, planting clues more and more obviously until I finally got it; it was as if I was destined to discover myself as being subject to my subject.

As Borges suggests, this is often the way tradition comes to us, conspiratorially, seemingly ours and yet alien. It is a message that we come upon and recognize as such, although it appears to be written in a curious code that we cannot finally decipher even after an intriguing memory comes to us . . . of having written such a message, perhaps even this very message, ourselves. It is this aspect of tradition that can make an endless journey around the world a shorter way to seeing oneself than the step or two it would take to look at oneself in a mirror.

If tradition were not opposed to the miracle, we could not pretend to draw any rules, customs, and ways of life from it; if it were not a miracle in disguise, we would have to know and admit that it is our own doing. In either case, it would cease to be tradition.

If the miracle were not opposed to tradition, we would not stand still for it; if it were not tradition in disguise, we would consider it madness and see no way out of it. In either case, it would cease to be miraculous.

In other words—still figuring things in this way—we would have to conclude that language, reason, materiality, and history (among other things) would all be destroyed in an instant. So long as such an end is unthinkable, so long as their identity cannot be avowed, the miracle and tradition must be perceived as being engaged in a conspiracy.

This thought snakes its way through many of Borges's works, such as "The Babylon Lottery" and "The Congress," but it may have been most finely developed in his early and perhaps most famous story, "Tlön, Uqbar, Orbis Tertius" (17–35). In this work, individual and cultural memory come to seem the effect of a secret society, a conspiracy, whose boundaries cannot be precisely measured even though there are certain quite precise evidences of a disturbance. These include an article about the country of Tlön which appears in but one copy of *The Anglo-American Encyclopaedia*—"Tlön" apparently being absent from all other copies and from other reference books as well. Furthermore, these evidences include certain uncanny objects, such as an "intolerably heavy" metal cone. Finally, there is that little matter of an all-encompassing "intrusion of the fantastic world into the real one" by which this conspiracy promises to leave no object, image, or idea unturned. "Now," says the narrator, "in all memories, a fictitious past occupies the place of any other. We know nothing about it with any certainty, not even that it is false." The entire conspiracy is traced to a benevolent secret society of the early seventeenth century, of which George Berkeley was a member, as this was renovated nihilistically by Ezra Buckley, a citizen of the nineteenth-century United States who was "a freethinker, a fatalist, and an apologist for slavery." In passing, the need to "submit to Tlön [*someterse a Tlön*]" is compared to the compulsions exacted by "dialectical materialism, anti-Semitism, Nazism." The narrator calmly notes that soon, without any other languages or traditions to challenge it, "the world will be Tlön." Nonetheless, he concludes unprotestingly, sequestering himself from the world while occupying himself with a translation of Sir Thomas Browne that he does not intend to see published.

To the many resemblances between this story, "Theme of the Traitor and the Hero," "The Sect of the Phoenix," "The Circular Ruins," and "The God's Script," which make these and other works by Borges seem repeated conversions of an elusive *ur*-text, "Tlön, Uqbar, Orbis Tertius" adds the note of an overwhelming, all-pervasive conspiracy. In keeping with the allusion to Berkeley, this conspiracy observes no difference between imaginary, ideological, and physical bodies.[68] The effect is not to illustrate Berkeleyan metaphysics, however, so much as it is to illustrate the genealogy of tradition. Tradition is shown to be born of the denial of its invention, to be dressed up in signs of misleading precision, to be communicated through corruption, and to be remembered by a process of forgetting: "Contact with Tlön and the ways of Tlön have disintegrated this world. Captivated by its discipline, humanity forgets and goes on forgetting that it is the discipline of chess players, not of angels."

Virtually alone among all others, the narrator identifies this conspiracy in which tradition and the miracle, chess players and angels, share the same atmosphere. Yet simply to come to this conclusion is, of course, not to betray the conspiracy. Instead, to come to this conclusion is to submit oneself to its betrayal. As Borges admits through the fatalism that comes to subdue the narrator as well as all others (at least as the narrator sees them), the description of the conspiracy is not opposed to its revelation. In point of fact, the very notion of the conspiracy depends on a productive relationship between these terms, just as the duality of a duel (as between Martín Fierro and the Moreno in "The End") depends on the cooperative engagement of two opponents.

In the facile way it conflates totalitarianisms of the left and of the right, this portrayal of conspiracy might be read as a barely disguised conservative reaction against any desire for activist political organizations or for the building of rebellious social alliances in the modern Western world. The possibility of this reading cannot be eliminated, and its cogency ought not to be underestimated if we do not wish to be so captivated by the pleasure of this work that we end up unable to draw any distinctions between, say, the pig Roberto d'Aubuisson and the butchered Archbishop Romero. To dismiss this reading out of hand would be unconsciously to accept "Tlön, Uqbar, Orbis Tertius" as an idealization of the triumph of the global capitalist marketplace, in which any hope for social change is discredited in advance because all totalities are taken to bear the same motivations, the same monotonously enticing commercial hue.

In other words, were this a tale in which readers were supposed to identify with the narrator, considered as an insightful critic of cultural, historical, and political mystification, it would be nothing but the most conventional detective story imaginable, returning us to a truth we are always already supposed to have known. As one might expect, however, from an author who had such a respect for good detective stories, this is not at all the case. Like the ecstasy of Tzinacán, the successful creation of the magus in "The Circular Ruins," the discovery made by the narrator in "The Sect of the Phoenix," and the imaginary tale unfolded from the date in 1944 on which "Theme of the Traitor and the Hero" is said to be composed, the narrator's identification of this conspiracy does not mark a simple point of insight. Instead, it marks the precise point at which tradition is revalorized through its seeming opposition to the miracle. In showing Ezra Buckley to be a disturbing double of the similarly surnamed George Berkeley, the narrator betrays his own kinship with Buckley. He too is a "fatalist," as in his final quietism; a "freethinker" inasmuch as he possesses just as much right to that oxymoron as anyone else; and an "apologist for slavery" in his tolerance for the world becoming Tlön and in his submission to isolation and futility. One may remember that the objects defining the Tlön conspiracy include "the *ur*, which is a thing produced by suggestion, an object brought into being by hope"; for the conspiracy can only be this narrator's *ur*-object, which represents his desire for despair, which this story is designed to show as the utterly terrifying desire that motivates some of the most powerful traditions of the twentieth century.

In this portrayal of despair, Borges was reworking an image suggested by Leibniz, who has long been popularly seen as the philosopher of optimism in this, the best of all possible worlds. (I would guess that Borges was doing so knowingly, but his precise awareness of this point of reference is irrelevant to my argument.) In his writings Leibniz repeatedly cited Hippocrates to support his argument that "the present is big with the future and laden with the past, and there is a conspiration of all things. . . . In the least of substances eyes as penetrating as those of God might read the whole succession of the things of the universe."[69] This passage allows one clearly to see the connection between the conspiracy of Tlön and the inspiring Kabbalistic "aleph" in the story of that title; and spelling out one of the implications of this conspiracy, Leibniz further noted, "There is an infinity of present and past forms and motions which go to make up the efficient cause of my present writing."[70]

In his own writings Borges did not simply cut the final cause out from underneath Leibniz's efficient causes, thus turning a good into a bad infinity. Instead, he took the issue of causality, as addressed by Leibniz and Nietzsche and Hume, among others, and the issue of totality, as figured in various theologies as well as in the work of Leibniz, Spinoza, and Schopenhauer, among others, so as effectively to propose a new understanding of tradition. The fact that the writings in which he made this proposal will scarcely submit to be classified according to traditional literary distinctions—stories? tales? essays? meditations?— is by no means the least important consequence of the desiring reality that these writings breathe forth.

As Borges tells the story, the conspiracy theory is the form logically taken by the thought of those who fail to observe the intimacy between tradition and the miracle. Assuming that questions and answers must be truly connected, such people are bound to interpret uncertainty as hostility, mystery as malevolence, and history, in its uncertainties and mysteries, as a representation "contaminated with fiction" ("The Babylon Lottery," 71). Assuming that tradition is supposed to grant a coherent sexual identity utterly opposed to feelings of animality and to the effects of modern technology, they are bound to sense betrayal reaching into their very bodies from somewhere beyond themselves. Like the hapless lover who is the narrator of "The Aleph," they will find signs of their experience being manipulated and perversely distorted, at once elevating them and reducing them to the condition ascribed to animals; and even in the precise details of their own memories they may find alien machinery intruding. ("I do not know whether there were two or three emptied bottles on the floor or whether an abuse of cinematography [el abuso de cinématógrafo] suggests this false memory to me" ["The Meeting," 180].) As with sexual, so with racial, national, and class identities, among others: there where they name what is their own, they will find the haunting and compelling Other. Since those who think through this sense of tradition assume that repetition should always bring a renewal of the same, they are bound to find their "own" identities being atrociously trifled with—translated, conquered, or converted—even as they themselves try to communicate these identities in the clearest of words, such as *world* or *all* or *I*, as in "Borges and I."

Similarly, in assuming that tradition must be unified, those who fail to observe the intimacy between tradition and the miracle are bound to find powerful plots arrayed against them by agencies beyond their ken, for nothing less will suffice to maintain this sense of tradition in the face of all the infinitely precise quotidian evidences of broken conversations, irreparable losses, ravishing interruptions, and irrational jumps in ideation and identity. The more one insists on this sense of tradition, the stronger must be the counterplot, the conspiration, by which it breathes, with the logical culmination being "an enterprise so vast that in the end it becomes confused with the world itself and with the sum of daily life" ("Afterword," 124). And logically, very logically, since tradition in this understanding is assumed to be unified, these plots opposed to oneself must be felt as corruptions, not as mere differences or even antagonisms, as they might have been during the time we can only imagine at the dawn of tradition, before Homer went blind: "In bustling marketplaces or at the foot of a mountain whose hidden peak may have sheltered satyrs, he had heard entangled stories, which he accepted as he accepted reality, without attempting to find out whether they were true or imaginary" ("The Maker," 155–56).

Furthermore, in assuming that a radical difference between humans and other animals must be sustained by tradition, those who think this way are bound to experience the effects of letters as a conspiracy. Definitively closed to animals and to all that animality is taken to connote, and yet communicating by means of "an infinity of present and past forms and motions" that brings them alive, like any animal, letters are bound to rise up in rebellion against the faithful upholders of this sense of tradition. Any book may then become "a nightmarish object, an obscene thing that affront[s] and taint[s] reality itself" ("The Book of Sand," 122), as what is denied in the animal returns out of the gulf in humanity's own bespelled being.

And finally, because this sense of tradition assumes that social consciousness must entail power, and conversely that any experience of powerlessness must signify a loss of identity and meaning, those who adhere to this sense of tradition must find their only hope in despair. As Borges tells the story, we are bound to experience some sense of powerlessness even—and even especially—in our most masterful moments of action, utterance, and thought. Therefore, to the extent that we must believe this powerlessness to be alien and corrupting to tradition, we must desire to feel a despair great enough to assure ourselves that we do exist over and against this powerlessness. Those most powerfully aware of the attraction of powerlessness will then find the only adequate image of their desire in a despair over a universal conspiracy.

As Borges tells the story, there is always another story, a dream, to which we can never own up because it leaves us something other than ourselves. *You see,* he says, *you can do things that are more than you can do: it happens all the time. It is just that afterwards you are not exactly you anymore.* And so what the labyrinth is to space, fire to identity, and repetition to time, conspiracy is to plot: the entrance that is not an entrance at all because the one who passes through it always turns out to be other than oneself. As Borges tells the story, that is the miracle, the tradition.

Unpardoning Tradition

Coming to Grief in Shakespeare, Brontë, and Artaud

IN THE MOMENT IN WHICH we are introduced to the grief of Titus Andronicus, he stands in a place of public ceremony, before the Roman Capitol and the ancient tomb of the Andronici, with the leaders of nation and empire gathered around him and their troops marching onstage.

In the moment in which we are introduced to the grief of Heathcliff, he believes himself to be unobserved and addresses a figure he himself is unable to observe out in the tumultuous air of a stormy winter night.

In Antonin Artaud's writings there is no moment in which we are introduced to grief. Either completely absent or all-pervasive, as in a moment of frantic Romantic desire endlessly reverberating, it has no point of reference. Marked as a ceremonious, public, and political issue in Shakespeare's work, a willfully private and spontaneously emotional one in Brontë's, grief is virtually unmentionable in Artaud's.

Yet in the moment in which I introduce them here together, with a grievous inattention to mortal boundaries of chronology, genre, style, gender, and nationality, these moments may suggest the historical dimensions within which grief is commonly felt even today, and not only by those who have read Shakespeare, Brontë, and Artaud. In other words, this introductory moment may convey a certain sense of tradition.

In saying so I am supposing that you who read this have experienced grief, or what might be called grief by such a one as I. I must wish to enter into that grief, exploring some of the ways tradition has prescribed and illustrated its dimensions, which are described in what follows in terms of ritual, gift-giving, death, burial, decorum, feeling, and writing. In effect, my purpose is to show you tradition in a moment of grief, which I spell out through remarks about the writings of Shakespeare, Emily Brontë, and Artaud. My hope must be that some part of what follows will strike a responsive chord in you, as we are given to say, and in that moment carry you away into the grief of the contending times you carry within yourself. My argument supposes that such transports exist as a kind of occult connection among people, or as a hermetic tradition, as would be the case if we belonged to a secret society but without quite knowing how we came to join it, or what its rules were, or who could and could not be counted among its initiates.

In other words, my introduction to this point says no more than that this work is the kind of experiment in being that people make every day in activities such as pledging their love, forming alliances, casually passing the time, reading, eating, and delivering one another unto death. It follows that this introduction cannot but be hypothetical, or composed of a ritualistic structure of supplications—of mournful suppositions. Yet I cannot suppose that in making it I am abusing the methods of those who offer ideas within boundaries that seem free of any discomposure. After all, at a minimum, to scrawl any sentence one must reach out a hand in a gesture no less imploring for being unthinking, practically as natural as cashing a check. In even the most traditional scholarly and critical writings there are primitive ceremonies and also, yes, storm-swept windows—not to mention the unmentionable.

And so, for instance, I may suppose that if we think of grief as an issue of ritual, we may say that in ritual a culture represents itself to itself. At the same time, it must threaten the organization, coherence, totality, and power imagined unto itself, transporting us through realms of understanding in which the terms *ritual* and *culture* can have meaning out to those points where they must appear simply brutal in their impertinence.

The problem is that when representing itself in ritual—in allowing identity to be put at risk somewhere between presumptuous essence and soothing performance—culture cannot help but display the vulnerabilities of that which it seeks to celebrate. The contradiction is precise, unavoidable, multifoliate.[1] As every lover of mystery must know, taboo and transgression are tattooed into our suspenseful flesh in the same moment, and they stay intertwined throughout all the reversals in the rhetoric of cause and effect through which we tell sensational stories about them. (This illogic is the same that drives priests to linger eloquently on sin, commissions against pornography to issue reports whose penetralia are studded with descriptions laying bare the bodies of evidence in need of their passionate chastisement.) Despite itself, culture cannot help but offer all comers the opportunity to see that its identity has always been brought forth by the caresses of dissimulation. It cannot forbear even from measuring and displaying, with ritualistic precision, its most violable entrances. As Oscar Wilde suggested when he found occasion to comment on the death of Charles Dickens's Little Nell, anyone who does not have a heart of stone must know that the cultural body is hysterical.

Founded on repetition, on a rhythmic imitation of itself that sounds the note of identity, culture must suffer the ineradicable difference in repetition, which is at once the condition of all communication and its unconscionable enemy or "other side." Ritual seeks to subsume history, in which culture sooner or later must come to grief as the spoils of migrating customs, social cataclysms, international trade and travel, re-bellions, and war, among other forces; but in order symbolically to subsume history, ritual must become historical. Taking on the pulse of history, it discovers the bleeding dispossessions within the culture it is supposed to represent. Therefore, through its very own rituals culture is bound to face the prospect of its future death as a past that is already and irredeemably decided. It finds itself battened upon by the past, maddeningly haunted by the very terms, images, and narratives that bring the past to life in its nourishing traditions, such as those that Ovid helped furnish to the dominant literary culture of Renaissance England. And therefore, as through the haunting refrain of Ovid's nightingale in *Titus Andronicus*, culture is bound rhythmically to divide, punish, mu-tilate, and destroy the very members that it claims for its own incor-porate and incorporeal identity.

It was this recognition that drove William Blake, in *The Marriage of Heaven and Hell*, to suggest that one has not really read a cultural work unless one has somehow passed through it to another side, suffering a transformation in the process, as when its privileged consumers raise their eyes from a book and find life even in what they had supposed to be insensate stone. Similarly transformed, "I've dreamt in my life dreams that have stayed with me ever after, and changed my ideas," says Brontë's Catherine Earnshaw; "they've gone through and through me, like wine through water, and altered the colour of my mind" (62).[2] As if this figure were my charactery, she reminds me of cultural works to which I have repeatedly returned and from the experience of which I sometimes feel lucky to have emerged in one piece. A similar suffer-ance of culture is evident in all the acts of transformation—literary, artistic, religious, political, and so on—in which we submit to have ourselves burnt, devastated, confined, overwhelmed, or otherwise ravished in the hope that when we emerge from the event, close the book, turn from the painting, rise from the bed, whatever the case may be, we will have become unaccountable things at last.

Shakespeare turned to this point in *Julius Caesar* when he had Cassius exclaim, "How many ages hence / Shall this our lofty scene be acted over / In states unborn and accents yet unknown!" Brutus is then made ritually to repeat this prophecy of repetition: "How many times shall Caesar bleed in sport, / That now on Pompey's basis lies along / No worthier than the dust!" (3.1.111–16).[3] In thus insisting on a certain theatricality in the assassination of Julius Caesar—a theatricality portrayed as being intrinsic to the act, the plotting that preceded it, and its predictable historical resonance—Shakespeare did more than broadly wink at the artifice of his own dramatic work. At once closing and opening an eye, a curtain, an orifice of visions, he drew attention to the grief of ritual, which lies in the fact that it can maintain itself only insofar as it foresees its own disappearance into innocuousness.

Julius Caesar suggests that the difference between "butchers" and "sacrificers" (2.1.166), or between "murderers" and "purgers" (2.1.180), or between "a savage spectacle" (3.1.223) and the carving of "a dish fit for the gods" (2.1.173) is a matter of justice only inasmuch as justice is the coming to grief of repetition. Antony repeatedly offers Caesar the crown, and Caesar repeatedly refuses it: this piece of business is all the justification necessary to the conspirators. Like the statue of Caesar that appears in Calphurnia's ominous dream, spurting out blood in which Roman citizens bathe their hands, this imperial gesture invites conflicting interpretations. In fact, in the way this gesture takes place offstage and in its formal, hieratic, statuesque decorum, as of a manufactured figure that comes alive but then remains forever doomed mechanically to repeat the same motions, it is remarkably dreamlike itself. Shakespeare emphasized this aspect of the gesture by showing it exciting disturbed apprehensions in the conspirators in the same way Calphurnia's dream proved upsetting to her and to those around her.

In this context Calphurnia's bleeding statue becomes an emblem of classicism made grotesque, carnivalized, like the human bodies on which Aaron writes with a knife in *Titus Andronicus*.[4] The result is that grief in this dream, as in this play as a whole, bears almost no resemblance to its conventional understanding, which may be represented by the Duke's jingling platitudes in *Othello*: "He robs himself that spends a bootless grief" (1.3.209). Instead, grief is made out to be an all-encompassing ritual of rituals, overleaping all bounds. *Julius Caesar* suggests that grief can be rationally accounted for and profitably "ended" (1.3.202), as per the Duke's recommendation, only through submission to just such social, economic, religious, and political institutions as the Duke is designed so pompously to represent, so hollowly to sound.

A similarly dreamlike condition prevails throughout all the perfervid action of *Titus Andronicus*, as Titus recognizes in an exclamation in the middle of the play: "When will this fearful slumber have an end?" (3.1.252). The nightmare is introduced from the very first moments of the first act, as the audience finds a mutilated body, "headless Rome" (1.1.186), awhirl in acts of warning, appeasement, violence, and betrayal. Given the almost farcical pace of events, the sense of the moment is such as to suggest a carnivalesque hurly-burly of things tumbling over one another, each struggling to find some meaningful space for itself but finding only displacement, manic changes in temper and dimensions, so that it is virtually impossible to perceive any distinctions on the stage among words, thoughts, bodies, images, and settings, as in a theatrical *Finnegans Wake*.[5] The opening of the play introduces Titus as a noble warrior, a father, a merchant ship, and a figure of the legendary Roman past, among other things; and if we are expecting these figures to be easily integrated with one another, we had better think again.

The anachronism of my comparison to James Joyce's work is deliberate; for as the opening of this chapter suggests, anachronisms are fundamental to the haunted structures that yield such a nightmarish sense of the moment in *Titus Andronicus*. A brutally succinct definition of grief would be *an assault on one time by another*, as a grief-stricken person is one assailed by a brutal conflation of *thens* and *nows*; and it is at a grievously anachronistic juncture of histories, genres, styles, genders, and nationalities that *Titus Andronicus* begins. As the play continues, this sense of the moment is emphatically reconfirmed by the hectic collating and reworking of different sources—especially in Ovid and Virgil—through which the life of texts in tradition, like the blood of the statue in Calphurnia's dream, issues in events that make a mockery even of the most profound grief. The opening disequilibrium of *Titus Andronicus*, in the question of succession, is dramatically echoed in the succeeding contest over the possession of Lavinia, which divides Saturninus from his brother, Bassianus, and Titus from his remaining sons; but it is also echoed in these classical references that demand citation and fight for precedence throughout the play, with a wounding inattention to the boundaries supposed to define the internal and external forms of Roman civilization.

It has become traditional to regard the use of classical models as, among other things, a distancing device—in the instance of this play, one that might be presumed to detach its audience from the terrible immediacy of Lavinia's rape.[6] But, if this play is to have any emotional resonance whatsoever, I must suppose that this derives in large part from its insistence on the immediacy of its allusions to tradition, which would appear to have a status on the stage equal to that of any character, speech, or act. That is why the allusions in this play are treated in such a matter-of-fact manner: because its drama does not for a moment pretend that tradition has ever been anything but an agency of terrible violence. From the very beginning we are made to see that bookishness, like the ceremoniousness of the opening of this drama, is as bloody a business as any with which one could ever wish to meet.

It was just such a vision of the brutality of tradition that Artaud was seeking to display when he came to conceive of his ritualistic, magical Theater of Cruelty. His theater was premised on the demand that repetition not be rendered innocuous and that words not be separable from deeds, bodies, images, and inspiration; it was not for nothing that he instanced Elizabethan revenge tragedy as one of the sources of his work.[7] For just as "theft" was Pierre Proudhon's argot for property, "revenge" is the revolutionary term for repetition. Revenge is repetition's repetition, its monstrous ideal. (Hence the proverbial irony that "to pardon is divine revenge.") In revenge the identity signified by repetition is fully accepted and yet transformed by this acceptance, which convulsively scatters the constitutive differences of this identity across unsettling categories of being such as history, genre, style, gender, and nationality. Far from restoring an anterior state of being to its presumed original purity, the *lex talionis* proves to be a formula for revising and infinitely extending the constitutive conflicts in woefully preconceived plots. To put it as simply as possible, revenge teaches that identity is defined through ravishing tradition.

Thus it is that human life may actually turn to stone, as did Ovid's Anaxarete, or may be found in stone, whether in tombs or in some other cultural form. It is only logical that when Lavinia is pleading for Chiron and Demetrius to disobey their mother's sanguinary commands, she should tell her assailants, "The milk thou suck'st from her did turn to marble" (2.3.144). Undeterred, they perform an exuberant version of the rape of Philomela, as if working out the implications of W. Jackson

Bate's rather too casual observation that the classical example "often proves a Trojan horse."[8] Yet Lavinia's failure is no reason for not addressing oneself to stone, as Titus makes clear when one of his sons, Lucius, finds him lying in the road and imploring mercy for Martius and Quintus, his other surviving sons. "O noble father, you lament in vain," says Lucius, adding, "The tribunes hear you not; no man is by; / And you recount your sorrows to a stone" (3.1.27–29). To this characterization, Titus responds,

> Yet in some sort they are better than the tribunes,
> For that they will not intercept my tale.
> When I do weep, they humbly at my feet
> Receive my tears, and seem to weep with me,
> And were they but attired in grave weeds,
> Rome could afford no tribunes like to these.
> A stone is soft as wax, tribunes more hard than stones;
> A stone is silent, and offendeth not,
> And tribunes with their tongues doom men to death.
>
> (3.1.39–47)

Picture if you will stones melting onstage, stones weeping, stones being sucked into the mouths of babes, stones dressed up in clothes of mourning and performing the administrative tasks of a state, stones opening their mouths to show the bleeding stumps of their tongues—and you may get some sense of what that opening scene is designed to represent through the tomb of the Andronici, which is prepared to swallow and hallow the body of a young man. (Hazlitt nods, forgetting his beloved Shakespeare, when he says that "we do not quarrel with a stone.")[9] These sorts of metamorphoses exemplify the issue of grief as ritual, in which bodies appear as stony tablets animatedly telling of tradition.

Centuries later the sight of the grieving Heathcliff would lead Nelly Dean to say, with all the monstrous innocence characteristic of her tone, "I did not feel as if I were in the company of a creature of my own species" (124); but *Titus Andronicus* suggests that such transformations of species are a matter of course. In fact, it suggests that the rituals of grief regularly transform inanimate into animate matter and vice versa. In this play it would appear that such changes are even banal compared to some others, such as metamorphoses of bodies into tropes and corpses into cuisine. In the issue of grief as ritual, *Titus Andronicus* tells us, we must take these transformations quite literally if we do not wish to put our own bodies at any greater risk than that which they already suffer.

Or if we think of grief as an issue of a particular sort of ritual, that of gift-giving, we may say what Charlotte Brontë's Jane Eyre says: that "a present has many faces to it."[10] Legend tells of Trojan citizens who rued their failure to come to this realization in a timely manner, but grief itself is not a simple present and is never simply present. (After all, we may remember that Jane Eyre would come to regret even the seeming timeliness of her own ironic banter.) The same is true of other gifts besides grief; for how can one look at the many faces of a gift all at once, especially if each of them is looking back, searching out a recognition that must be mutual and yet impossibly multiple—and all the more impossible when the offering in question is the living soul of an inanimate thing such as a manuscript, statue, crown, or wedding ring? Shattered, the time of grief may be shattering even to the most familiar sort of offering. Can human eyes see all the faces of such a thing at once, or must we submit to the overwhelming vision of tradition in this regard? What can we possibly make of these fetish-objects, these grief-eaters that are the things we are supposed to know and love, these glorified greedy scars that we are? Can there be a gift that is not also ravishment, theft, revenge?

With these questions we may remember that although some offerings may seem intended to serve specific purposes, such as propitiation, thanksgiving, or seduction, many cultural traditions associate offerings with the suspension of differences between statement and response, giver and receiver, desire and demand, or subject and object. In modern Western ideals of love, for instance, informed as they are by the structuring of offerings in religious, political, and social practices with hundreds and even thousands of years of tradition behind them, the gift of love is commonly evaluated according to its success in figuring forth this suspension. Conventionally one wants neither to be a cringing supplicant nor a blind tyrant. This suspension, then, is not nothing (although Shakespeare's Lear mistakes it as such) but rather, precisely, everything in the presumptively universal offering of imagination, which appears in this context as the very possibility of culture through which we are to give ourselves one another and the world. (So Titus characterizes himself and his beloved Lavinia: "I am the sea; hark how her sighs doth blow! / She is the weeping welkin, I the earth: / Then must my sea be moved with her sighs" [3.1.225–27].) This imaginary suspension of terms is a recognition of communication as being nothing else if not fundamentally the shattering transcendence of sociality through sociality.

This is why we are supposed to make an offering of our ideals to the dead: because only the dead can be imagined fully to feel the irrationality of this immortal transcendence through mortal identifications. If the dead cannot feel it, or if our ritual offerings to them are not allowed to take place in a satisfactory way, then the irrationality that has not been suffered to be felt must instead be acted out dramatically, as in incestuous civil war. Then the genitive ambiguity in "the transcendence of sociality"—a phrase that may suggest either an absolute identification with or dismissal of society—can no longer be contained. It becomes a psychotic oxymoron, its presumed suspension of differences an unpardoning *sparagmos*, as we ourselves become offerings made by and to our inhuman exhumed tradition. The sacrificial excess that defines repetition as such—the *more and less* that defines the *same*—no longer serves as a stable ground.[11] Instead it arises from the ground, hauntingly, upsetting the material sense and efficacy of signs and so upsetting the very difference between words and things—and so rendering Artaud just as absolutely central to cultural history as he felt himself to be.

If the dead refuse our offerings, we become as the dead; sustaining tradition then comes to devour us; we are eaten from within by that which we no longer are able to recognize as part of ourselves. The philosophy of the boudoir is revealed as the rituals of the abattoir, and the pitilessness of psychotic violence is shown to be the unacknowledged and yet undeniable premise of the state and of the patriarchal identity traditionally taken to be coterminous with it. The repetition that constitutes tradition shows itself as rollicking revenge, incoherently proliferating. In Shakespeare's insufferably platitudinous Duke we then may come to see the likes of Gilles de Rais, Richard Nixon (a classic mass-murderer with state sanction), or Jeffrey Dahmer, the "serial killer" made famous for his sentimental, cannibalistic preservation of human remains. Similarly, in the noble Titus, "the woefull'st man that ever liv'd in Rome" (3.1.289), we may come to see one who stabbed his only daughter, who directly or indirectly encouraged the slaughter of twenty-four of his twenty-five sons, and who found gladness in promoting butchery and cannibalism among his fellow citizens as a way of taking revenge not only upon a specific woman but upon maternal nature in general.

"And bid that strumpet, your unhallowed dam, / Like to the earth swallow her own increase," Titus says to Saturninus of his wife, Tamora. "This is the feast that I have bid her to," he adds (5.2.190–92). Lest "Rome herself be bane unto herself" (5.3.73), the procreative matriarch must meet her match in the homicidal patriarch. This is the same logic momentarily teased into the open when Vittoria Corombona, in John Webster's tragedy *The White Devil*, finds she must "personate masculine virtue" if she is to defend her "modesty / And womanhood" (3.2.132–36).[12]

If the male idea is not there to distinguish life-giving from death-dealing agencies through the measure of its deliberate violence, one cannot hope to know what the ritual of a feast or the gift of a stone might be. ("And this ruling Male," said Artaud, "poets hitherto have called him Spirit" [7:160].) The wife of Titus Andronicus need not appear in Shakespeare's play;[13] her presence could only distract us from this lesson in the humanity of stones taught to us by tradition. Grief as an issue of gift-giving thus must return us to a genitive ambiguity of genitalia, violently divided as they traditionally are in their functioning as possessions and gifts, givers and receivers, males and females. The cultural logic at work here draws a parallel between the ritual entombment of the dead son and the sacrifice of the living enemy while basing both on the display of the daughter's raped and murdered body. As Sandra R. Joshel puts it, in writing of the woman typified by Livy's Lucretia and Verginia, "Her raped or almost raped and stabbed body kindles thoughts of men's own sufferings and feeds mass male action" so that "in an almost vampiric relation, the living are enlivened by the dead."[14]

Or, if we think of grief as an issue of death, we may say that grief is a repulsive emotion. It must be so because even when our traditional tales of cause and effect attribute certain deaths to disease, old age, or other "natural causes," we know that death is always an unnatural act. If it were otherwise, mortality would take its place in the universe of human beings just as we imagine it does among flies—whereas the fact that one can produce a striking simile by comparing human actors to flies tortured for men's sport indicates why death can never be a natural occurrence. ("Thy griefs their sports," says Saturninus' messenger to Titus [3.1.238], returning him his amputated hand along with the heads of his sons and, incidentally, anticipating Gloucester's famous outburst in *King Lear* [4.1.36–37].) In a more contemporary form, this lesson was also suggested by the great Vincent Price film, *The Fly* (1958), and by its fine 1986 remake: that for a man to die as naturally as a fly would require cultural resources that can only be imagined as available to a godlike genius. Obviously—all our traditions tell us so—there is nothing more unnatural than death. Death is always a social and cultural act.

Therefore it is eminently logical that this act, when turned to grief, should be regarded as a murderous decision. No one truly believes that death ever occurs innocently: when Artaud titled an essay "Van Gogh, the Suicide of Society," the title was striking only in its unimpeachable banality. If death is so perverse that the only satisfying form in which it can be imagined is the conspiratorial plot, as of gods or natural laws manipulating men, then it is only logical that grief should be found to be totally repulsive. Imagine the frustration of Artaud as he strove to assert a point so obvious, visible in every sign of grief—tears, fists, wails, weeds, stoic features, whatever the case might be—and yet still unrecognized as long as people would persist in representing grief as a conventional sign and thus as bounded within a satisfying form. So he wrote in *New Revelations of Being*:

> I am really identified with this Being, this Being that has ceased to exist.
> And this Being has revealed everything to me. . . .
> Dead, the others are not separated. They still turn around their cadavers.
> I am not dead, but I am separated. (7:151)

The living are dead because they do not experience their alienation, they do not know their nonexistence, and so, unlike Artaud—who is an "unpardonable Brute" (7:199)—they can find satisfaction in grief. By contrast, Artaud's is a nameless grief, a grief universal and entirely unselfish and so prophetic, apocalyptic, and pitiless. It communicates that it is our losses that bring us together, not our understanding, asserting in so many words that we are joined most profoundly by our traditions of brutality.

In the deadly earnestness that characterizes his writings of the 1930s and 1940s, when Artaud felt himself, like Don Quixote, surrounded by tormentors who enchanted him, conspired against him, beguiled him in his sleep, distorted the appearances of things, and tortured him, with a remarkable attention to his genitals, one sees the banalities of the social and cultural act of death for once taken seriously. Refusing to allow grief to dissipate itself in grief, respecting culture too much to allow it to hide itself in nature, so completely accepting mortality that he could not allow it to rest at ease in the deceiving signs of the corpse and the grave, Artaud prophesied an end for himself that could serve as a précis of the stories of Heathcliff in *Wuthering Heights* and of Titus Andronicus in Shakespeare's play:

> This means that Man is going to regain his stature. And that he will regain it *against* Man. This also means that a Man is going to reimpose the Supernatural. Because the Supernatural is man's reason for being. And man has betrayed the Supernatural.
>
> This also means that in a world surrendered to the sexuality of the woman, the spirit of man is going to win back his rights. (7:156)

In the war of Titus against Tamora, as in Heathcliff's sadism toward Isabella Linton—toward the desire of a woman who has the effrontery to dare not to be identified as identical to his own spirit—we see the tradition that demands Artaud's madness. Like the Heathcliff who finds himself degraded when he cannot see a "counterpart of himself" in the "bright, graceful damsel" (41) that is Catherine Earnshaw returning from the Lintons', the Artaud who regarded his genitals and saw a map of the iniquities of modern civilization was seeing again, repeatedly, the "map of woe" that is Lavinia raped for reasons of state, culture, history, and tragic art.[15] As if recalling in an especially loathsome way the condition of Marsyas after he lost his bet with Apollo, the people around him appeared to Artaud as nothing but wounds, death-in-life.

So it is with unimpeachable cultural logic that Artaud found conspiracy in ritual as in death. All of culture (of "his own" culture) was implicated in this conspiracy, which Artaud's ridiculous metaphysics was designed to counter. In *New Revelations of Being*, for instance, he invoked the tarot, prevision, numerology, the Kabbala, and a phallic cane and sword, among other eclectic things. In this way he sought to counter the brutality lurking in the ceremonious turns of causality and temporality commonly taken to justify this culture in which he felt his body threatened with dismemberment.

This sense of conspiracy, of course, implied that his culture had once been other than it now was. Like Titus and Heathcliff, Artaud could not imagine, except in fury and despair, a culture that would not mirror what he took to be his own male spirit. So when he wrote to a friend of a conspiracy against his desire to return "to an ancient pregenital notion of being that all sects and religions have abandoned" ("To Henri Parisot," 9:201), as when he cast about among the Tarahumara of Mexico for traditions, maintained with the use of hallucinogens, that would not be a matter of "legend" or "illusory fable" ("The Country of the

Magician-Kings," 7:78), he did not see himself as entering another culture so much as excavating what was buried in his own. In other words, he was searching out a fundamental and ongoing betrayal in Western cultural tradition, as he explained in a letter to André Breton that included laudatory references to Plato, Lao-tzu, Anaximander, and Hindu theology:

> There are Gods, though there be no God. And over the gods the unconscious and criminal law of Nature, of which the gods and We, which is to say *We-the-Gods*, are mutually victims.
> Paganism made sense, but Men who are eternal bastards have betrayed Pagan Truth. Hence christ has *come again* to return to the light of day this Pagan Truth, on which *all* christian Churches afterwards have ignominiously shit . . .
> Because the only secret is to learn to destroy the law so as to fall back into Non-Being *even over Eternity*.
> AND THIS ALSO IS THE LAW. (7:265–67)

Of course, Artaud was given to drug use, was judged to be mad, and resided for many years in a mental institution. Yet this history only makes it all the more striking that he should have hit upon the central plot of both *Wuthering Heights* and *Titus Andronicus* in his prophecies of the coming apocalypse of Western civilization. Similarly, it is notable that in his identification with paganism, with its echoes of his erstwhile surrealist brethren and also of Thomas Hardy, Algernon Charles Swinburne, Friedrich Nietzsche, and Sigmund Freud, among others, he was teasing out a sadomasochistic conception of law that *Wuthering Heights*, in its blaspheming protagonist, and *Titus Andronicus*, in its revivification of pagan legend, could also be said to promote. (In this regard it is only logical that in English *to grieve* is at once a transitive and an intransitive verb.[16]) And it is also significant that in 1943, while he was confined in the hospital at Rodez, Artaud dedicated a copy of his *New Revelations of Being* thus:

> To Adolf Hitler
> in memory of the *Romanischès café* in Berlin one afternoon of May 1932
> and because I pray GOD
> to give you the grace to remind yourself of all the marvels with which HE GRATIFIED (RESUSCITATED) YOUR HEART that day

kudar dayro Tarish Ankhara
Thabi

(7:430)

This was accompanied not only by a dedication of himself and the book to "THE ETERNAL INSTRUCTION OF CHRIST," but also by marginalia announcing the presence of the Antichrist and the war soon to be waged by this figure.

In the context in which I have introduced it here, what can possibly be made from his glossolalia, which Artaud practiced assiduously and included in many writings of this era? If we think of grief as an issue of death, or more particularly of death in a holocaust whose historical agents sought to justify themselves in the name of Western, Christian, pagan, and natural principles, with a pitiless disregard for what intellectuals often quaintly suppose to be logical boundaries, we may be led to see the very notion of tradition tearing itself apart in Artaud's language with a tortuous precision. Here as elsewhere, Artaud's glossolalia is the impossible sign of an apocalyptic end to the repulsiveness of grief, which in the absence of this sign would not allow him to bury the connections between what makes sense in civilization and what makes war upon it.

Considering grief as an issue of death can then allow us to see that in his anti-Semitism as in his misogyny, Artaud was a genius at following the logic of powerful cultural banalities all the way through to their mortal end, where grief finds its origin not in love but in death. Thus, in the living death of his persecuted genitals, which he could not or would not yield to Sonia Mossé, a woman who later died in a German concentration camp, Artaud suffered the historical persecution that he was driven to encourage and reproduce in his own writings.[17]

Or if we think of grief as an issue of burial, we may say that James Joyce got it right in "The Dead." Within our bodies and between them and the bodies of others, delineating their differences and distances, defining even the *feel* of these articulations, are the dead. We are graves, but so are these others, and so is the very air we breathe, like the other elements of our lives and the rituals by which we live. To focus one's attention on this state of being is to appreciate grief as the most brutal of all emotions, far more so, for example, than hatred or rage. Even in its milder forms it is a challenge to the very lineaments of the world. For what grief tells us is that we have graveyards, tombs, funerary urns, and the like only so long as they will suffer us to possess them. Maybe we are allowed to amuse ourselves by pretending that the place of death is a fine and proper place, one that is covered, walled in, mortised, nailed shut, sealed, or otherwise contained, but we can do so only by disallowing our knowledge that there is no place proper to death and no propriety in it. The grave is an essential marker of culture, and we may add that Nathaniel Hawthorne got it right in *The Scarlet Letter*: the grave is as one with the stones of the prison. The peaceful grave is a site of intense and unending cultural activity.[18] The multiple identifications that converge at the grave site—of names, relations, statuses, tastes, spatial and temporal orientations—radiate out from it to secure for cultural life the only markers of security it can have, as pathetic as they may be. Through disavowal the grave vouches for the truth that we acknowledge playfully, incidentally, or fearfully elsewhere: that the dead may walk among the living, and even as the living, making demands upon us; that we may be the dead, or possessed by the dead, while yet seeming to live; that far from being an ultimate bourne or eschatological event, death may be a piece of jewelry, an example of writing, a dream, a statue, or the very and entire world we think of ourselves as inhabiting, just as Artaud would have had it.

It was some such sense of things that brought Nietzsche to argue throughout his works that tradition is as much a burying and forgetting as it is a handing down of riches. To preserve the past in tradition means properly burying that past and thus, of necessity, not burying some things. (Obviously, the only things we ever truly suppose to be dead are those we leave unburied.) This is the sense of tradition marked at the end of *Titus Andronicus*, when the devilish Moor, Aaron, is sentenced to be planted breast-deep in the ground and left there to starve while for "that heinous tiger, Tamora," queen of the Goths, the following orders are given:

> No funeral rite, nor man in mourning weed,
> No mournful bell shall ring her burial,
> But throw her forth to beasts and birds to prey:
> Her life was beastly and devoid of pity,
> And being dead, let birds on her take pity.
>
> (5.3.196–200)

This situation reverberates through its parallel to the opening scene of the play, in which Lucius Andronicus, the same character who pronounces the foregoing sentence, proudly announces to his father the dismemberment, disemboweling, and cooking of Tamora's son, "the proudest prisoner of the Goths" (1.1.96):

See, lord and father, how we have perform'd
Our Roman rites, Alarbus' limbs are lopp'd,
And entrails feed the sacrificing fire,
Whose smoke like incense doth perfume the sky.

(1.1.142–45)

This demand for blood-sacrifice at the opening of the play is historically inaccurate only in the most literal, pedantic understanding of tradition. This is precisely the kind of understanding whose brutality this play is designed to expose, just as its allusions expose the wedding of Aeneas and Lavinia at the fabled origin of the Roman state as a composition of violent powers, not their conclusion and transcendence.[19] *Titus Andronicus* shows that the opposite term to grief is not happiness or joy, as a popular gloss might suggest, but rather sacrifice, which eliminates loss by pretending to choose it and by this pretense stuffing it full of repetition. (Obviously, death as repetition, the banality of death in general, can never be our concern.) *Titus Andronicus* further suggests that the opposing terms of grief and sacrifice create, support, and elaborate each other within the cultural poetics of the patriarchal, imperial, religious state, which always advances in a killing state of mourning.

No wonder the opening sacrifice in this play is performed to the life of the past, which is tradition: "To appease their groaning shadows that are gone" (1.1.126). Or we might say that it is made so the first words Titus Andronicus utters in this play will not seem paradoxical: "Hail, Rome, victorious in thy mourning weeds!" (1.1.70). Or more generally we may say the sacrifice is performed, the rites are fulfilled, the tradition is transmitted so death can be known in the only way possible: through the oratory, architecture, rituals, elections, and other arts that let culture represent itself. In overlooking the paradox to which Titus' opening words are vulnerable, these are the arts that will also turn away other figures, threatening figures, such as the irony in the comment on Rome that is offered by Chiron, a son of Tamora who will later return as murderer, rapist, and foodstuff: "Was never Scythia half so barbarous" (1.1.131). Figures of speech are ordered in accordance with the arrangement, derangement, and rearrangement of human flesh: it is thus that culture cooks its books to make all its accounts seem unaccountably to balance perfectly. It is thus that bodies are cut up, dressed, and served as ideals for our delectation.

In the opening of *Titus Andronicus*, Shakespeare emphasizes this relation between bodies and tropes not just once but repeatedly, as befits the relation that he presents as crucial to the functioning of ritual. Having been articulated in terms of the sacrifice of Alarbus, it returns al-most immediately in relation to Lavinia. After the sacrifice, when Titus agrees to throw his influence behind the claim of Saturninus to the position of emperor, Saturninus tries to seal the proceedings by pro-posing to Lavinia, Titus' daughter. She accepts but is abducted by Bas-sianus, the brother of Saturninus and a rival for the throne, who is aided in this rape by Titus' sons, who contend that Bassianus has a property in Lavinia that by right of tradition takes precedence over the claim of Saturninus. Outraged, Titus kills one of his sons, Mutius, and pro-nounces them all traitors (1.1.283)—a word that stems, of course, from the same root as *tradition*. When he then wishes to refuse Mutius a burial in the monument of the Andronici, he reluctantly allows himself to be argued out of his position by Marcus, another son, who offers the following words:

> Thou art a Roman, be not barbarous:
> The Greeks upon advice did bury Ajax
> That slew himself; and wise Laertes' son
> Did graciously plead for his funerals.
> (1.1.378)

Rhetorically Marcus recalls the bodies of Mutius and Titus to tradi-tion, here invoked so as to bury its internal betrayals or contradictions. By contrast, when Tamora leads her sons to stab Bassianus before en-couraging them to rape Lavinia, the latter will say, "Ay, come, Semi-ramis, nay, barbarous Tamora, / For no name fits thy nature but thy own!" (2.3.118–19). Her correction of herself in midsentence is the sign of the contradiction that she will not allow to have a name in tradition, which would imply a precedent bound to be repeated. In this context one could not say anything more killing than that someone has a name of her own. Tamora, who has pronounced herself "incorporate in Rome" (1.1.462), is thus expelled from her own body, as from the stones of nation and empire, without any possibility for a burial.

In seeking to strip Tamora of any name but her own, Lavinia seeks to deny her a sacrifice, a meaningful ritual, in the killing of Bassianus and in her own rape. She would have these acts appear only as butch-ery or senseless, innocuous play. She thereby seeks to refuse Tamora a sign and a burial for herself (foreshadowing her eventual fate), since a name that cannot be identified with any other must be particularized into meaningless particles, even as the dust in which the weeping Titus will scrawl his pleas and the bloodied Lavinia, with a phallic staff stuck in her mouth, her rape. And yet the way Lavinia takes note of contradiction is itself contradictory, as is made evident by her use of the term "barbarous," which Shakespeare by this point has caused to reverberate with the voices of Chiron and Marcus, among others. Lavinia's attempt to expel Tamora from tradition faces the contradiction of these reverberating voices, which give "barbarous" the impenetrable quality of glossolalia. Moreover, it meets with contradiction in the means by which Lavinia will communicate what has come to be her fate: the pages of Ovid's *Metamorphoses*, in which Tamora does after all bear other names, as traditional as they come.

In this respect the word "barbarous" proves to be of a kind with "rape," which is also torn apart, even as Lavinia's body is, in the opening acts of this play. To Saturninus' angry claim that he is a traitor for carrying away Lavinia, Bassianus replies, "Rape call you it, my lord, to seize my own, / My true betrothed love, and now my wife?" (1.1.405–6). He thus echoes the defense of Marcus, who seeks to forestall his father's claim that he and his brothers are traitors by saying, "*Suum cuique* is our Roman justice: / This prince in justice seizeth but his own" (1.1.280–81). So one man's tradition is another's rape, while in either case a woman can count on being abducted, plotted over, and toyed with, like a fly or dirt, as a preliminary to her remembrance in the ritual renewal of society. As Shakespeare recognized in alluding in this context to Aeneas, Virginius, Junius Brutus, and Procne, it is a story so often repeated as to have become commonplace, threatened even with innocuousness. The "many unfrequented plots" of the leafy forest that Aaron declares to be "[f]itted by kind for rape and villainy" (2.1.115–16) are the plots in fact frequented by classical literature and myth, as Titus and Marcus recognize when Lavinia "turns the leaves" of Ovid so as to tell the tale of *stuprum*.[20] Titus exclaims, "(O, had we never, never hunted there!), / Pattern'd by that the poet here describes, / By nature made for murthers and for rapes"; and Marcus replies, "O, why should nature build so foul a den, / Unless the gods delight in tragedies" (4.1.45, 56–58).

The quibble on "plot" in this play allows it to signify both a conspiracy and the innocent natural site ravished by it. We have the "obscure plot" in which the assault on Bassianus and Lavinia takes place (2.3.77) alongside the "fatal-plotted scroll" that is forged to implicate Martius and Quintus in the murder of Bassianus (2.3.47), even as Tamora herself speaks of the "complot of this timeless tragedy" (2.3.265). This quibble is of a kind with the reversals of agency and sufferance in the discussion among Demetrius, Aaron, and Chiron over the evidence, in the form of a dark-skinned infant, of what Aaron has "done" or "undone" with Tamora (4.2.73–77). It is also of a kind with the outright differences voiced in this play over what constitutes "barbarous" conduct and the act of "rape"—and this association is crucial. Through it Shakespeare suggests that in matters of place, character, and event, nothing is one's own save that which is unspeakably buried. (Obviously, the present that is one's own happens only once, ungraspably, while the past is endlessly repeated, endlessly transformed.) Lavinia's experience of violation may be imagined to be her own only until she communicates her story, at which point it is expropriated by Ovid even as she undergoes a metamorphosis, for good measure, into the slaughtered daughter of Virginius.

It is significant in this regard that the pit into which Lavinia's ravished body is thrown after she is abbreviated as to her hands and tongue is compared to Cocytus, the legendary river of lamentations in Hades (2.3.236). In this spot, as in the plot of the play as a whole, Shakespeare refigures grief as the consecration of filth, the heroic entombment of the son as the violation of the daughter, funerary commemoration as animalic defilement, ceremonious burial as savage plunder, and nurturing tradition as devouring violence. This is the sight from which the audience turns away in the views that are most common in the critical literature on this play, which wishes to derive at least a good portion of its violence from a tragic flaw in Titus. These views block out all the tortured signs with which Shakespeare suggested that the brutality at issue here derives quite logically from the highest ideals coursing through the blood of the idealized Roman state—that in this context there is nothing erroneous about it.[21] In other words, in this play Shakespeare suggested that what was unspeakably buried in Elizabethan culture, what presently was most its own, was the innocuousness of the relation between the rape of women and ravishing tradition, which paralleled a more general plotting of arms and lordly power against what might be called, if this trope could ever be returned from the status of an innocuous cliché, common humanity.

Therefore, the soothing promise Titus makes to Saturninus in the first scene of the first act of the play—"I will restore to thee / The people's hearts, and wean them from themselves" (1.1.210–11)—by the end appears as the fine words of a man whose idea of weaning involves knives. (Asking for a sword to chop off his own hands when he first sees Lavinia's dismemberment, Titus says that his hands "have nurs'd this woe, in feeding life" [3.1.74].) As Lucretia weaned herself from her shame, restoring heart to the Roman state, so Titus will plunge a knife in the breast of his daughter. Similarly, the end of the play merely spells out more explicitly the assumption that Titus makes in demanding the sacrifice at the beginning: that one best restores a heart by consuming it.

Titus Andronicus begins with the fatherland deliberately consuming its male children and ends with a father and mother inadvertently snacking on their sons.[22] In this way it suggests that tradition is cannibalism, as in the old sow eating its farrow of Joyce's *Ulysses*, which of course is itself a work preoccupied with classical tradition in ways that go beyond the merely titular. Furthermore, *Titus Andronicus* suggests that what gets raped in the woman of tradition is not the honor of the father and the son, as tradition would have it, but rather their own barbarously alienated, furiously plotting, terribly revolting flesh— the genitals of their own hands, as it were. It is not for nothing that Virginia Woolf came up with the device of Shakespeare's sister when she wanted to revolutionize the notion of what is one's own as it was handed down by what Titus calls the "pattern, president, and lively warrant" of tradition: "Die, die, Lavinia, and thy shame with thee, / And with thy shame thy father's sorrow die!" (5.3.44, 46–47). Woolf understood that this murderous coupling of the father's grief with the daughter's shame was a rape that moved all of tradition unless one insisted on betraying it, and so she put Judith Shakespeare on the page to honor Shakespeare through the transforming repetition of figures traditionally associated with his name. Such is grief as an issue of burial: this terrifying turning of mother's milk to stone, despoiling monumentality, the consuming nourishment of patriarchal social structures.

Or if we think of grief as an issue of decorum, we may say that the sleep of grief breeds monsters. "What bleeds leads" is a joking catchphrase among journalists at the moment I write this; and as I think of such officially unavowable mottos, in all their grim risibility, I am brought to remember a time many years ago when I worked in a hospital in the hinterlands of Minnesota. I met Heathcliff there in the form of a patient who had been brought in for observation while arrangements were made for a transfer to a psychiatric facility upstate. He was a white, plump, middle-aged woman who would not have stood out in any gathering of rural Midwestern types, as far as I could see. The story had it that her husband had died about six months previously, and ever since she had been bringing his dinner to his grave; the community tolerated this behavior for a while, but something had to be done when the caretakers at the cemetery complained that the dishes were piling up.

As I suppose my readers must feel if they have ever read *Wuthering Heights* with any sympathy, the monstrosity here lies in the reasonableness of these offerings and in the corresponding madness of the graveyard decorum called out against this Heathcliff who was unwilling to swallow clichés about "accepting loss," "getting over it," "learning to cope with grief," and "moving on." For there is a kind of grief that is not grief, or which requires us to recognize the ruthlessness of rue, the pitilessness of pity, by refusing to utter the official mottos of loss. For in this grief nothing has been lost; instead, one is missing something. Because one is there, the other must be, no matter how many silly persuasions or so-called forms of evidence may be marched out to assert the contrary. To deny this would be to deny the social nature of language, consciousness, and identity right on down to the ground, leaving one standing completely alone in an otherwise uninhabited abyss of a world. It is unimaginable, as it were demonstratively disproven by one's own continuing existence, that the other might not be there. Heathcliff thrusting his anguished face out of the window overlooking storm-swept moors, like Heathcliff shooing flies away from her potato salad and pot roast in a graveyard in Shakopee, would be perfectly willing to accept the conventional terms of grief if they had anything to do with his situation—but they do not. It is all some kind of dreadful, impossible mistake. To paraphrase William Faulkner, the other is not gone; it is not even the other.

So we have the counter-ritual, the offering of the cursing prayer, spit out through the "sharp cannibal teeth" (136) of Heathcliff:

> "And I pray one prayer—I repeat it till my tongue stiffens—Catherine Earnshaw, may you not rest, as long as I am living! You said I killed you—haunt me, then! The murdered *do* haunt their murderers, I believe. I know that ghosts *have* wandered on earth. Be with me always—take any form—drive me mad! only *do* not leave me in this abyss, where I cannot find you! Oh, God! it is unutterable! I *cannot* live without my life! I *cannot* live without my soul!" (129)

If I were this Heathcliff (as Catherine Earnshaw knew she was), this grief that is not grief could be described by saying just this: *She is here, and I miss her.* There is nothing to get over: it is just that somehow I am doing something wrong, or I am making a terrible mistake, because I am missing her. She is not missing; it is I who am missing her. What is missing is my fault, a fault in me, as those who study stones speak dispassionately of faults in the earth. And so Heathcliff gives Catherine a lesson in the grammar of cause and effect: "I have not broken your heart—*you* have broken it—and in breaking it, you have broken mine" (122).

From this perspective, it is so-called normal mourning that appears as a melancholic abjection of the self. Moreover, it may appear that in distinguishing mourning from melancholia, Freud did not allow himself this perspective only because he did not consistently take to its logical conclusion an idea that actually is scattered throughout his own writings, even as a dismembered foreign body. The idea is this: that in considering how subjectivity is implicated in specific social formations, we need to take into account how the formation of the patriarchal state always advances, through obsessional rituals, in a state of killing mourning. Logically, then, the narcissistic, sadistic, self-tormenting melancholic must be seen as simply impersonating the nature of the state—even though this conclusion decapitates Freud's distinction between mourning and melancholia and sends it gibbering out of control.[23]

To accept the notion of loss would involve an irrevocable change, a time opening onto the logic of tradition. One could come to terms with that, even if the only really adequate way ever to pay one's respects is to die. (So his wife taunts Heathcliff with his survival of Catherine's death [136], and Artaud comes to the conclusion that his survival is imaginable only if the others around him, who seem to be living, are all dead.) But, to refer to the notion of loss in the circumstances of which I write here would be grotesque. Obviously, for a Heathcliff, she is here; obviously the notion that she might be gone is unimaginable. To think otherwise would be to allow one's own existence to disprove itself or pitilessly to mock itself. It would mean submitting oneself to the imperceptiveness that those around one brutally suggest to be the stuff of merciful reason and triumphing morality.

Knowingly or unknowingly, in doing so they follow in the tradition of *Titus Andronicus*, in which the title character's first line—it demands repetition—is "Hail, Rome, victorious in thy mourning weeds!" Yet I might note that Shakespeare shows the vulnerability of Titus' rhetoric when he counterpoints it to Aaron's disdainful reference to "slavish weeds" in the opening of the second act of the play (2.1.18). Spotting this wound would enable me to argue, were I Heathcliff, that those who say this other is gone are persons besotted with normality, self-consuming cannibals, slaves of a despicably comforting grief. They cannot live without their reason, which is the confined and mutilated condition of perception through which they would deny the most in-controvertible reality—that of one's very existence—which comprises, of necessity, the existence of this other.

And so just like me or anyone else, you may find yourself suddenly returned to the inaugural moment of culture, at which point you must see that every determination of tradition is a gross political division and an insult to the plain light of day. This grief beyond grief, from which one cannot return except as someone else, or even something else, such as a god-touched bird, the alien species of Heathcliff, or the glossolalic Artaud—we cannot fully admit this if we are still in any way to entertain tradition. It is not tradition's opposite or antithesis; it is not even its doing or undoing; it is a way tradition will never be.

After all, despite all that I have said here of it, have I been able even to begin to introduce it? Am I not, as a traditional saying would have it, just banging my head against a stone wall?

She is right here, and I am missing her, or I am right here, and he is missing me . . . we call out to the night, let's say, or maybe we try to feed each other something of ourselves as if nothing is awry, or maybe you simply raise your eyes from this sentence . . . and what would one have to be not to recognize in these images, in our very blood, the vertigo one feels when loss casually takes a seat at the dinner table or stretches its imploring hand out of the book of a dream? What recourse is there but to insult perception right back with all the edgy cultural resources at one's disposal? Is there ever any other reply to the issue of grief as decorum?

Or if we think of grief as an issue of memory, we may say that in individual memory, as in cultural tradition, the activity of preservation and recall is really a form of interment. We murder to select, and what is selected does not live any more than what is not: it simply merits entombment while the rest is laid waste. That which is selected is also consecrated, of course, through the symbolic forms and associations that mark out a resting place to which our rituals thenceforth may return us. In this way grief is buried not only as the substance of memory but also and equally as pattern, typification, and rule. As such, it serves at once to confirm and extend the cultural formulations with which we are preoccupied. And yet, when its memory is not a burial but rather a bringing back to life—when the mottos of grief come alive and so cease to be clichés—grief, no longer grief, reveals the glossolalic ecstasy of cultural tradition.

Then we can see how far phrases like "the acceptance of loss" are pleonastic. We see how far, in its common acceptance, *grief* signifies not something that may be buried but rather an act of burial that has already taken place—that is even banal, as in the commonness of the commonplace to which Alfred Tennyson made reference in his elegy to Arthur Hallam. For as Tennyson would come to recognize, as he fled back into Christianity, jingoism, racism, and a willed stupidity in all things but brilliant poetic melody, a grief that is not already memorial in its very conception must be horrendously appalling. It is a violation that all of culture rushes in to label "denial" . . . as if all of culture were not itself a labor of denial, and as if all the suppositions of reason were not the elaborately embroidered articulation of our grief, and as if the instauration of culture were imaginable on a basis other than the shock of mourning attendant upon the loss of an imaginary paradise. Memory may remind us that whatever else they may do, cultural institutions such as religion are designed to teach grief as a technique of nostalgia in the same way that perspective might be taught today by an art school still invested in a Renaissance invention of tradition. Without this nostalgia, what bleeds leads, and no joke about it.

Thus, when Titus addresses Lavinia after her rape and mutilation—"Thou map of woe, that thus dost talk in signs!" (3.2.12)—he is addressing Rome and all of the cultural tradition with which he is taken through her. "I, of these [signs], will wrest an alphabet / And by still practice learn to know thy meaning" (3.2.44–5), he says, recognizing that his task is to learn all over again what it means to read and write. This lesson in grief as alphabets, signs, maps, and classical texts points to sacrifice as the ultimate material ground of society, which manages its members through those perspectives, caught up in the heady perfume of sacrifice, which are commonly termed *feelings*. And thus, through the map of woe that is Lavinia, we see the defilement of self in and through traditional social structures, including the structures of desiring, bleeding genitalia.

This is the pitilessness of pity: this technology of feeling, which makes life over into the image of death, demanding that it be undertaken through the guidance of sepulchral memory. As opposed to this technology, the brutality of grief is bound to seem demonic even as it may seem, as in Heathcliff, monstrously attractive in the simplicity of its offering. *For once in our lives to experience a loss not repaid, accounted for, experienced in advance* . . . such is the attraction offered by Heathcliff; but is such a Heathcliff even imaginable as a "realistic character," or must we readers deliver him over to characters that spell out pathology, stereotype, the conventions of gothic fiction, and the like?

In the memorial nature of culture everything about us, including our tongues and limbs, chatters hysterically with grief, ensuring that no sane person can truly miss anyone or really feel the Frankensteinian rending that would be adequate to one's passion. (This is the rending that Artaud insanely sought to face down through his identification of the legendary passion of Christ with the passion of Adolf Hitler, much as Christians had confronted it more decorously, at least to some minds, by identifying the figure foretold in Virgil's fourth eclogue with their savior.) And so, for all practical purposes, all articulate speech is grief speaking as technique. Hence the hatred of speech in the repetitiveness that defines those rituals that in turn define such things as religion, marriage, patriotism, the family, and, not incidentally, the formal calendrical framework, at once spiritual and nationalistic and marital, around Tennyson's so-called outpourings of feeling in "In Memoriam."

Whether we admit it or not, we all know that we are closest to animalic and psychotic states not when we are "expressing ourselves," as the saying would have it, or when we are "acting out" in a yowling, bashing, socially disruptive way, but rather in our most carefully elaborated rituals in all their compulsive, autistic splendor. Nothing is more civilized in its attention to ceremony than the brute beast blindly driven by instinct. In ceremoniousness the boundary of civilization is a grief beyond grief in which there is no way to distinguish love from cruelty. In metaphysics this vanishing difference between love and cruelty may be marked out on the scale of epic struggles between informing law and formless matter, master and slave, Eros and Thanatos, or the like, but these epic portrayals may actually have served more importantly as traditional distractions than as challenging insight. They distract us from all the intimate gestures and everyday acts invisible to tradition but constitutive of its most perdurable rituals, such as the reaching out of hands or the turning of flesh to stone. Nevertheless, these definitively indistinct acts have still shown up even in the most widely marketed forms of emotion, such as "love," insofar as they are touched with an angelic rigor that asks us to "be cruel only to be kind," as Hamlet puts it (3.4.178).

However plainly or indistinctly it may be felt, this grief beyond grief is an unbearable experience that we cannot touch save through the very traditions that bear it away. Liberty and the pain of survival look at each other as we stare at our images in a mirror. In this grief we find how ravishing tradition delivers us, in all senses of that word: at once giving birth to us, rescuing us, and handing us over to the defilement of a predetermined destination. This is the deliverance we see in the first line Titus speaks in the opening scene of *Titus Andronicus*, which dramatizes an act of entombment as the birth-scene of tradition. Some three hundred years after the writing of this play, when Napoleon crowned himself emperor of France, his act came to be seen as a dramatic breaking with tradition; but the opening of *Titus Andronicus*, which also involves the crowning of an emperor, would suggest that Napoleon got it exactly right. If anything, the Corsican's performance ought to be seen as fulfilling tradition by making explicit the imaginary beginning in which it must be conceived as having given birth to itself. This point is suggested by the way Shakespeare's play opens on a question of succession, with Saturninus protesting against "indignity" (1.1.8) before any such has been introduced or suggested onstage; and this suggestion is reinforced by the way this play shows the very mechanism of succession—by primogeniture, election, or some form of martial accomplishment—to be radically in dispute.[24]

Through this opening, this birth-scene, this violable entrance into the body of Roman culture, the ultimately incoherent relation between tradition and culture is put on display. Insofar as they may seem to make sense, each of these aspects of identity is supposed to authorize the other, the consecrated history being secured through the proper bodies, tropes, and rituals and these latter, equally, being secured through the former. And yet—as the opening funeral attended by ominous troops and shades makes clear—each can be known only through the prospects of generalized war, both natural and supernatural and both international and internecine. This is not to say that violent force decides the matter but, on the contrary, that violence is shown to be the most civilized of arts.

Thus it is that H. Rap Brown beautifully made Shakespeare our contemporary when he said that violence is "as American as cherry pie."[25] One may note especially the gustatory image, a cliché of modern American popular culture that so smoothly incorporates the Senecan pie that the woeful Titus arranges to have baked for Saturninus in the regenerative conclusion of Shakespeare's play. In this regard it is notable that this play was written and first performed at a time when torture, dismemberment, and execution were regular instruments and signs of sovereign justice, that divine revenge. (And by saying so, of course, I do not mean to downplay the existence of such practices today—quite the contrary.) Historically speaking, one can understand nothing of this play if one does not recognize that the gore in it appears as definitively *not* barbarous. So Jonathan Goldberg notes that "in the Elizabethan and Jacobean period among the favored public activities of the populace were theatergoing, bearbaiting, sermon attendance, and witnessing public executions and tortures." He goes on to add, "These are cognate activities; all are moral mirrors and displays of power."[26]

Anticipating Artaud's reading of revenge tragedies, Emily Brontë read this spectacle off the body of the Renaissance when she had Heathcliff appear "like a savage beast getting goaded to death with knives and spears." "I observed several splashes of blood about the bark of the tree, and his hand and forehead were both stained," says Nelly Dean, concluding, "Probably the scene I witnessed was a repetition of others acted during the night" (129). Yes, one might add, probably so; probably such repetitions are well known even to the theater of daylight.

Violence is the most civilized of arts in that it is utterly selfless, unlike the arts of war, religion, literature, and other fields of endeavor. Violence demands nothing in the way of honors and institutions for itself, being perfectly content to submit itself to any language, culture, and social order, content in the knowledge (and who among us does not share this knowledge in his or her heart of hearts?) that it is always there at the origin, no matter how that origin may be imagined. That is why the opening scene of *Titus Andronicus*, which gives birth to a new body to replace "headless Rome," is a scene of death and sacrifice; and that is why the only birth within this play, of the child of Aaron and Tamora, leads to a quibble in which the giving of birth and the suffering of ravishment are confused. ("She is delivered," says the nurse of Tamora, leading Aaron to ask, "To whom?" [4.2.61–62].) This is also why the birthing of this play focuses on a patriarch who has managed up until that point to have had twenty-one of his twenty-five sons killed, and this is why it ends with this father murdering another man's sons and feeding them to him. To put it succinctly, this play suggests that the entombed body is a sweetmeat for tradition. According to Titus Andronicus, Hamlet's eloquent outrage on this score—"the funeral bak'd meats / Did coldly furnish forth the marriage tables" (1.2.180–81)—shows his complete misunderstanding of tradition, wherein he grievously takes what amounts to its general rule as if it were a terrible violation of ceremony. Brontë knew better, as when she had Hindley Earnshaw show his grief over the loss of his wife by threatening to cut off his son's ears and break his neck. She further showed this knowledge when she had Heathcliff both displace and repeat the character of Hindley, just as Hareton Earnshaw would displace and repeat him. The civilized ending to *Wuthering Heights*, which sees Catherine Linton regenerating Hareton by teaching him his letters, is hardly soothing in this regard, unless we can hope against hope that they will not be reading anything remotely resembling the works of Shakespeare, Virgil, or Ovid.

But we need not turn to classical literature for this suggestion, given that even in love of the most banal *moon-spoon-June* sort there is always an offering to something else, to unknown powers and forms beyond the beloved. So too in the most "civilized" mourning we can glimpse, at least sometimes, a storm of grief that bears no resemblance to the force that Hamlet thought ought to be installing a teleological technology, a posture of foreordained cultural submission, in our deepest feelings. Finally, this is why it is important to think through grief as an issue of memory: because this path may lead us into the rough magic of everyday experience and out the other side, where we may remember some of that which is lost in our traditional forms of deliverance.

Or if we think of grief as an issue of feeling, we may say that grief reveals sympathy, the feeling with and for others, as barbarism. "O, what a sympathy of woe is this," exclaims Titus, "As far from help as limbo is from bliss!" (3.1.148–49). As surely as Cathy is Heathcliff, sympathy is cruelty: a terrible indignity, an insufferable identification, as when Heathcliff is outraged by Lockwood's fumbling attempts to excuse his intrusion into Cathy's bedchamber and the nightmare into which he wandered there. In this scene Heathcliff repeats himself, having already been outraged at the sympathy Nelly offered on the occasion of Cathy's death; obviously the repetition itself is the outrage, in that it threatens him with innocuousness.

Yet this reaction to having one's grief observed so stupidly, ridiculously, and pompously is what makes Brontë's Heathcliff, in comparison to Shakespeare's patriarchs, so curiously feminine. (By way of contrast, recall the composure with which Brutus and Cassius foresaw the impending innocuousness of their representations.) Through his identification with Cathy even beyond the point of death, which leads him to arrange to have their rotting bodies intermingled, Brontë showed that although Heathcliff usurped the role of the male head of the house, he saw and felt as a woman. In this respect, as in others—one may remember his legendary haunting—there was no obstacle to his reincarnation as a housewife in rural Minnesota in 1973. It is not for nothing that Heathcliff's son is repeatedly accused of being more lass than lad. In the dissimulated form of Linton, we see his father's character repeated in terms of the vengeful desire for sadistic domination and, yes, in the terms of femininity. In this way Brontë, following Shakespeare, portrayed the patriarch as being at the mercy of the very female figure that he must kill, and to such an extent that *his* idea is revealed as *her*

natural feeling, even as Titus' policy was made from Tamora's impulses—again, a disturbing point to anyone inclined to sentimentalize
the final scene between Hareton and Catherine, which finds her playfully, as we say, taking pleasure in her pedagogical control over him.

Since to feel grief sufficiently, monstrously, must be an act of brutality
against all the world sufficient even to change one's gender or, as Artaud had it, one's genital state of being, the soothing of this feeling
through the pretense of understanding must be barbarously inhuman.
Culture is then a tear of grief, but a tear that is also a slashing sword.
And it then appears that while in pious acts we swallow all our pride,
in mourning we kill. We are brought to recognize our traditions as
traitors to us not incidentally or coincidentally to their spiritual functioning but thoroughly, all-pervasively, in every possible experience in
which we may be implicated. Logically, then, one might conclude that
to love one's sons, one must bury them; to avenge the rape of one's
daughter, one must kill her; to show sympathy, one must slaughter.
Similarly, one might conclude that the only place where one can hope
to find true sympathy is in a Theater of Cruelty.

All of which is to say that in the feeling of grief we may come to
recognize that the past must have its revenge upon the present. In its
identification with the past through tradition as in its assumed transcendence as the here-and-now, the present is a continual insult to the
past, and the past must have its revenge. That is why in our lives we
are bound to meet with living stories, or elements of our cultural heritage that demand life, as in the way figures such as Hecuba, Lucretia,
and Philomela haunt Titus Andronicus, or as in the way Heathcliff
came before my senses in Minnesota. The power of tradition is the
power of haunting examples that will ravish us, silence us, even cut
away our tongues, hands, or breasts—assuming that cultural tradition
even allows us to tell the differences among these body parts and parts
of speech.

The present is defined by sacrifice, for we must give up some portion
of the present to appease the dead who would otherwise demand all
of it. For it is in the act of memorializing that we at once mark and
remark boundaries such as those between the living and the dead, the
past and the present, the public and the private, the victor and the
vanquished, and the text and the present event. In this way one takes
life as being in, as, and of signs (of which the tomb and the funeral
oration are exemplary) instead of taking life as Tamora urges Titus to
seize it: as sympathy. In the context of this feeling of grief, sympathy
can only mean degradation, unthinkable satisfaction, a meaningless lev-

eling of distinctions, the Christian shit against which Artaud railed, in fact a general collapse into chaos in all realms of life. It can only suggest a death without Solon's happiness, which is the pleasure anticipated in and through death.

The feeling of grief is then a story, a plot of earth, handed down to us, and to release ourselves of this feeling we must repeat it. This is the awareness to which Titus comes after the rape of Lavinia.[27] *Revenge* is the conventional term for this situation, but the conventional understanding of this term does not begin to touch upon all that is comprehended within it. We need to ask, for instance, what kind of revenge is involved when Titus says to his daughter, in the aftermath of her rape and mutilation, "Lavinia, go with me. / I'll to thy closet, and go read with thee / Sad stories chanced in the times of old" (3.2.81–83). What kind of revenge seeks out grief for grief?

Here as elsewhere in Shakespeare's play, what we see is grief as the object of desire. As the most eminently social of feelings—the ground of imagination and the foundation of the state that advances in killing mourning—grief must always be a state that is anticipated, desired in advance of its appearance, if it is to make any sense when it does in fact appear. Therefore, strictly considered, the loss to be mourned is a loss that has been desired, and in any given case of grief we must recognize our appetite for destruction. If we do not in some way see as our own kind these others whom we sacrifice, then the sacrifice becomes innocuous, even as flies to gods or Roman stage plays to clowns in the Elizabethan audience. For cultural rituals and reproductions to have any meaning, we must desire the destruction of the very thing that we mourn even to the point of experiencing a mad grief beyond grief. This is the logic to which Artaud took a shortcut when he announced the apocalypse already at hand in his *New Revelations of Being*: "It is thus that from all sides the Destruction sought everywhere has been unconsciously desired by everyone and I maintain that it is occultly *wanted* by everyone as the only means of saving ourselves from a world where life no longer can exercise itself" (7:165). This is the logic that leads the dying Catherine Linton to tell Heathcliff, who ostensibly has come to grieve her impending loss, "You have killed me—and thriven on it, I think" (122). And this is also the logic that can lead us to see in the repeated attack on Lavinia—repeated in the first instance through her status as an overdetermined classical allusion, then by way of her *two* attackers, then when Titus kills her in the last act of the play, and then again in the works of Brontë and Artaud, among others—an admission that the destruction that comes upon her has been desired in the first place by her own father, who could not profitably mourn her otherwise. Through its anticipation already to have survived death: as Shakespeare represents it, this is the formula for both murder and masterpieces.[28]

When Marcus first leads the ravished Lavinia to Titus, he says, "I bring consuming sorrow to thine age," thus leading Titus to reply, "Will it consume me? Let me see it then" (3.1.61–62). In this desire to be consumed by grief—as by the earth that swallows her own increase, as by the Rome who devours her martial sons, as by the pie in which Procne will forever serve up Itys to Tereus, the rapist of her sister Philomela—Titus admits a desire for mournful death that is already within him but that is still formally to be withheld until he stabs Lavinia, thus completing in deed what he, as a good Roman citizen, has always had to desire in imagination. His subsequent death at the hands of Saturninus is, strictly speaking, redundant, like the punishment that he had earlier ritually carried out on the corpse of a fly (3.2.71–75); for Titus has shown that in reality he is already scattered elsewhere, as in the bodies of Chiron and Demetrius that were baked in the pie consumed by Saturninus. And so in stabbing Titus, Saturninus must also stab himself—as his own redundant death will immediately remind us. All this seemingly excessive violence is the sign of repetition recognizing and renewing itself in the love of death that so moves it. Or to put it in other terms, all this seeming excess is the sign of a scar in the process of assuming a phallic cloak of dignity for itself.

If we take seriously these tropes and their movements in this direction, then the feeling of grief must appear as something of a joke. And this is precisely Shakespeare's suggestion; hence the significance of Titus's "determin'd jest" when he says of Tamora and her sons that he "will o'erreach them in their own devices" (5.2.139, 143). The feeling of grief is something of a joke because one will have repeatedly acted out, in desire, precisely the plot whose effects one will claim to regret. All of what is called cultural tradition contributes to this joke—indeed, *is* this joke—as this play suggests through the eerie equanimity with which Lavinia, her assailants, and her mourners all recognize themselves as participating in a revival of Ovidian literature.

Tamora and her conspiring sons, Chiron and Demetrius, especially take this lesson to heart. That is why they can present themselves to Titus at the end of the play as the allegorical figures of Revenge, Murder, and Rapine: because they wish to offer themselves to Titus as the image of his own desire. The fact that he sees through their device in no way lessens its cogency, as he himself admits in his eagerness to advance its consuming plot. Their failure is simply the mirror image of his success, its openly acknowledged and yet playfully disavowed identity, as with the Ovidian mirroring in the play as a whole, while what triumphs over all is the deathly cultural ideal of a sorrow that would consume itself and thus free the imperial ego from its mortality. Such is grief as an issue of feeling: an artistic task.

Or if we think of grief as an issue of writing, we may say that it is indeed the sign of life as being in, as, and of signs. Logically prior to and irrationally exceeding its functioning as a technology of communication, writing's moment of origin is imaginable only in terms of the selfless, generalized violence of grief beyond grief. To draw attention to this issue, *Titus Andronicus* presents its spectacularly overdetermined villain—the black, foreign, adulterous, atheistic, conspiratorial, and forever *un*grieving Aaron—as the figure who writes the words of undying tradition:

> Oft have I digg'd up dead men from their graves,
> And set them upright at their dear friends' door,
> Even when their sorrows almost was forgot,
> And on their skins, as on the bark of trees,
> Have with my knife carved in Roman letters,
> "Let not your sorrow die, though I am dead."
> (5.1.135–40)

Although bound to appear as the figure of the alien who would violate all that culture and tradition hold dear, Aaron is also bound to appear as the sedulous agent of tradition. That is why he understands Roman culture even better than its adherents, as when he demands that Lucius swear an oath, knowing that even in the face of his enemy's open derision Lucius will still be held fast through these words. Aaron is not laid waste at the end of the play simply because he is evil, or even because he represents specific acts (as of atheism, adultery, and miscegenation) deemed evil by the dominant culture of Shakespeare's time. Rather, his real crime is that he figures forth a social contradiction as repellent to the technology of writing as it is to the technology of grief. The figure bound to be misrecognized so that cultural recognition may seem attainable, Aaron must die that grief may live; he must be inhuman so that inhumation may take place; he must be turned forth from the body of Rome so that Lucius may return from the Moors with the tropes of Rome incorporated within his body:

> I am the turned forth, be it known to you,
> That have preserv'd her welfare in my blood,

And from her bosom took the enemy's point,
Sheathing the steel in my advent'rous body
(5.3.109–12).

In effect, Aaron is Shakespeare caught in the act of manufacturing a fantasmatic identification between himself and Roman civilization, Shakespeare spurning and punishing the illegitimacy of his own dramatic devices—with their exhumations, miscegenations, and competitive recarvings of classical writings—and thus Shakespeare ritually repeating the violent act through which he pledged allegiance to the imaginary configurations of Elizabethan social order in all their nightmarish splendor.

At the same time and through the same gestures, Shakespeare was doing battle in this play with the image of a past that was bound to seem pagan and merciless in the context of Christian ideals. He was seeking to incorporate this past into his art, thus making the crimes of the play figure as *idealized* crimes, ravished ravishments. In this respect, he was repeating a figurative act that goes back at least as far as Pliny's telling of how Zeuxis carried away the art of Apollodorus;[29] and so in this respect, too, his authorship was bound to suggest a similarity between the usurping Aaron and himself.

This resemblance is emphasized by the way this play shows writing coming to grief in its every appearance. All signs come to appear as of a kind with the "martyr'd signs" (3.2.36) of Lavinia's handless, tongueless dumb show. In addition to the engraving of corpses practiced by Aaron, we are offered, for instance, the example of Titus with "the bloody battle-axe, / Writing destruction on the enemy's castle" (3.1.168–69). Titus also writes in the dust, with his body and his tears, as he begs in vain for his sons' life; in the air, with arrows that have letters addressed to the gods stuck on them; and with his own blood (5.2.14).[30] As these examples should indicate, when Lavinia makes signs with her handless "arms," she is a dramatic rebus illustrating the identification of signs and weapons, imploring and destructive arms. This is the commerce between letters and arms displayed in a more comic but still gruesome manner in *Don Quixote* and, of course, in our own journalists' motto: What bleeds leads.

This identification of imploring and destructive arms disturbs the funeral ceremony at the opening of this play precisely so the audience may seem to have faced an anomalous disturbance, and not the agonizing agency of living tradition, by the time it witnesses the obsequies that Lucius Andronicus pronounces over Titus at the end of the fifth act. This violently self-subverting trajectory is epitomized in the scroll Demetrius and Chiron, Tamora's sons, find wrapped around a bundle of weapons sent to them by Titus: "*Integer vitae, sclerisque purus, / Non eget Mauri jaculis, nec arcu*" (4.2.20–21). In asserting that the pure and innocent man does not need the Moor's weapons of war, these words from Horace's odes (and from William Lily's Latin grammar) deny an identification of cultural with martial arts even as this denial functions, covertly, as a weapon in Titus' plans for reasserting his idealized cultural identity.

Demetrius and Chiron represent a more commonplace sort of thug than Aaron and so seem oblivious to the endless suggestiveness of these lines, but the Moor has a different reaction. He recognizes these "weapons wrapp'd about with lines" as a threatening "conceit" (4.2.27, 30)—which is, one might add, the conceit that structures the entire play. This conceit is armed with a memorialized literature written in disdain of others' arms; it is literally supported by arms offered freely to these others; and it figuratively serves to prepare a more effectively composed, because ironically pointed, violence. Thus, this device shows tradition to be a form of identification based on a denial of the communications that take place between "arms" and "arms," quills and arrows, records and wreckage, purity and violence. When Titus says of his enemies that he "will o'erreach them in their own devices," the apparent contradiction between this and the Horatian statement is consumed in the larger structuring of denial that is tradition set forth, ritually represented. In other words, this device displays the educational, nationalistic, martial, gendered nature of the feeling traditionally called grief. In this regard, it is notable that it is Lucius, he of the opening sacrifice and the closing funeral oration, who delivers (and thus is delivered by) this conceit.[31]

To clarify this final point about the politics of grief, I might offer here the example of a *New York Times* headline, "In a Tiny Haitian Port, Even Grief Is Political"[32]—a very traditional headline in a sense, in its assumption that it is only in aberrant, foreign, Third World circumstances that grief could be political—as if there had never been such a figure as Antigone—as if Sophocles' classic play were still waiting to be read for the first time, along with the works of Shakespeare, Brontë, and Artaud.

Or—well, yes. For all that I have essayed to suppose here in the name of grief, all of which has seemed deserving of my time and that of others, I must also suppose that it has all been a waste. What might not be the transformations that I would have undergone—and you, too, who read this—if the structure of suppositions that I have entertained here were imaginable only as a kind of fantastic, dreamlike play? If the words of Shakespeare, Brontë, and Artaud could not so much as begin to touch us, could be at most so much rich gibberish, like the screeching of a tropical forest to one raised in regions of rattling winds and creaking, squeaking snow? If my hand confessed no cunning, my pulse no rhythm, no matter how obscure?

I do not know that I am glad to have been able to write this, and I do not know that it matters much at all, either this or the attendant uncertainty. This sense of the moment, too, might be supposed to belong to the haunting feeling with which I have been preoccupied here.

Unpardoning tradition, I know nothing of time.

Captioning the Image of Tradition

Phillis Wheatley and Preposterous Authority

THROUGH ITS ETYMOLOGICAL RELATION TO *captor* and *captive, caption* is a term that might be expected to convey some sense of violence. Nevertheless, the common understanding of this term is oblivious to any such thing; if violence once was rooted within it, it would seem to have become illegible. This word no longer serves as a caption to its historical derivation. It has been carried away from that and taken somewhere else to serve a different meaning.

Such a history of deracination certainly befits the term, which has come to signify an identification accompanying a work on which it is dependent. In other words, the caption is popularly understood as a willing captive to its rightful captor. An object, image, illustration, document, or printed text stands before us, and the caption attends upon it, as Ganymede upon Jupiter. If the establishment of such distinctions must presuppose an act of violence at some point in time, as in the abduction of a beautiful youth by a fierce divine eagle, it would seem to be an act with which we are unconcerned. If violence there has been, it has been totally sublimated, as in the history of *ravissement*, which signified a forceful abduction before medieval French carried it away from that to suggest various kinds of religious, emotional, and romantic transport.[1]

In the common understanding of the caption, a past any different from the one that leads to the present distribution of properties appears virtually unimaginable. It would seem that certain distinctions have been destined to be put into place; and so just as there is no captive without a captor, we can say that the caption would have no reason for being were it not for the work to which it owes its obedience. This servitude may take the form of naming, explaining, describing, clarifying, highlighting, criticizing, praising, or in some other way supplementing the work supposed to dominate our attention, but in any case the caption is seen as logically posterior to the work, following upon it in a more or less inessential, adventitious, and humble way.

To be sure, in some instances captions may be altered, as with paintings scholars judge to have been misattributed or misidentified by the benighted souls who came before them. They may also be subject to abuse, as with Robert Capa's most famous photograph, "Death of a Loyalist Soldier" (1936), which has been suggested to be some kind of fake.[2] Or they may be played with in various sorts of games, as in the "art of reading" by the technique of "deliberate anachronism and erroneous attributions" that Jorge Luis Borges describes at the end of "Pierre Menard, Author of Don Quixote" ("Would not the attributing of *The Imitation of Christ* to Louis Ferdinand Céline or James Joyce be a sufficient renovation of its tenuous spiritual counsels?").[3] Furthermore, captions may range from an indeterminate minimum—for instance, in the numbering of a catalogue raisonné—to an indeterminate maximum, which may have been approached by the Smithsonian Institution's 1991 exhibition "The West as America," which offered wall texts that were roundly condemned for intruding on or misrepresenting the works of art on display.

Despite the diversity of cases, and even as it is expected to remain subject to possible examination and correction, the caption is still commonly thought of as a humble servant. It would seem that nothing but empirical happenstance, formal conventions, or pragmatic contingencies should stand in the way of works' being properly captioned. By the same reasoning there would seem to be no logical impediment to objects, images, or texts standing alone, by themselves, uncaptioned. Indeed, many would argue (in so many words) that we can measure the progress of our understanding by the extent to which we can do without captions in our apprehension of a given object. Handbooks are for beginners, they might say, and docents for vulgar tourists, glosses for tyros, footnotes for pedants, wall texts for those interested more in politics than in art—whereas what *finally* matters is our grasp of the thing itself, informed as it must be by traditions we have "made our own."

Of course, this understanding of the caption has never gone entirely without question,[4] and especially over the last several decades it has been extensively criticized, most notably in the writings of Jacques Derrida. Yet even in these writings, this sense of the caption cannot be rejected out of hand. Instead, it proves to be as unavoidable as it is inadequate to its own logical presuppositions and entailments. The caption of tradition proves neither entirely necessary nor entirely dispensable. Or so I would claim, even as I recognize that there is nothing particularly captivating about the formulation that I have just offered. If it is to be meaningful, it will have to be made at least as compelling as the seemingly unimaginable violence through which the common understanding of the caption has been established.

To this end I might begin as modestly as possible by noting that, formally, empirically, and pragmatically speaking, a caption often precedes the thing it is supposed to follow. A patron might commission a painting on a set theme, such as "The Rape of Europa"; an event, such as a death, might yield a title to a poet before she has any idea of the poem that ought to go with it; or an entrepreneur may try to invent a thing by throwing out a name and hoping the reality will follow, as in the practices of modern advertising ("Oh, no, I have *combination skin!*"). However trivial they may be in themselves, such examples suggest the possibility of a more general reversal of the logic that structures the common understanding of the caption. It seems that ravishing captor and willing captive may revert to the status of wary strangers jockeying for precedence; and once they have appeared, what is to restrain the revisionary possibilities offered by this image? Are they not bound to seem terribly immodest in their potential effects, so much so that all communications between captors and captives—and even the very sense of these terms—may suffer a metamorphosis before our very eyes?

After all, whether or not a caption appears to have preceded a given thing, that thing is always subservient to the very conception of the servile caption. The thing in question must have been classified, captioned in that fundamental sense, before it was apprehended as any kind of thing at all. As J. B. Baillie noted in his translation of Hegel's *Phenomenology of Mind*, the word *perception* has its roots in taking (*capio*).[5] To say "artwork" rather than "fetish," "curiosity," "frame," "ornament," "relic," "instrument," "urinal," or "trash" is already to caption a thing, no matter what else one may do to represent it; to say "elegiac poem" rather than "autobiography" or "story" or "nonsense" is already to seize hold of the thing in question, which cannot even *be* a question outside of such generic considerations. Rightly or wrongly, for good or ill, for an hour or an eternity, things come to us as they came to Adam, in kinds; in this regard it is important to remember that *kind* and *unkind* once meant "natural" and "unnatural." Whether or not a caption in the ordinary sense of the term is visibly attached to it, all objects of our apprehension bear the caption of being "of a kind" in this classificatory sense, which therefore can be said to delimit all formal, empirical, and pragmatic rules, including my own formulation of this limit. Captioning establishes both the possibility of these rules and the inadequacy and excessiveness of that possibility, which is bound to confound itself in historically telling forms.

Despite all their differences, which certainly are not negligible, all such rules strive to keep the caption in a fixed orbit around the master work. They do so either by forever multiplying epicycles of explanation—arguing that the caption only *seems* to come first in some instances—or else by cutting off explanation at crucial points through a dogmatic stipulation of a delimiting ethics or ethnos. Yet in order to have been developed at all, these rules must have presupposed objects to be marked out before them, or captioned in advance, no matter how provisionally; and so the unofficial history contained in such presuppositions, no matter how much it may be denied, internalized, and repressed, is bound to belie the common image of the caption as an entirely subservient and naturally dependent kind of thing. Instead there arises the possibility that the divisive, violent roots of all things may be betrayed, as if in a moment in which the composure of one's thought were suddenly interrupted by someone else's moving memories. In such moments that which is taken to be original shows itself to be a figure imagined out of the movements of fundamentally incommensurable preoccupations and aftereffects.

One result is that as we face the future, we are driven into the past, like a boat failing to make headway against a river's current or (let us say) against all that would distinguish the luminous promise of a New World from an Old. Like Nisus in the *Aeneid*, who wonders whether the gods put desires in men's minds or whether these desires become men's gods,[6] temporal, hierarchical, and causal orders show themselves to be implicated in one another and, therefore, subject to radical questioning. History becomes a pressing issue as the appearance of so-called natural kinds turns out to be a kind of cultural production, only one among many real and imaginable others, and thus an appearance that puts us in a peculiar bind.

On the one hand, a given caption is likely to be very much under the power of a work's mastery, which it will not be able to appropriate to itself except through what is perceived to be error, abuse, or ritually sanctioned play. This, one might say, is a matter of history, undeniable history. On the other hand, the caption can serve in this position only because of its definitive capacity for unintentional detachment: its profound rootlessness, which Derrida has described in terms of the iterability of the mark.[7] Therefore, paradoxically, the caption is always liable to detach itself from its root in the Latin word for "taken" and to assert itself over its associated work, which then will appear as in some part its captive—and this possibility, too, is history.

Although my purposes here have brought me to linger on an explication of the caption in relation to the work of Derrida, which so many persist in taking to be aberrant or destructive in relation to tradition, there is nothing more traditional than this paradox epitomized in the etymology of *caption*. For instance, when Shakespeare described Tarquin in "The Rape of Lucrece" as "a captive victor that hath lost in gain" (730), it was in this historical bind that he was wrapping his words.[8] This was a familiar point for him, as is evident in the figure it also made in one of Aaron's speeches in *Titus Andronicus*: "And now, young lords, was't not a happy star / Led us to Rome, strangers, and more than so, / Captives, to be advanced to this height?" (4.2.32–34). Or one might instance in this regard the exegesis played out in the drama of *Cymbeline*, which opens with a gentleman imitating the ravishing role of Tarquin; dwells upon the theft, or ravishment, of the heirs to Cymbeline's kingdom; and comes to a conclusion through the precipitate image of the ravishing eagle of Jupiter and Roman empire. "Although the victor," Cymbeline is brought to say, "we submit to Caesar" (5.5.460).

John Milton is another who found cause to dwell on this paradox, as when he played on the relation between "rapt" and "rape" by using them to begin phrases only ten lines apart in a passage in *Paradise Lost* in which Michael is enabling Adam to foresee the stories of Enoch and Noah (11.706 and 11.717). One might instance as well the concluding line to one of John Donne's most famous poems: "Take mee to you, imprison mee, for I / Except you enthrall mee, never shall be free, / Nor ever chast, except you ravish mee."[9] Examples such as these indicate why certain scholarly debates that continue to this day—for instance, as to whether Rembrandt's *Rape of Ganymede* should be read as exemplary of or parodic toward classical tradition[10]—are bound to remain unresolvable in some respects. For tradition—as tradition has been bound to recognize—can be identified as such only through its captioning, an act in which the caption ruptures identities even as it constitutes them by seizing, transporting, or ravishing things.

As he recognized in pointedly captioning one of his fragments

"Danaë and god in gold," Friedrich Nietzsche was writing in this traditional vein when he commented on the capitalist desire of his era: "In this impatience and this love . . . there turns up again that fanaticism of the *lust for power* which was in former times inflamed by the belief one was in possession of the truth and which bore such beautiful names that one could thenceforth venture to be inhuman *with a good conscience* (to burn Jews, heretics and good books and exterminate entire higher cultures such as those of Peru and Mexico)."[11] In effect, Nietzsche's caption spells out the task of any historical criticism of tradition, which is to grasp the struggle in things that captions can never completely seize, no matter how truthful or beautiful they may be. He might have been commenting on John Keats's "Ode on a Grecian Urn," from which there emerges a captioning statement, "Beauty is truth, truth beauty," which has proven to be remarkably impressive even though readers have never been able to agree on its proper punctuation, source, reference, meaning, or value.[12] From Nietzsche's perspective, and given that Keats's poem is concerned with the interpenetration of cultural tradition and rape, desire, death, and religion, this textual situation does not seem accidental but rather predictable and even in some sense necessary. For along with whatever else it may say, what caption does not spell out "Danaë and god in gold"? What caption can keep itself from pointing to the social practices on which all ideals depend—such as rape, appropriation, canonization, sacrifice, and extermination—even while seeking to contain and neutralize their force?

Insofar as we are creatures of tradition, we forever find ourselves taken with the caption. For instance, as a consequence of this situation readers are bound to learn, with reliable hermeneutic circularity, that a poem is a poem if it is taken to be a poem in a sufficiently ravishing way somewhere, somehow, by someone. Similarly, it makes sense to say that a woman is made, not born—although she is also born, perhaps "as a young plant by hurricanes up torn," as Phillis Wheatley put it ("To a Lady on the Death of Three Relations," 52).[13] It also makes sense to say that slaves are never simply slaves in and of themselves, but only within a dialectic of master and slave that cannot hope to be all-encompassing even within the domain over which it is supposed to extend. Simultaneously and incorrigibly, startling reversals, violent reclassifications, and entirely different orders of captioning will carry themselves into experience.

To understand the caption is then to confront the possibility that what is last may be first and what is first, last—a possibility in which understanding must engage in a preposterous struggle to stand over against its own structurings and energies even as it is embroiled with certain quite specific historical tasks. For instance, an eighteenth-century poet in this situation, one who is driven to find her end in her beginning by the very same terms that bar her from that origin, might lead her readers—or might herself be led—to emphasize the limits of what is commonly labeled "imagination." Having addressed imagination in familiar images as "the leader of the mental train," the "sov'reign ruler" of "subject-passions," a power capable of making "gay scenes arise" even while *Winter* frowns" ("On Imagination," 66–67), this poet might conclude (if she is Phillis Wheatley) with the alien, inhospitable winter of a northern climate suddenly reversing this supposed precedence. In the place of imagination she might put instead, as in one of her elegies, sublimely unimaginable "pleasures without measure, without end" ("A Funeral Poem on the Death of C.E.," 71). In other words, she might lead us to wonder at other climates, other realms of imagination, as when she wrote of "Afric's blissful plain" in a moment of revisionary drama: "And pleasing Gambia on my soul returns" ("Phillis's Reply," 144).

More generally this confrontation may lead us to conclude that for a caption truly to succeed, it must precede the work it follows. In other words, the caption can owe a work its obedience only insofar as that work is indebted to the caption. Or again: to speak of the unimaginable violence that establishes definitions is to speak of the representational violence established by those definitions. And then again: in the desires of our gods we find the gods of our desires.

Obviously, the foregoing formulations are not exactly historical, since they fail to speak of particular conditions—for instance, the force held in some circumstances by specific definitions of *master* and *servant* and their attendant rules, laws, practices, technologies, and violations. Yet this is not to say that these formulations are ahistorical unless one pledges allegiance to certain formal, empirical, or pragmatic rules that one imagines to be limitless—and thus truly ahistorical—in their application. Not quite historical, these statements are also not quite paradoxical, if by paradox one understands a statement that logically cancels itself or a figure that yields nothing meaningful through its reversals. For if they are worked through, these formulations transform and transport the caption. They enable us to see how historical change becomes possible through their turnings—and how this possibility has been limited by the captious practices of those cultural orders that have attained a certain historical dominance, no matter how contingent. These formulations then take us out of the binding lockstep of before

and after, in which we can imagine only one origin, center, and progress in history, by calling our attention to upsetting aspects of identity
that cannot be made uplifting by any kind of figuration, historical or
paradoxical or otherwise. In describing what might be called the rapt
damage of the captioning ideal, an ideal that breaks forth only through
its own violation, these formulations lead us to see captioning as a
taking up of an object that is not pregiven—and thus as a ravishing
event in which we are implicated together with all our properties. The
logic of the caption demands that in taking note of things, we must
also see how we take charge of them; in rendering things, seizing them;
in asserting ourselves, impersonating others.

In short, these sorts of formulations give us a way to reexamine how
the things of our world, such as authors and their images, are bound
to the caption—and at the same time they serve to discourage any sense
of detachment from the historical violence to which the caption is
bound through all its unwilling detachments. For instance, they remind
us that the captioning logic of humility and mastery does not preclude
the former from penetrating the latter, as Wheatley had occasion to note
in a letter to Samson Occom, a Mohegan convert to and minister of
Christianity. "How well the Cry for Liberty, and the reverse Disposition
for the Exercise of oppressive Power over others agree," she took some
pains to tell Occom and the world at large, "I humbly think it does not
require the Penetration of a Philosopher to determine" (177).[14] To bear
witness is still to be borne away by the caption, but saying so does not
mean that Wheatley's writings do not in fact bear witness to historical
events and issues with which we are still preoccupied today.

It is not only Wheatley's poetry that has suggested these remarks on
the caption, although it certainly is what I have been leading up to—
and following. And though I certainly have not written of the caption
solely because her 1773 collection of verse bore a frontispiece, an engraving of the poet at work, with a caption engraved within it, that
caption does bear some remark. In her poetry Wheatley was very much
concerned with the question of what comes before and what comes
after, and especially so in her elegies, which account for fully a third
of the poems in her 1773 volume; but this question is already raised by
the crisp, delicate engraving of the frontispiece.

Facing the title page of *Poems on Various Subjects, Religious and Moral,
by Phillis Wheatley, Negro Servant to Mr. John Wheatley, of Boston, in New
England,* the portrait of Wheatley is set in an oval frame superimposed
on a horizontally ruled square. Within the frame the poet is pictured
sitting at a table, which supports a book, an inkwell, and a sheet of

paper, on which she is writing with a quill pen. (It may be important to note that she is not looking at either the paper or the book, which is closed, but instead seems to be glancing slightly upwards, as if in the act of being imaginatively inspired.) Under this engraving—in the traditional place for a caption—there appears instead the formulaic notice of the book's publication date ("according to Act of Parliament") and the name and address of the publisher. The portrait's real caption, in the traditional sense of the word, appears on the oval frame within the engraving, mirroring the identification on the title page: "Phillis Wheatley, Negro Servant to Mr. John Wheatley, of Boston."

The pages that follow include a dedication to the countess of Huntingdon; a brief preface that describes the poem as having originally been written solely "for the Amusement of the Author" (4), without any intention of publication; a brief "Letter sent by the Author's Master to the Publisher," which begins by stating that "Phillis was brought from *Africa* to *America*, in the Year 1761, between Seven and Eight Years of Age" (6); and finally an "Attestation" bearing the caption "To the Publick." In this document eighteen "Judges," as they style themselves, "do assure the World" that the poems in this volume were, they believe, "written by Phillis, a young Negro Girl, who was but a few Years since, brought an uncultivated Barbarian from *Africa*, and [who] has ever since been, and now is, under the Disadvantage of serving as a Slave in a Family" in Boston. Those subscribing their names to this document include the governor and lieutenant governor of Massachusetts, seven clergymen, John Hancock, and "*Mr.* John Wheatley, *her Master*" (7).

In Wheatley's *Poems* this authorizing document appears neither wholly dispensable, since "it has been repeatedly suggested to the Publisher" that without it many people might "suspect" the writings, nor wholly necessary, since the writings are, after all, by someone "thought qualified to write them." With the exception of the letter and the "Attestation," which anticipate the prefaces that were to become a conventional part of slave narratives published in the nineteenth century, the elements of this textual apparatus are completely formulaic. For instance, there is nothing unusual about a frontispiece with an engraving bearing a caption, even a caption made part of a frame within the background of the overall design. But then again this caption still may be remarkable, as we can see if we consider it in relation to the letter and the Attestation directed to those who recognize themselves as "the Publick."

In this portrait, consciously or unconsciously, one is bound to con-

front complexly overlapping determinations of precedence and obsequence that involve mastery and subordination, activity and passivity,
relief and indebtedness, interiority and exteriority, and, always, genre
and occasion. For instance, this image is authorized not only by Wheatley, who presumably agreed to sit for it and gave it her approval, but
also by the "Judges" who testify that this image is, indeed, an image
of an author, and of *this* author. In fact, although the design of the book
has the Attestation coming after the portrait, this document logically
must be considered to precede Wheatley's image, since we can infer
that the book would not have been published or even attributed to
"Phillis Wheatley" if the judgment of these men had gone against her.
The portrait has its place at the beginning of the volume, then, but then
again, it is there only in lieu of the real placeholders, who determine
its proper position to be after and under their own names. (It is notable
in this respect that John Wheatley's letter is dated 1772—apparently
also the year when the Attestation was drawn up after Wheatley submitted to an oral examination—whereas the book's dedication is dated
June 12, 1773, and the publication date is September 1 of that year.)[15]
So the image of the author is there, heading the volume and serving as
a kind of caption; and then again, it is not quite there, since it is not
permitted to stand on its own and identify itself—quite the contrary.
Henry Louis Gates, Jr., has pointed out that "the almost quaint authenticating signatures and statements that prefaced Wheatley's book"
would become the "authenticating color description" used by later African American writers "as a political as well as rhetorical strategy";[16]
but the possibility of this figuration is already prefigured in Wheatley's
Poems, in which the features of her image form a drama in themselves.

The resultant complexities of agency, time, and place, which all develop within the logic of the caption as a signifying device, are further
compounded by the specific words of the caption borne by Wheatley's
portrait. These words identify Wheatley not as the author but as "Negro
Servant to Mr. John Wheatley, of Boston." Her identity as a writer is
subordinated to this other identity, which curves around the oval frame
above her image, in the very place where she seems to be looking for
inspiration; but then again, the image shows Wheatley in an act of
writing, not an act of apparent servitude—or at least not of the same
kind of servitude. (This contrast is all the more striking in that literacy
was historically denominated a sign of reason and, indeed, seems in
this case to have led to Wheatley's manumission in the year of her
book's publication.) Thus one finds that while it is figuratively bound
to the relation of mastery and servitude, and in this instance literally

inscribes such a relation in the book, the caption cannot entirely say what it in fact says. How can one hope to measure the extent to which Wheatley's name is first and foremost her master's, according to a familiar history spelled out in their formally identical last names in this caption? And then again, reversing his priority and superordination, how can one measure the extent to which his name is one Wheatley might meaningfully have appropriated, refigured, so as to make it her own?

John Wheatley himself may be said to have raised this question, since his letter, like the Attestation, follows the common practice of granting the African American only a first name, thereby cutting her off from the supposed completion offered by his surname. But does "Phillis" really come before this last name—"Phillis," the name her mistress assigned to the author-to-be, which also happened to be the name of the ship that brought this child away from Africa and into slavery in the American house of John and Susanna Wheatley? ("What her African name was," Benjamin Thatcher noted, "never has been ascertained.")[17] And the poet had still other names, appearing in a 1774 advertisement for her book as "A Negro Girl" (not servant)[18] and then as "Phillis Peters" after her marriage in 1778. Here one may also remember Phillis Wheatley's attitude in the portrait, looking not to the closed book but either to her muse or to the superior caption: How can one measure what was her own in this stereotypical posture of literary obeisance, which is bound up with Western traditions that go back to Plato and that often have been intimately related (as in Plato's dialogues) to defenses of slavery? (This portrait was commissioned and used as a frontispiece at the request of Wheatley's patron, the countess of Huntingdon, who was a slave owner, as was "almost every identifiable white person in Phillis's writings," including most of the testators to their authenticity.)[19] In her poems this young woman expressed her indebtedness to Homer, Virgil, Ovid, Terence ("one alone of *Afric's* sable race" [11]), Milton, and Pope: here, too, it does not require the penetration of a philosopher such as Derrida to determine that there is an issue of servitude in the name of liberty that is by no means easy to circumscribe.

This point becomes all the more pressing if one considers how the extreme instance of servitude that we call slavery was historically related, by way of rhetoric both colloquial and formal, to the general system of literary production in the eighteenth century. In the dedication of her volume to the countess of Huntingdon, Wheatley inscribed herself as the countess's "much obliged, Very humble, And devoted

Servant" (3); similarly, she professed that she had "humbly submitted" her poems to the public (5). How are we to understand this posture of submission, which might seem to make the muse very little, if at all, her own? This question is all the more important because critics so often have faulted Wheatley's poetry, both formally and ideologically, for supposedly bearing the sign of her submission to eighteenth-century English models, especially the measures of Pope.

In other books the formulaic deference of this dedication might remind us of the traditional hierarchies, established institutions, economic conditions, and cultural figurations that subtended the production of art in this time, not simply as an enabling but as a structuring system of relationships. If not identical, aesthetic and social decorums would at least appear to be implicated in and responsive to one another in some crucial aspects, effectively inviting us to analyze the historical grounds of contemporary representations and theories of representation—as of course many have done and continue to do, and as I am doing here. In Wheatley's *Poems*, though, this question of the ways in which art is formulaic, or a recognizable codification of powerful relationships preexisting its production, meets with the image of a poet who in her own social existence was signed, sealed, and delivered over to the very notion of a serviceable code. According to her captioned image in the engraving, the letter from her master, and the Attestation, she was the code made flesh, the formula incarnate, in that servitude for her was considered not a figurative but a literal, continuing, legally articulated and authoritatively certified condition of being. That is why, when George Washington wrote her a letter and subscribed himself her "obedient and humble servant,"[20] his words were of a different kind than hers when she so subscribed herself, even though in this instance the radical difference was bound to be formally unmarked.

The deference of the eighteenth-century dedication, which depends for its value on the conventional assumption that the writer is freely submitting herself to the respectful formulas comprised therein, cannot remain undisturbed when it is professed by a writer said not to have control over herself physically, legally, economically, socially, linguistically, and, in general, imagistically. True, one might want to suggest that Wheatley's situation in this respect was a terrible but logical extreme of a more general human condition, since all individuals (and even the historical notion of "the individual") must be presumed to be subject to the articulation of society; but the difference in this case is more than a matter of degree.

To be denominated a slave, to bear that kind of caption, foreclosed the possibility of truthfulness in communications with one's captors even where this was not legally cut off, as by rules disallowing or putting under a disadvantage the formal testimony of slaves. This is true not only in respect to the ways African Americans practiced various forms of disguise and Aesopian language or maintained a "double consciousness" (in W. E. B. Du Bois's famous term), but also in the sense made clear, however unintentionally, by the authorizing documents placed at the beginning of Wheatley's *Poems*. Their seemingly narrow concern—to establish that Wheatley truly wrote these works—takes for granted that her own word is insufficient, and not simply because of the pronounced suspicions of others but in an essential way. Were this not the case, the testators would not have had to submit her to an examination; instead they might simply have taken her word and affirmed that they had done so, thus adding their names to it as her servants, as in a kind of authenticating caption. In doing otherwise— very formulaically, to be sure, as in what we might say is a very natural kind of thing to do—they made themselves incoherent.[21] They granted her the status of the indisputable *"Original"* only insofar as she would remain eccentric to her aboriginal ("Barbarian") and current ("Slave") condition—and thus in a posture that would have to be thought of as secondary to, dependent on, and internally constituted by her defining master, who is represented in this instance by the kind of person that can be abstracted from a group of free, white, socially and economically distinguished American men. Even the question of the author's gender is drawn into this incoherence, since—as John C. Shields notes in her collected *Works*—Wheatley's "publication venture was supported, both financially and intellectually, almost exclusively by other women" ("Notes," 273), whereas all her testators (as if to recall the derivation of *that* word) were men. In this situation, having been taken captive, converted, and renamed, somewhat as Pocahontas had been in the previous century, and having been forced to submit to an oral examination to establish her authority, much as Sor Juana had been in Mexico a century earlier, Wheatley might well have seemed destined to become a symbol and an allegory of American cultural history in her own person—just as her poetry suggested she was.

In the letter to Samson Occom written in the year after her book's publication and her legal emancipation, the same letter in which she wrote of the reversible disposition of liberty in language, Wheatley called the kind of persons who had been her testators "Modern Egyptians." This term was formulaic, to be sure, and in that sense one that showed her indebtedness to others before her; and yet her use of it neatly reversed several ideological sequences of "before" and "after" (historical, cultural, racial, and religious) so as to use the biblical word, the masters' source of conversion, against them. A few years later, in her poem "On the Death of General Wooster," Wheatley even felt free to put words into the dying general's mouth which again raised the question of "the Reverse disposition" in language:

> But how, presumptuous shall we hope to find
> Divine acceptance with th'Almighty mind—
> While yet (O deed Ungenerous!) they disgrace
> And hold in bondage Afric's blameless race?
>
> (149)

To be "presumptuous," of course, is to get ahead of oneself or to take on credit something for which one may not be able to pay. In other words, it is exorbitantly to bind oneself to something other than oneself, something over which one has no right, and thus—in Wheatley's payoff for this reversal of priorities—it is to define oneself as the only kind of slave deserving of the name, which is the one without any hope of redemption.

But even in her earliest compositions Wheatley was aware of how her fate was bound up with the presumptuousness of language, which never could be trusted not to make the first last and the last first. In "America," a poem composed when she was approximately fourteen years old, she wrote, "Thy power, O Liberty, makes strong the weak / And (wond'rous instinct) Ethiopians speak / Sometimes by Simile" (134). Given such evidence, how can one hope without presumption to determine the time and the place, the before and the after, of the simile in Wheatley's poetry? Or what kind of caption could possibly befit her image?

In evaluating what Sondra O'Neale has called "a slave's subtle war,"[22] it is important to remember that in her 1773 volume of poems the very measures that granted Wheatley any authority in language also served, literally and figuratively, to alienate that authority from her. In subscribing herself the humble servant of a countess or of the public at large, Wheatley could not help but appear absent from "her own" words, since it was only on this condition that she could have any property in them. Thus, in confronting the issue of literary codes, Wheatley was bound to confront the image of herself as a slave. She was bound to see herself as one of a kind with the logically dependent and seemingly unnecessary caption, which is said to exist only through the mercy of a transporting origin and center of value. Therefore, it was forcefully brought home to her that if she were to prove she could understand them, she would have to understand literary codes as alienable and convertible human property—and thus, like herself, as the subject of an ongoing historical drama rather than the idiom of an unquestionable tradition.

So while Wheatley shared with other writers of this time a rhetoric of servitude with distinct social, sexual, romantic, and religious registers, she was bound to write herself in this language in a way distinct from these others. They were privileged to come to language with a sense of difference between themselves and its conventional formulas that was categorically forbidden to a woman who had to find her freedom through slavery; and this distinction made all the difference, as one can see in her most famous poem, "On Being Brought from Africa to America" (18). "'Twas mercy brought me from my *Pagan* land," it begins: "Taught my benighted soul to understand / That there's a God, that there's a *Saviour* too: / Once I redemption neither sought nor knew."

Concerned as they are with the complexities of how one may be taken, transported, transformed, or otherwise carried away to act as a servant, these lines are not at all simple, although they have often been taken to be so. For if these opening lines, by themselves, leave the impression of a humble, submissive, utterly compliant servant to the Christian doctrine often used historically to support the institution of slavery in particular and the extension of imperialist designs in general, this impression is brought into question by the concluding quatrain, which abruptly carries the reader away from the topic of redemption to which the poem had seemed to be immediately heading. "Some view our sable race with scornful eye," Wheatley writes, breaking with the isolated image of herself to imagine her identity communally and dialogically, as it is taken by "some" others. "'Their colour is a diabolic die,'" she quotes them as saying, and then concludes, "Remember, *Christians, Negros*, black as *Cain*, / May be refin'd, and join th'angelic train."

Thus, through a detachment from herself in the formal center of this poem, several sequences and consequences of "before" and "after" are reversed and transformed. For if the first quatrain tells of the before that is Africa, in contrast to the America to which she was brought, it also testifies from its very first words to the after of a conversion subsequent to her abduction from this place. And if the second quatrain tells of the after that is America, which represents understanding and the hope of redemption, it also represents just such a benighted state of mind as was attributed to the "*Pagan* land," which was supposed to stand before this other. Those who are reproached for their scorn—a category in which she generously includes *all* Christians by the time we arrive at the penultimate line of the poem—still have yet to learn, or at least to remember, what she had yet to learn before she was brought to America. And so although she appears as a servant, it is as a servant teaching her master, as a Negro teaching whites, or as a child teaching learned doctors in their own temple. In fact, she shows the sign of diabolism that she supposedly wears as actually being internal to the eye and voice of the very persons implicated in the social, political, economic, and religious forces that transported her into her present state of knowledge. In this representation she penetrates them with her perception. The "die" or mark of sinfulness is portrayed as an imaginary projection: a confused reversal of subject and object, of primary and secondary concerns, of activity and passivity, and in general of what comes before and what after.

Such reversals, of course, were already familiar in debates over slavery[23] (as they were in almost two millennia of Christian tradition, on which such debates often depended). It is not Wheatley's originality in the invention or choice of this trope that is at issue here but rather the striking intelligence in her use of it, as through it she wrote herself into traditions of authority that must have seemed to be categorically closed to such a one as her.

In this context it is notable that one of the captions most commonly assigned to Wheatley's "kind"—the simile "black as *Cain*"—is accepted as an idiom precisely so that it may be rejected as an insult. Because of the way she places it in the poem, it allows her to transport the determining grounds of identity, value, and community from a particular race to a retrospective and proleptic morality and thus to turn a seemingly established similitude into a simile detached from its usual service and converted to a very different sense of priorities.[24]

It becomes apparent, then, that when Wheatley says "mercy" brought her to America, she does not do so to thank her masters. Instead, she denies them any credit for her knowledge and hope of redemption, which (in a perfectly orthodox way) she makes out to be owing to a God that is neither "before" nor "after" Africa and America. Moreover, Wheatley calls into question the very name of mercy. For within this context the "mercy" of the opening lines must be seen as lacking in those who think themselves already "refin'd" even as they demonstrate by their racism that they have forgotten (if they ever knew) the religion on which they drew to give names to themselves and others. It is as if Wheatley's "mercy" appeared somewhere between the viewpoints of William Blake's "Songs of Innocence" and "Songs of Experience," testifying to the dwelling of God in "the human form" while also taking note of patterns of super- and subordination that upset this redemptive sense of identity and universality: "Mercy no more could be, / If all were as happy as we."[25]

All the terms of the poem must then offer themselves to a reading in which their ideological aspects are no sooner expressed than they are coolly recited, as by a detached observer of her own experiences. "'Twas mercy brought me from my *Pagan* land," the poet says, utterly submitting to the mastering terms of her experience—or blandly reciting those official terms so as to make manifest the violent bondage commonly denied, internalized, and repressed within them. "Remember," says the penultimate line of the poem, demanding that her readers look back if they are correctly, redemptively, to look forward; and if one looks back at it, the very title of the poem is transformed. Rather than being euphemistic or a sign of submissiveness, as has sometimes been claimed, the title appears as the poem's most profound site of reversal. The passivity it might seem to exemplify even grammatically—"On Being Brought from Africa to America"—is converted by the poem into an active representation of Christianity, which, if its implications had always been taken to their proper conclusion, would never have allowed Wheatley's enslavement and subsequent conversion in the first place. The poem must then appear to be undoing the occasion of its entire performance and erasing the name of Phillis Wheatley in favor of one that is both gone before and yet to be found. As June Jordan has pointed out, this poem says, among other things, *"Once I existed on other than your terms."*[26]

Therefore, since the supposed agents of redemptive mercy are also the agents of scorn, erroneous self-understanding, and contradictory teaching, the opening quatrain must open itself to radically conflicting readings. This mercy that carried Wheatley away, first in the form of an enrapturing God and later as the eagle of revolutionary America, is it such mercy as transformed Io into a heifer and Daphne into a laurel tree when divinities sought (and succeeded or failed, as the case would have it) to rape them? Although Johann Winckelmann was arguing around the time of Wheatley's birth that any artist "who has a soul, who has learned to think, finds himself useless and without occupation in relation to a Daphne and an Apollo, an abduction of Proserpina, a Europa and the like,"[27] Wheatley had good reason to find that these images still had some life in them; and certainly the "decided taste for the stories of Heathen Mythology" that was noted in Wheatley's poetry by her first biographer suggests the possibility of such a reading.[28]

Or is the mercy in "On Being Brought from Africa to America" represented as a metamorpheme in its own right, so that its traditional conception, in which it is understood equally to bless the giver and the receiver, must be accounted preposterous? Given that what may at first appear an expression of submissive thanksgiving may also be read as a cool, distanced reflection on a forceful ideology, this mercy must appear not only as once having been unknown and unwanted by the poet but also as not knowing and not wanting *itself*. It must appear as itself its own oppressor, and in this form as standing in need of the one who can stand in memory before it, outside its power, whence is shown the truest mastery of its refinements. The one supposed to receive must then appear as the one who gives, the patient as the agent, as if Daphne had transformed her own flesh to bark, amazingly rooted herself in the earth, so that men and gods might be gifted with a vision in which they would be ravished by their own violence. Such an image may be necessary to grasp a life and a poetry such as Wheatley's, and it is there to be read if one is sufficiently attentive to the upsetting configurations of her writing. If we take the foregoing considerations into account, the image of Shakespeare's Prospero, "transported / And rapt in secret studies" (*The Tempest*, 1.2.76–77), is certainly no more marvelous than the image in the frontispiece to Wheatley's collection of poems.

The case is similar with Wheatley's very early poem "To the University of Cambridge, in New-England" (15–16), which also begins by speaking of the "mercy" that "brought [her] in safety from those dark abodes"—from "the land of errors, and *Egyptian* gloom." This initial characterization no sooner is posited than it is effectively reversed and transformed as Wheatley universalizes her personal history. Sublimating this history in an allegory of the Christian injunction that one must be brought out of sin, the poet excluded from Harvard in at least four ways—by virtue of her age, gender, race, and economic condition—ends up in the position of instructing these students as to how they must let themselves be carried out of sin: "An *Ethiop* tells you 'tis your greatest foe." This is a defining gesture in her poetry, to make her color cover the earth—"earth's dusky shore," as she has it in one elegy ("To the Honorable T.H. Esq.," 98)—so that nothing and no one may fall outside the questions that may be raised by the way some others perceive her. The "*Egyptian* gloom" she attributes to her place of origin, one notes, she also attributes to the "*Modern Egyptians*" who practice slavery, so that if the former is mastered by the religion of the latter, the latter can gain no credit from that fact.

Similarly, in her poem "To the Right Honourable William, Earl of Dartmouth" (73–75), she includes an obeisance to the force of her abduction: "I, young in life, by seeming cruel fate / Was snatch'd from *Afric's* fancy'd happy seat"—so as to make herself exemplary of enslaved North America: "Such, such my case." The apparent negations of the opening lines—"*seeming* cruel fate" and "*fancy'd* happy seat"—have led many critics to follow the lead of J. Saunders Redding, who saw them as signs of Wheatley's capitulation to the enslavement of her people.[29] Since, however, the authority for her argument in favor of North America's emancipation from "tyrannic sway" is premised on her sorrowful memory of being ""snatch'd" and "seiz'd," these lines must bear another reading, in which they appear only as marking out a change in her order of perceptions, without any prejudice as to their reality or relative value. Certainly one is led to presume that the author, in retrospect, would be forced to give a different account of Africa and of the fate that carried her away from it, but at the same time one is led to presume that the changes consequent on this abduction cannot be taken to legitimize it.

Especially when one notices that "raptured" is one of Wheatley's favorite words, invariably used to suggest heavenly bliss, it is important to remember such moments in her poems. Etymologically related to *rape*, *rapture* is a traditional term for the power of poetry, as in Milton's *Paradise Lost* (7.35–36), because it suggests the experience of being seized and transported, as by a god. "Such, such my case": the repetition serves formally to fill out a line, but it also appears there as if to measure out the cruel distinction between historically experienced and artistically imaginable abductions. As Wheatley presents it, this is the distinction that makes all the difference as she struggles, through all kinds of formulaic overdeterminations, in trying to determine what comes before and what after in any moment of representation. Humbly to present the identifications with others without which freedom can be only a fancied "*Goddess* long desir'd": "Such, such my case." In making herself an allegory of transporting communication, which must pass through unwilling detachments and unforeseeable raptures, Wheatley showed that to bear witness is yet to bear the caption: a formulaic servitude that is unnecessary and yet unavoidable. As Chinua Achebe has said, speaking in a related context of cultural forms of identification, "Each of these tags has a meaning, and a penalty and a responsibility."[30]

Through words designed to measure the willing of identity and, then again, its unwilling detachment from itself, Wheatley called attention to the crucially differentiating repetitions in any petition—to the moving memories of others in ourselves—which form the question of tradition. She might have been following the logic of Milton's "Lycidas," which opens on a note of repetition ("Yet once more") and almost immediately speaks of a poet ravaging by reason of his own ravishment ("And with forc'd fingers rude").[31] "Such, such": as if to say *then, in that event, I must have been of such a kind, all else being unimaginable—but then again* ... "To do unkind things in kindness" is the definition of Satanic pity in Blake's *Milton;*[32] and by releasing her historical struggle in the words that would confine it, Wheatley showed the power of violence and divisiveness that constitutes the repeated "then again" of idealized cultural tradition. "Such, such": as if to say, in a formula at once sentimentally retrospective, philosophically critical, and morally preemptory, *of such an unkind kind am I.*[33]

The reversals of before and after in Wheatley's poems thus lead to a return that is *not* in kind, or to striking differences in communication. This is so in legal terms, if one remembers Wheatley's manumission; in an economic sense (for it is not to be forgotten that Wheatley had a pressing concern with earning money through her publications); in the imagistic register that allowed her to go back to Gambia, to childhood, and to liberty, among other places and conditions that stood "before" her in the paradoxical sense of that word, or at once in front of and behind her;[34] and also in all the senses in which establishing priorities, for such a one as Wheatley, could figure as different kinds of advancement. For it is important to remember that her poetry was vitally concerned with matters that ranged from the tables at which she would eat her meals to how and where her name might take on more than a nominal power of liberty in her world and in worlds yet to come.

To say so it is not necessary to fantasize the existence of a Wheatley who must have exercised her understanding in certain ways pleasing to one's own sense of the fitness of things, a Wheatley hidden in the formulas of her poetry like a princess in a prison of signs, awaiting her rescue. I am not inclined to follow the example of the fourteenth-century *Ovide moralisé* by conjuring up a *Wheatley politisée* for our time. Although it need not oppose this kind of fantasy, which often is important and in some respects is unavoidable, the argument here is that we should examine more carefully the priorities of Wheatley's poetry, its designs on what is before and after and all else that is wrought therein, since these offer us the greatest returns from her writing. In other words, rather than being obsessed with the question of the original or the real Wheatley, as reactions to her work have been from the time of her first publication to the present day,[35] we would do better to consider how this obsession is significant but also misleading for reasons explored within the poetry itself. As Cynthia J. Smith has noted, Wheatley "considered herself a full-fledged participant in the poetic tradition of Western writing,"[36] and it is important to consider her work in this context. For what Wheatley grasped through the accidents of her own "case," and what she made essential to her poetry, is the preposterousness of the very distinction between origin and imitation.

Of course, we cannot have done with images and captions; and, given the multiple orders of priority that preoccupy Wheatley's poetry—formal, social, temporal, political, economic, ideological, racial, national, religious, and so on—any determination of the order that caps the others at a given textual moment must have something willful about it. It may be important for some to identify Wheatley now as "in many ways the first representative African-American poet," just as it was important for Thomas Jefferson to define her as being no kind of poet at all but rather "below the dignity of criticism"; for Margaretta Matilda Oddell to imagine a wonderfully pious and poetically gifted Wheatley, an original genius who had "nothing forced upon her, nothing suggested, or placed before her as a lure"; or for some later readers, such as Addison Gayle, to imagine a totally antipathetic, passive figure.[37] But rather than viewing her as one who did or did not learn how to be a great poet—thus binding ourselves to an ill-formed question about tradition—we should consider how she was bound to learn her lessons both triflingly and all too well, in which complex state she would distribute these conflicting images of herself throughout her writings, where they have awaited their captioning. Instead of dismissing all the differing readings her poems have been given, we need to account for their possibility in terms of the multiple captionings to which her poetry lends itself, as of Wheatley as helpless victim, pathetic apologist, and brave rebel; sport of nature and wonder of education; historical anomaly, example, pioneer, and origin—and so on. And there is no better way to begin this analysis of captions than by focusing on the reversals that Wheatley's own poems show to be struggling within the formulaic nature of language and eighteenth-century poetry, for these points return us from the potentially infinite variations in the image of Phillis Wheatley, in accordance with its various captionings, to the specificity of her writing. Obviously this specificity does not inhere in a fixity of text or context, but rather in the responsibility—the modesty and carefulness of interpretation—that is enjoined upon us if we acknowledge that which cannot be captured in any caption: the historical life of the person who came to be called "Phillis Wheatley."

Within this approach it becomes possible to see that no matter how one imagines its author, "On Being Brought from Africa to America" always returns one to a logic of inordinate gain through submission, or to what I have called the return not in kind. And yet it is by no means simple to account for or even to sum up this gain. After all, in Western tradition the logic of inordinate gain through submission can be figured (to give only a very partial list of the contexts relevant to Wheatley's poetry) as metamorphosis in Ovidian fable, inspiration in Neoplatonic aesthetic theory, redemptive grace in Christianity, maturity in biological science, profit in capitalist economics, progress in Enlightenment pedagogy, independence in political theory, emancipation in social custom or legal doctrine, and, most generally, all that is deemed generically human as set off against the barbarous nature presumed to be lost and yet surpassed in it. To take a reference to any one of these orders of idealizing figuration as a point of simplicity in any poem, let alone in poems as uniquely circumstanced as Wheatley's, must then be a very foolish and violent exercise in captioning—as Wheatley's poetry is concerned to demonstrate. By the way it dwells on and within formulaic expressions, as by the history both lost to and remembered in it, it is always preoccupied with the issue of an unintentional detachment that is bound to be denied by, even as it is called upon to serve, all the priorities, hierarchies, and agencies of imitable tradition. A child's abduction from her family and language and native land so that she might be a slave, the carrying away of poems "written originally for the Amusement of the Author" into other eyes and voices, the names of the author being forgotten and truncated and examined and supplemented in the course of being established as genuine and singular and original—these submissions, too, figure inordinately within the poetry of Phillis Wheatley. It may be just to call her "a paragon of acculturation,"[38] then, but not if one fails to note the violent effects of captioning that are at work in acculturation in any case, and which are as carefully interrogated in her work as they were uniquely brought to bear in what little we can be said to know of her life.

The documents that preface her *Poems* offer Wheatley to the reader as a remarkable oddity or wonder, even as her master and mistress had encouraged her to go out and display herself as a prodigy in the drawing rooms of Boston; and until recently even her most sympathetic critics were given to treating her more as a tragic historical image than as a writer to be considered among other writers. As she herself insisted, however, Wheatley is not a writer sui generis, completely apart from other eighteenth-century poets or from the history of poetry in general. That is why my concern is with how the peculiar forces that brought Wheatley to poetry transported her into a fascinating engagement with the captionings, or unintentional detachments, of generic convention. Simply to treat Wheatley as an affecting historical image must be as limiting an approach as willfully to detach her poems from the history exemplified by their introductory apparatus so as to evaluate them according to traditional measures of aesthetic form and value—when it is tradition that is most in question in them. In terms of the history of eighteenth-century literature, the most distinctive interest of Wheatley's poetry lies in the way it represents the relation of art to history through multiple orders of precedence and obsequence—mastery and subordination, passivity and activity, debt and relief, interiority and exteriority, and genre and occasion above all—which are implicated in mutual transformations in a way that may seem blandly formulaic and infinitely upsetting in the very same poem.

To be sure, as if following a matter of form, some might object that in this reading I am bringing a complexity to the poems that they do not possess in themselves. Certainly many readers have seen nothing in Wheatley's poems beyond the formulaic impression of tradition—and a weak impression at that. Therefore, it might seem as if the reading being carried on here is an effort to do through criticism what the poems cannot do for themselves, which is to communicate a distinctive and appealing sensibility through codes that otherwise must seem unimpressive. One cannot hope to see what these poems possess in themselves, however, unless one has come to terms with this question of the orderings bound up in the caption—a question that, once looked for, must seize upon the reader in all the formulations of Wheatley's poetry. In this regard, it is important to remember that I do not write here of "true" or "false" Wheatleys or of passages in which the poet is more sincerely and appealingly herself and others in which she is not. On the contrary, my argument insists on the violence that these sorts of distinctions must do to the understanding of her work, which is so much concerned with the effects of unintentional detachment that figure in literature and language in general.

With their range of cultural references and their self-consciousness about simile, myth, allegory, and "Reversal," Wheatley's writings make it clear that it is not exorbitant to think that her representation of Christianity, for example, bears a face no more obviously interpretable than does the poet who portrays herself in the act of seeing herself being seen. After all, the argument that the truest understanding derives from a place outside the scope of Christianity is at once extrinsic and intrinsic to Christian tradition: extrinsic as heresy or disbelief, intrinsic in the centuries of rhetoric (Augustine's *Confessions* being a prime example) that seek to derive their authority at least in part from a condition anterior to that of submission. Wheatley's poetry everywhere testifies that there are mysteries other than religious mystery, among which the taking up of religion in the first place is only the most obvious. Her poetry asks of Christianity what it asks of the other subjects into which it enters and which enter into it: What do we talk about when we talk about that? This is the formulaic point at which so many readers of Wheatley have stopped, finding her work to be a weak and servile imitation of a culture not properly her own, as if there were ever a proper culture—as if imitation were the closed end rather than the vi-olently divided genesis of captivating communication in all its repeti-tions, reproductions, and striking measures. To be sure, Wheatley's poetry *is* imitative, composed of a hand-me-down sentimental, Chris-tian, neoclassical inventory of forms, in which the hallowed mastery that may be identified in someone such as Pope is certainly not in ev-idence—all of this is true enough, as far as it goes. What makes her poetry remarkable nonetheless is the preposterous self written through it, in its very professions of humility and obsequiousness.

"Preposterous," I write, because the wildly overdetermined cultural task that Wheatley took up—always to have converted unwilling de-tachment into a return of her own desiring identity—was literally and figuratively so. Literally, it was preposterous in its demand that what came after would always be, by providential (or foreseeing) rule, judged to be the proper outcome of what came before; and it was also preposterous in dwelling on its own impossibility. The overdetermined returns of cultural formulas would not allow Wheatley to say what she was supposed to say, even assuming what cannot be assumed, that she wanted to say just that; and so she was bound to say—was transported into saying—too much and too little. In this situation, learning the tra-ditional lesson that any code she used could function at all only through the possibility of its unwilling detachment from itself—its possible con-version to radically different codes—she saw her images and their cap-tionings as of an unkind kind, preposterously bound together.

It makes sense that this effect of unwilling detachment should be most evident in Wheatley's elegies. Arguably, it is in the modern elegy that the formulaic aspects of poetry—its cryptographies—face their greatest challenge. In no other kind of writing are genre and occasion so strikingly counterposed, since all the qualities that distinguish the former—identity, reproducibility, continuity, communicability, and so on—would seem to distinguish the latter only through their absence. Insofar as the very notion of loss presumes a revealed frustration, nowhere more than in the elegy is cryptography so evident and so abhorrent in equal measures. If the elegy is to succeed, it must find within itself its own oppressor and vanquish it. In this respect the opposite of the elegy is not the song of joy or thanksgiving, but rather the work that witnesses to oppression from within its domain, such as the "rude and apparently incoherent songs" of which Frederick Douglass told in his *Narrative*.[39] For insofar as the very notion of oppression presumes a withheld satisfaction, nowhere more than in the literature of protest against oppression is cryptography so invisible and treasured in equal measures. The code the elegy wants to vanquish is the code the protest wants to construct; the loss the elegy would reveal in remembrance is the gain the protest would conceal in anticipation; the same measures that figure in the one as the denial of a death in mourning may appear in the other as the affirmation of a life in desire; as opposed to the release of surrender in the public performance of obsequies, we have the restrained militancy in the encrypted rituals of protest; the community that the elegy would symbolically reconcile, the protest would historically divide.

It is at the point of this opposition between tribute and reproach, lament and rebellion, that Mark Antony situates his funeral oration in Shakespeare's *Julius Caesar*, playing one side against the other; this is also the point that is worked by Milton in "Lycidas," in which the Pilot's criticisms of the clergy border on digression and even threaten to turn the elegy into a different kind of poem. Even as they call forth its challenge, these works recognize that social criticism is supposed to be transcended, or at least dwarfed and momentarily set aside, by the elegy's consolation for the emotional protest of grief; for to protest too much in this context is to insist on the otherness of death, and so to reject the life of tradition, by harping on the code as an alienable and convertible human property in an ongoing historical drama. All kinds of things are put into question when genre and occasion are thus pushed to their limits at their point of intersection, and the fact that Wheatley's poetry is very precisely situated at this multiply disjunctive origin explains why it has given rise to so many captionings of her image—for which her poetry preposterously strove to give us an accounting in advance.

Consider, for example, "A Funeral Poem on the Death of C.E. an Infant of Twelve Months" (69–71). Like all of Wheatley's elegies, this one is especially concerned with diverting the mourners' attention from this world to another, the one that is to come, which is heaven and the site of unqualified bliss. Even more than the others, however, this poem dramatically insists on a certain sense of detachment, going so far as to characterize the grief of the dead infant's parents as a sign of "prepos- t'rous love." The characterization is precise and exacting: the love is preposterous because it puts before what should come after, the "post" in the place of the "pre." Of course, in terms of traditional Christian doctrine this means that the parents are valuing temporal concerns (in- constant appearances, selfish feelings, mortal flesh, and so on) over those that are eternal, as contained in God and the salvation offered through his grace. The formula is clear and recognizable enough, though it might be (for those not attuned to the Latin root of "prepos- t'rous") a touch indelicate; but there is more to be said on this point. For if there is a "raptur'd babe," one "snatch'd" to a better place, there is also (if we remember) a "high-raptur'd poet" ("On Recollection," 62), whose case thus far is of a kind with the child's. (And so we may remember—and "Can Afric's muse forgetful prove?" ["An Hymn to Humanity," 97]—that the poet has also been a "babe belov'd," seized and snatched away from her home ["To the Earl of Dartmouth," 74].) If the babe flying up to heaven is able to see the "universal whole," so too may the "vent'rous Afric" with her "great design," who sees with Mneme "the actions done / By ev'ry tribe beneath the rolling sun" ("On Recollection," 62–63). The child is a "Phantom"; Mneme is also a "heav'nly phantom" ("On Recollection," 63); and the poet identifies with them both, looking before her, one might say, and then again looking before her but in a different direction, turning on the other sense of the word. If the infant is imaged, contra Calvin, as being taken "e'er yet on sin's base actions [he] was bent," a similar characterization attends on "Afric's blameless race" ("On the Death of General Woo- ster," 149). If the infant's name appears in incomplete or altered forms ("C.E." and "Charles"), which call attention to a certain formulaic im- personality, from which the individual must be detached, so does the poet's;[40] and if the one-year-old child was carried away before it could speak for itself, so was she in a sense, as perhaps in a sense we all are in this darksome vale of tears. If we consider as well the historical, formal, and thematic relations that link the elegiac genre to love poems and epithalamia,[41] in which desire may seek various worldly ends (such as poetic renown) and yet figure them in spiritual terms, the connection between the living poet and the dead babe becomes even closer and, therefore, broader in its implications. Here, as in all the imitativeness of Wheatley's poetry, there is a "then" and a "then again" that still reverberate, producing returns not in kind.

In reading how Wheatley wrote herself into these lines, making herself as one with the "heir of bliss," who takes "a superior air" and answers his parents' voices "with a smile severe," we certainly can see her as a poet who has learned her lessons. These are the lessons of the elegiac genre (in which the poet often identifies with the figure being mourned) and more generally those of a genteel white Anglo-American Protestant tradition. Wheatley, however, also appears as a poet who has learned her lessons both inadequately and excessively. In a proverbial paradox, just as a little knowledge may be a dangerous thing, one can learn one's lessons too well; and Wheatley's poetry measures out these conflicting strains in communication, in which abject imitation may also prove to be an ecstatic identification with "nobler strains." For instance, how are we to evaluate the kindness and the unkindness in the last line of this poem, in which the parents are told to detach themselves from their "thoughtless wishes" and "prepost'rous love" in favor of preparing "to join [their] dearest infant friend / In pleasures without measure, without end"? It is as much as to say that they should prepare to die such a death as the poet has already died before them— such a death as they *owe* to the poet. There is something preposterous in this severity—something, I dare say, very like the opposite of an elegy—which is of a kind with the challenging of generic priorities throughout Wheatley's poems.

Because of its uniqueness, Wheatley's work is (as the formula would have it) absolutely contemporary: alive to the questions of race, nationalism, gender, cultural hybridism, and postcoloniality that have been at the forefront of current critical theory. At the same time it is thoroughly traditional in its preoccupations—of a kind with ancient images, such as the rape of Ganymede, which in Renaissance Neoplatonic interpretation symbolized "the enraptured ascension of the Mind," as Erwin Panofsky put it.[42] In the history of how this image has been taken, Wheatley's personal history, the symbols and allegories she made of that history through her poetry, and her elegiac interest in the dead child of "A Funeral Poem" all seem to have been prefigured, captioned in advance. For instance, when Margarita Russell describes how violent and sexually tinged abduction was taken to represent the willing "aspirations of the pure human soul" and "a kind of consolation for parents who mourned a dead child," she might almost be directing herself to Wheatley's image:

> Thus the Neoplatonic, christianized version of the Ganymede story resumes the idea already strongly implied in classical antiquity and in early Christian art, of the *Rape of Ganymede* as the symbol of the death of a mortal whose purity of soul makes him desirable to God. Since purity of soul is the attribute traditionally associated with small children, and since the antique Ganymede myth involves a child being taken away from his parents, the Ganymede symbolism became particularly meaningful with the death of a child and was already used in this sense on antique commemorative sculptures.[43]

As Russell points out, this treatment of the "rape," or abduction, was also followed in other cases. In addition to the examples she mentions, one might recall the case of Dante's Beatrice, who is this kind of abducted figure already transfigured, or carefully Christianized, so that its spiritual potential appears concurrently with but distinct from the erotic and grasping motivations that might otherwise define its rapture. Similarly, one might remember the quattrocento practice of decorating marriage chests with the image of the rape of the Sabine women, which was to serve as "an edifying scene."[44] Just as Wheatley, in her art as in her life, repeated the linguistic fates of *caption* and *ravissement*, and just as she participated in a history that effectively drew her into a symbolic connection to Terence, Pocahontas, and Sor Juana, among others, so too did she retrace the cultural designs bound up in these images—the designs (to borrow from Stephanie Jed yet another example) of "a humanistic tradition that has celebrated Lucretia's rape as a prologue to republican freedom."[45] It is notable that in some versions of this Roman legend, Lucretia is moved to her self-sacrifice only after Tarquin threatens to kill her African slave and place their bodies together in a compromising position: she becomes the image of the ideal in rejecting not simply the image of sexual violation but also the images of social degradation and miscegenation.

Given such a perspective, one may begin to appreciate how notable it is that in repeating such fates and designs, in ravishing ravishing tradition, Wheatley won her own freedom through them. In her art as in her life, Wheatley then appears always to have been an image destined to precisely those multiple intersections of preoccupations and

aftereffects that we can see exemplified in the history of reading occasioned by her poetry.

Where, then, is the before, where the after, in the rapture of this
poetry?

In a famous conclusion Victor Shklovsky declared the unconventional
Tristram Shandy to be "the most typical novel in world literature";[46] he
might have added that one of Sterne's contemporaries, Phillis Wheatley,
in her very conventional poems wrote the most untypical poetry imaginable.

Stereotyping Tradition

Charles Dickens and the Book of Fire

WE HAVE FIRE WITHIN US. Pop music tells us so; so do thousands of years of cultural tradition. Literature, philosophy, religion, and multifarious social practices all testify that we cannot so much as entertain a feeling or a thought, can scarcely twitch a muscle, without fire. It would seem that it glows immemorially in the blood and fibers of our being even as it is burnt into the English tongue. Like the Satan of *Paradise Regained*, we are bound to hear the *ire* in *fire* (as when we are incensed, from the Latin *incendere*, to kindle); like Shakespeare and others before him we are driven to find the rhyme between *fire* and *desire* natural, almost irresistible, and eminently just (as in the sense we make of our ardor, from the Latin *ardere*, to burn).[1] We recall that love is Cupid's fire, "the flame that burns everyone," as Jean de Meun had it;[2] in art in the Islamic tradition, Muhammad is sometimes represented as a flame; and if we like, we can cross-reference the Buddha on this point, even as he was quoted and footnoted by T. S. Eliot in "The Waste Land." Or just as some ancient theories suggest that our power of vision is owing to the fire in our eyes, we still may lend ourselves to this sense of things when we see these organs as being lit up, ablaze, or burning.

In these figurations and innumerable others, after defining the spaces of human habitation from prehistoric to modern times, fire can also be seen to have inhabited us. It is as if the *Timaeus* were physiologically unimpeachable when it tells of "an internal fountain of fire" at "the center of the body."[3] Whether we happen to be old flames or young sparks, firebrands or burnouts, blazing geniuses, shining spirits, spitfires, firebrands, or flaming queens, it is as if all of us, even those who have never read a word of Walter Pater, must burn with some kind of flame.

Thereby hangs a tale, at least. For this fire does have a history, an ongoing record of disruptive representations both within and without us. Despite the impression it may give of forever telling the same elemental story—"fire is time," said Hegel[4]—it has not always been what we now take it to be, which in itself must be a continuing matter of contention. As was learned too late by Nadab and Abihu, the sons of Aaron who took it upon themselves to offer "strange fire" to an incendiary divinity (Leviticus 10:1–2), fire has always involved itself in flaring disputes, contradictions, ambivalences, speculations, and material changes that have left their mark wherever flames may dwell.

This history, so complex and compelling, moved Charles Dickens to take fire as the very emblem of his storytelling. He conceived of his stories as being told by the fire, in both senses of that phrase, in which the hearth becomes at once the location and the source of narrative. As Dickens imagined it, fire tells us stories crucially resembling those we may read in a novel by the hearth; the book is always, in this sense, a book of fire.

So we are given a scene: a man, woman, or child gazing into a fire and deciphering what it has to say. This scene is repeated throughout Dickens's novels in such a way as to figure forth the imaginable conditions of their meaning, as at the end of *Hard Times* (1854), when the reader and the author are brought to join Louisa Gradgrind before the oracular flames of her hearth. Consistently, stereotypically, this scene served as Dickens's focus (from the Latin *focus*, fireplace or hearth) for burning questions about cultural life in the Victorian age. These questions can all be summed up in one: When the characters in Dickens's novels gaze into the fire, what do they see?

The Old Curiosity Shop (1840) was among the earliest works in which Dickens entertained this scene. In this novel, when little Nell is fleeing with her grandfather from the home that has become threatening to her, an anonymous laborer appears out of the night to take her in hand and lead her to his hearth, which turns out to be a factory furnace. The fire within it is his "friend," he says—"We talk and think together all night long"—and it is his "memory," too, showing him all that his life has been. What is more, it has taken the place of his mother, who died before he could develop any memory of her: "So the fire nursed me—the same fire. It has never gone out." And he offers Nell a simile that sums up these several characters of the fire: "It's like a book to me ... the only book I ever learned to read; and many an old story it tells me.

It's music, for I should know its voice among a thousand, and there are other voices in its roar. It has its pictures too. You don't know how many strange faces and different scenes I trace in the red-hot coals" (*OCS*, 11:66–68).[5] After her schooling in this encounter, one might almost have predicted that the next helper met by our fairy-tale waif, as she continues her wanderings, should be a poor teacher reading a book as he walks along the road.

For the rest of his career Dickens would find himself returning to the elements of this scene. At some times he did so merely to retrieve them in a line or two; at others to linger upon them, toying with them, interrogating and rewriting them; but always to dwell on the offering a fire may make to a reader. Thus, upon arriving back in England after he has traveled abroad to recover from Dora's death, when he is resting from his journey at an inn, David Copperfield sits before a coffee-room fire and falls to "tracing prospects in the live-coals" (*DC*, 15:47). The "haunted man," Redlaw, sees the ghost that represents his sorrowful memories in his hearth, among other places, and the narrator of his tale concludes by informing us that some people say he actually read this tale "in the fire, one winter night about the twilight time" (*HM*, 18:436, 524). In *Dombey and Son*, the younger Mr. Carker, in all his corruption, might have been observed "pondering over the blackening grate, until he rose up like a man who had been absorbed in a book"; the same novel finds the younger Paul Dombey, in all his innocence, "studying Mrs. Pipchin, and the cat, and the fire, night after night, as if they were a book of necromancy, in three volumes" (*DS*, 9:251, 8:129).[6]

As in these examples, a devotion to the book of fire is evident throughout Dickens's works, and yet it also seems obvious that Dickens had his doubts about the value of this devotion. For instance, *The Battle of Life* found him striving, with what must seem a deliberate heavy-handedness, to make explicit this connection between the reading of his novels and the reading of a fire in the hearth. One might infer some anxiety that his insistence on this scene was failing to light up his readers' imaginations in the way he desired. At the very least, we can see his concern to bring this fire home to the reader and thus to bring the reader to book.

Laboriously, then, the scene is arranged: a young woman, Marion, sits before the family hearth and reads aloud from a book while her sister Grace sits beside her doing needlework and her father, the Doctor, relaxes in his easy chair, contemplating them. "Two better faces for a fireside," the narrator notes, "never made a fireside bright and sacred." As if further to ensure that no one will miss the point, Dickens has

Marion reading a story that mirrors her own immediate comfort and imminent tribulation, which will result from her elopement with a man other than her long-absent betrothed. " 'And being in her own home,' read Marion, from the book; 'her home made exquisitely dear by these remembrances, she now began to know that the great trial of her heart must soon come on' "—at which point in her reading Marion begins to weep. The reason she gives for being unable to read any further—"The words seem all on fire!"—greatly amuses her father, who prides himself on being a philosophical cynic:" 'What! overcome by a story-book!' said Doctor Jeddler. 'Print and paper! Well, well, it's all one. It's as rational to make a serious matter of print and paper as of anything else. But, dry your eyes, love, dry your eyes. I dare say the heroine has got home again long ago, and made it up all round—and if she hasn't, a real home is only four walls; and a fictitious one, mere rags and ink' " (BL, 18:352–54).[7] This scene prepares us for the vanquishing of the father's cynicism and the attendant moral: that the home of the home is the book, whose story is told by the fire, which is feminine in gender, sacred in spirit, suffering in attitude, and a heart in point of anatomy. (It is significant in this respect that some of Dickens's working-class characters, such as Mr. Peggotty in *David Copperfield*, pronounce "heart" as "art.") Be it ever so dreary, this is a stereotypy fundamental to Dickens's fiction.

As Dickens has its own image turned to letters of blinding fire, however, this scene must also suggest something other than what is conveyed by its formulaic exposition. If it is to be consumed in fire, the code of heartfelt, suffering, sacred femininity may still be an unavoidable result of Dickensian logic and yet only a very partial accounting of that logic. So if we attend well to the burning of the Dickensian book, we may be able to appreciate the relation between this scene and the more fascinating instances of this author's obsession with fire, such as the book he makes of Lizzie Hexam's brazier in *Our Mutual Friend*—a novel whose conception of heart, attitude, spirit, and gender, as of art itself, requires a more unsettling understanding of the institution of the hearth.

At first, to be sure, even *Our Mutual Friend* may lead readers today to see only that any mention of the hearth is bound to call forth the all-too-familiar words flickering within it: the *ear* attuned to the voices and sounds of human fellowship, the *heat* of material comfort and pleasure, the *heart* of gentle feelings, the *tear* of human sympathy, the *earth* whence we come and to which we shall return, and, by no means the least among these, the *art* that would tell of all this so as to succeed in treasuring the hearth and holding it sacred. Indeed, when a term has been taken for thousands of years as a point of reference for familial, social, economic, political, and metaphysical understanding—and even cross-referenced as their common center or ground—it is difficult to see how it could ever not have seemed fully known. Such, of course, has been the fate of *hearth*, which may appear to have known no vicissitudes between the era of Plato's *Laws*—"Now the soil and the household hearthstone are sacred, in our universal conviction, to all gods that are"[8]—and the England of Charles Dickens.

But even if we believe we have disabused ourselves of this faith in the hearth—as when we think of *hearth* as a tired formula signifying a substance, experience, feeling, or mode of life that now essentially belongs to the past—we may be dreamily imagining the very thing on which we pride ourselves for having gained a historical perspective. For when elements of the past seem all too familiar to us, all too clearly stereotyped, it is likely that we are losing ourselves in what we take to be our distance from and knowledge of that past. In other words, we may be acting like philosophical cynics who are naive enough to think they can read a story of fire without feeling its searing effects.

Our Mutual Friend attends to this point throughout its drama, but nowhere more so than in the way it allows John Harmon, under an alias, to draw Bella Wilfer into the dramatic fictions of hearth and home from which she had tried to separate herself. So Bella comes to say of Lizzie, whose pyromancy had foretold her destiny, "I have often thought I would like to tell her how right she was when she pretended to read in the live coals that I would go through fire and water for him" (OMF, 24:331).[9] As this whole episode in the novel makes clear, whatever else Dickens thought and believed, he was not so naive as to think that the act of reading and the truth of life were necessarily distinct.

So fire is not so easily dismissed, despite the naive overfamiliarity that may still show itself in our own day, as when people speak of television displacing the hearth (not to mention the book) from the center of the household. What these would-be historians think they know is that the fireplace is still with us, to be sure, but only as a luxury or vestigial survival. It is a token of a bygone age, often fronted with glass like an exhibit in a museum, sometimes fed with gas beneath its blithely impervious logs, and serving in any case as a carefully ventilated sign of ornamentation, tradition, and semiotic "warmth." Having read this sign with a sense of the past nourished by Hollywood movies and *Masterpiece Theater*, these latter-day cynics feel assured that real fireplaces, of which this present one seems but a sign, belonged to the nineteenth century—that first great age of the novel and last great age of the hearth.

There is no gainsaying the position held by the hearth as a central institution in nineteenth-century life. It is important to remember, however, that even then it was a manufactured thing. In fact, long before the development of motion picture and television technologies, the hearth drew meaning from popular representations disseminated through the contemporary media, as by writers such as Dickens. It was not for nothing that the historical novel was virtually invented in the nineteenth century by Walter Scott and popularized by Dickens, among others.

No matter whether one mourns or celebrates television's displacement of hearth and book, one misses a crucial point: that the hearth has a history beyond its stereotypical nineteenth-century image in twentieth-century representations. By the Victorian era, with many an irregular tempo and local variation but with a tendency gradually made unmistakable, the hearth had spent centuries shrinking away from the central ground it had held in European dwellings prior to the Renaissance. Having formerly occupied the center of the domicile, it had first retreated to one side of the main room; subsequently it had withdrawn even further, recessing all but its front side within one of the walls of the dwelling. While chimneys were improved, fireplaces distributed in other rooms, the primary fuel changed to coal from the earlier wood, charcoal, or peat, and freestanding stoves invented and sold on an ever-widening scale, the hearth had grown yet smaller.

None of this was news to Dickens and his readers. In 1861 a writer for *All the Year Round* could refer offhandedly to "the present diminished receptacles for fires,"[10] taking for granted his readers' sense of the hearth as an item of architectural and social history already laden with nostalgia. As he knew, it had lost not only much of its grandeur but also many of its functions. It is significant in this respect that Dickens did not bother to focus much attention on the Calibans stoking the fires of his novels, despite the crucial role played by the smoke-blackened *focarius* in *The Old Curiosity Shop*; it is also significant that the characters in his novels almost never see a place of work when they stare into the fire. (Grandfather Smallweed, who occupies himself in observing the family hearth "and the boiling and the roasting" [BH, 16: 360], is an exception.) In the dwellings of those beyond the ranks of the poorer working classes, most food preparation had long ago come to be restricted to a separate kitchen fire; the invention of matches early in the Victorian era was making the hearth, and the tinderbox, less vital to the lighting of pipes, candles, and lamps; and the gradual spread of gaslight during this century was coming to suggest a modern sense of illumination almost completely divorced from the flickering fire of the hearth.

George Eliot implicitly alluded to such changes when she wrote in 1860 of "that familiar hearth where the pattern of the rug and the grate and the fire-irons were 'first ideas' that it was no more possible to criticise than the solidity and extension of matter."[11] In this evocation of the sentiment of Tom Tulliver in *The Mill on the Floss*, one should note that Eliot was writing not only of an England a generation removed from her own day, but also of that England in one of its most decidedly provincial corners and as it was being experienced by a relentless blockhead of a young boy. Eliot's philosophical and scientific allusions remind us that the fireplace of the Victorian era was already most definitely a place of irony—and not only to those who had a scholarly knowledge of Aristotelian and modern physics, as Eliot did. After all, would the hearth-felt sentimentality of Dickens's fiction have been so popular had it not been bound to the cynicism shown in his readiness always to reconfigure this sentimentality as vapid affectation and destructive manipulation? (Someone of "a sentimental turn," Dickens noted in *The Old Curiosity Shop*, is likely to respond to an injustice in the world "by going home again, in his grief, to kick the children and abuse his mother" [OCS, 10:141].) The understanding could not have been spelled out more clearly if it had been written in letters like those on Belshazzar's wall: if there were to be gods of this nineteenth-century hearth, they would have to be latter-day gods, conscious of the Penates they had displaced and thus drawn to recognize the precariousness of their own tenure—the precariousness even of their names.[12]

To refer to the centrality of the stereotypical Victorian hearth must then be to tell stories of central displacements and of death and the destruction of names; and in this regard it is notable that by the middle of the nineteenth century, even the substance of fire was losing the place, and the names, it had formerly occupied in the natural universe. As *All the Year Round* put the matter, "Earth is a thing, Air is a thing, Water is a thing; Fire only is now no longer a thing, although, previous to 1778, it was considered to be a material substance."[13] Having lived through its earlier incarnation as phlogiston and the subtle fluid of caloric (and this is not even to mention its conceptions prior to the eighteenth century), fire was coming to be seen as a movement rather than a material—albeit a movement conveyed through that subtlest of materials, the ether, which was not to become an unmeaning name in scientific theory until the work of Albert Einstein early in the twentieth century. This history in science is but one of the many stories through which fire came to Dickens, Eliot, and others of their time, and any understanding of the nineteenth-century hearth must recognize the extent to which its stories are multiple and often incompatible or incommensurable; but it is important to see what the Victorians knew very well, that in their day the institution of modern science had entered quite thoroughly into the nature of the hearth. It had taken a place in its physical conception as much as it had in its design, which had been influenced, for instance, by the innovations of Count Rumford in the eighteenth century—the modernization that Jane Austen's Catherine Morland was so dismayed to find in the drawing room hearth at Northanger Abbey.[14] Although the fire in the nineteenth-century hearth could not have foretold the coming of television (on which one may now watch a videotaped record of a fire from its kindling to its peacefully glowing embers), it certainly was not oblivious to the modern possibilities of technological artifice.

In the age of Victoria, famously, one result of this awareness of science could be an arrogant silencing of the old gods, as when one of Dickens's writers went to the Zoological Gardens to see a salamander, the creature ancient legend had characterized as living in fire. The "vile ancients," in this account, are proven to have been "arrant liars" when "the Salamander of the nineteenth century" is found actually to be living in a tank of water, which to the happy, blustering, commonsensical modern must seem the very antithesis of fire.[15] But this consciousness of the historical nature of knowledge could cut another way, no less characteristic of Dickens's fiction than the first, as when another contributor to *All the Year Round* observed that if an early proponent of gas lighting had lived "in the fifteenth instead of the eighteenth century, he would most probably have been tortured as a wizard."[16] In this case the past does not appear as a simple lie in benighted contrast to the present; instead, it is a threat of violence in the name of dogmatic truth which might conceivably reappear at any time. In and of themselves the different conceptualizations undergone by fire evidenced the potential for such violence, which might well have found its exemplary figure in fire, and did, not only in the martyrdoms of earlier centuries but also in the book Dickens placed in the hearth of his own time.

Of course, there were other reasons why it was natural—fully as natural as the worship of sun gods, the practice of torture, and the experience of a self-flattering warmth in one's heart—for fire and book to be identified with each other. Much like a mug of purl or a snack of toasted cheese, a book as Dickens knew it was a thing likely to be consumed both next to and thanks to a fire. Throughout the nineteenth century this relation was so unremarkable as almost to go without saying. Where it was made explicit, as with the "Fireside Poets" in the United States or in anthologies with titles such as *Home Words for Heart and Hearth*, a special emphasis was placed on the values of domesticity, which must be of interest in themselves; but it is important first to note this association, once unremarkable because it was so common but now, perhaps, because it is so foreign to our experience of the book— if we still even speak of books and not of textuality or bytes of information. To describe the naturalness of this relation in which the book is bound with fire is, then, not to deny that there is a story of culture here, even many stories, all fluttering and flaming through the various cross-references within the Dickensian hearth; on the contrary, it is to recognize how Dickens took the lead for us in raising the question of the language of the hearth, which is the question of "household words," to use the term he lifted from Shakespeare.

"Hear me!" demands the Cricket on the hearth—itself a bit of language from Milton's "Il Penseroso"—when he addresses John Peerybingle, who is distraught with suspicions about his wife's fidelity. "Hear everything that speaks the language of your hearth and home!" (*CH*, 18:276). Like the narrator of *Martin Chuzzlewit*, the Cricket knows full well that "home is a name, a word," albeit "a strong one; stronger than magician ever spoke, or spirit answered to, in strongest conjuration" (*MC*, 7:160). And so here as elsewhere Dickens emphasizes the homely, the peculiar, the grotesque, the puny, the misshapen, the cute, and the sloppy, in all of which we are urged to see the consumable, mortal devices of language, not its supposed transcendence through some form of empyreal sublimity. It is because of this focus that Dickens is so lousy at conveying any sense of religious emotion (a weakness one may well consider a strength) and so good at conveying the posturings and puerilities of grief. Could there be any greater emphasis on this point than to call upon an insect, a fictional creature of no more elevated a status than our own latter-day Jiminy Cricket, to pronounce the moral of a story about "Voices in which the Spirits of the Fireside and the Hearth address themselves to human kind" (*CH*, 18:239)? Yes, Kafka is close by, listening in on this tale.[17]

Dickens's chatty insect is called upon to explain how Dot, Peerybingle's wife, has made "a few stones and bricks and rusty bars" into "the Altar of [his] home," a place of daily sacrificial offerings "with a better fragrance than the richest incense that is burnt before the richest shrines in all the gaudy temples of the world!" (CH, 18:275–76). Yet Dickens apparently foresaw that his readers, absurdly mistaking fictional voices for established human identities, might take the words of the insect for his own. Therefore, he was careful to end this work on an unsettling note of pathetic, sentimental isolation in which the narrator, in effect, is betrayed by the very hearth that but just this moment had been loving and nurturing him: "A Cricket sings upon the Hearth; a broken child's-toy lies upon the ground; and nothing else remains" (CH, 18:305).[18] Here as elsewhere, Dickens's hearth could become unfaithful or even "mercenary . . . a very courtezan" (BR, 12:104) because it was not a primary element of nature but rather an alienable, marketable, pyrotechnic matter of language. It was a work, a commodity, that he was producing but that certainly had not begun and just as surely would not end with his own contributions to it. Consequently, in telling of the naturalness of fire, Dickens retold a cultural history of shrines and temples and associated arts quite different from and even opposed to those with which he might seem most immediately concerned. To Dickens, what came to be accounted as nature was never a simple thing but rather a compound of emotional perversity, outmoded history, and sheer fantasy. Thus, as figured in his novels and in comparable works, such as Charlotte Brontë's *Jane Eyre*—that autobiography of fire—the burning book so distinctive in Victorian social history was always fed with the materials of ancient traditions, no matter how arrant their lies may have been.

In *Paradise Lost*, for instance, Raphael had told Adam that the sky set before him, with its fiery sun and stars, was "the Book of God" (8.67). Dante had written to a similar purpose when he imagined, in the last canto of the *Paradiso* (33.85–87), a book made visible in the burning light of heaven: "In its depth I saw that it contained, bound by love in one volume, that which is scattered in leaves throughout the universe."[19] In Dante's system of figuration, this burning book would be the very image of *The Divine Comedy* if the impossible could be imagined, that Dante's work might be adequate to its otherworldly conception; hence the way Dante had Saint Bonaventura compliment Peter the Spaniard, referring to him as he "who shines below in twelve books" (*Paradiso* 12.34–35).

In images such as these, long before the development of the coal grate, the blazing furnaces of the industrial revolution, the extension of literacy to the middle classes, the mass production of books, the popularization of the novel, and all the other historical turnings that made it possible for Dickens to figure his storytelling in the image of a book of fire, this work was being prepared by innumerable others. (One could further instance the illuminated manuscripts of the medieval world, such as those that illustrated the blazes expected of the apocalypse.)[20] To say so is in no way to impugn what Dickens liked to refer to as his inimitable self, for no one was more aware than he of this scattering of the leaves of earlier volumes within the nature of books such as his own, inciting them to flicker and leap into cross-references. He showed this awareness most obviously in his frequent mockery of those who would make a cult of nature, most subtly in the way he made the image of reading in his books one that substituted silence for speech and vanishing, dancing, unpredictable flames for ordered rows of letters. The valued experience of reading is then made to resemble the condition of being illiterate and yet knowledgeable, like Joe Gargery at the beginning of *Great Expectations* or Lizzie Hexam at the outset of *Our Mutual Friend*, and the scene of reading is made to register the most demanding irony of Dickens's sentimentality. One reads with confidence because of, and to the extent of, one's admission of the unreadable into this experience. As in a baptism of fire, it is as if one were undergoing a regression to an imaginary infancy in which sensation and divination, desire and repletion, would know no division before the name that Dickens preferred to write as GOD; at the same time, as in a trial by fire, it is as if one were anticipating the experience of death.[21] This irony is dramatized throughout Dickens's novels, as in the illness Pip suffers in *Great Expectations*, in which fire plays a notable role, or as in the violence inflicted on Eugene Wrayburn in *Our Mutual Friend*. Confounding seeming opposites, this attack is portrayed as surrounding him in images of fire ("flames shot jaggedly across the air" [OMF, 24:348]) even as he is plunged into water, and it results in injuries from which Wrayburn might well have died—if his name, like Lizzie Hexam's reading of her coals, had not promised a different story.[22]

Even where it was not identified with the book, fire had traditionally been identified with vitality in general, as with the Democritean soul or the burning brand of Meleager, and with the life of spoken language in particular. Both of these characterizations are carried over into the Dickensian hearth. A commonplace analogy—hearth is to house as spirit is to body—encouraged Dickens to write of the "embers of his soul" in a description of Mr. Carker the Junior (DS, 8:94) and of "the now-extinguished fire within" Nemo, the copyist in *Bleak House* (BH, 16:182). When Dickens tells, in *Martin Chuzzlewit*, of "the soul's bright torch" (MC, 6:275), we are invited, if only through countless mediations and indirections, to recall the shade of Anchises telling Aeneas of "the ethereal sense and pure flame of spirit."[23] Similarly, when that "fire-spirit," Jane Eyre, fears what would become of her if she were to marry St. John Rivers—"forced to keep the fire of my nature continually low, to compel it to burn inwardly and never utter a cry, though the imprisoned flame consumed vital after vital"[24]—she is communing, whether knowingly or not, with the beloved addressee of one of Shakespeare's sonnets.[25]

Within the line of tradition thus exemplified, it was a commonplace variant of the aforementioned analogy—spirit is to body as language is to humanity—that allowed "fire" to become a formulaic term for eloquence. (By extension, one could speak of "flaming out" at somebody or of "taking fire" in a conversation.) The contexts contributing to this analogy included the Old Testament, in which the word of the Lord is figured in "flames of fire" (Psalms 29:7), and the New, which offers, among other images, the association of Pentecostal fire with the Holy Spirit, inspiration, and communication in diverse tongues. Of course, the great medieval encyclopedist of fire was careful to mark out this line of tradition at every stage of his journey, as with the speaking flames that are revealed to be Ulysses and Guido de Montefeltro in the *Inferno*; with Guincelli and Arnaut in the *Purgatorio*, when they address Dante out of the fire by which they are being purified; and with Aquinas discoursing from within his "blessed flame" (12.2) in the *Paradiso*.

In his own book of fire, what Dickens remembered most from this tradition was the intimacy between vitality and eloquence on the one hand and destruction on the other. In remembering that fire was "the subtlest of the elements," according to the tradition that descended from Aristotle, he also remembered that it held the distinction among the elements of being identified with plague or pestilence and of leaving its mark in especially scarifying forms.[26] Like Augustine, who had written dismissively of those who "wish to see, but not to be burnt,"[27] Dickens did not believe one could consume a printed page with any understanding unless one risked being consumed by it. As he always portrayed it, reading in its origins is an astounding, striking, violently affecting experience. In drawing on the conventional phrases that associated fire with vitality and inspired language, Dickens did not stop at the conventional images of revitalization through fire that one could find in traditions stemming from Hindu, Greek, Islamic, Persian, and Christian mythologies. He also drew attention to his sense that "conventional phrases are a sort of fireworks, easily let off, and liable to take a great variety of shapes and colours not at all suggested by their original form" (*DC*, 15:185). This is as much as to say that he felt it necessary always to insist, with his resolute distaste for the popularized attitudes of Romantic aesthetics, that the language of men and women is not as the language of God is imagined to be. He knew the old saying, that fire is a good servant but a bad master;[28] and so another story told by his hearth was that of the violence of fire in a world of bad masters. This is the author, after all, who did not hesitate to send one of his characters to meet his maker by way of spontaneous combustion.

In other words, Dickens always remembered that fire is also associated with the sword: in the imagery of popular culture, as in the fairs at which performers would swallow both items; in idioms, such as Virgil's formulaic association of these terms, which would be taken up by Dickens in his *Child's History of England* just as it had been by multitudes of others before him; in the various locutions that allowed flames to be tongues and tongues to be instruments of language both cutting and incendiary; and in Western religious tradition, which told of an angel's flaming sword guarding the entrance to postlapsarian Eden. With this sense of things in mind, Dickens, like Blake, wrote with "corroding fires" and, like Artaud, knew that "the Fire is going to go out of the Hearth."[29] Often, if not at his most simplistic, sanctimonious, and saccharine moments, he knew that the book of the hearth, as an experience of reading, involved destruction and scarification. ("As fire drives out fire, so pity pity" was the sententious reminder of Brutus in *Julius Caesar* [3.1.171].) In memorializing the sacred fire of the hearth, Dickens also remembered such things as the legend of Empedocles, book-burnings, the auto-da-fé, Guy Fawkes's insurrection, and the hayricks set afire by "Captain Swing."[30]

So the good servant always labored under the threat of the bad master—or mistress—as Dickens perhaps most vividly suggested when he described the arson committed upon a house during the Gordon riots of *Barnaby Rudge*. He made it out to be a home engulfed by the hearth, as it were, and so suffering all its values to be turned inside out. What might have been its sanctified maternal nursing of a boy is traded for an image that conjoins infanticidal and suicidal impulses, and so "the book of life," in accordance with the biblical prophecy (Revelations 20:15), is exchanged for "the lake of fire":

> There were men who cast their lighted torches in the air, and suffered them to fall upon their heads and faces, blistering the skin with deep unseemly burns. There were men who rushed up to the fire, and paddled in it with their hands as if in water, and others who were restrained

by force from plunging in, to gratify their deadly longing. On the skull of one drunken lad—not twenty, by his looks—who lay upon the ground with a bottle to his mouth, the lead from the roof came streaming down in a shower of liquid fire; melting his head like wax. (BR, 13: 135)[31]

This fire recalls its mythological heritage as a stolen gift: an element in some primordial way illegitimate, like a servant turned master, and thus bound to communicate suffering in whatever else it may convey. A further analogy is revealed, in which the hearth is to the house as the mouth is to the body: an *opening* of the body, and as such a potential danger to its integrity. In itself both inside and outside, the hearth might appear not to be a proper place at all.

Fire is then a language that speaks interminably of the danger it poses, of the impossibility of anyone controlling it once and for all, and of the consequent necessity (and inevitable failure) of attempts to tame it. As in *Beowulf*, this fire comes to be seen as the "greediest of spirits."[32] It forever threatens to violate its own sanctuary, the property of the host, the walls of civilization that offer it its only definition—even as the spirit of the letter of "conventional phrases" may take fire in unpredictable ways, resulting in damage all around.

As is shown by *The Cricket on the Hearth* or the scene of arson from *Barnaby Rudge*, certain traditions may bring us to envision chaste Vesta—"the milder fire of the world," as Augustine put it—surrendering herself to Vulcan, "the more violent."[33] Eve falls, shall we say, and catches Adam with the "contagious Fire" of her eye (*Paradise Lost*, 9.1036). Or in a nineteenth-century characterization, having noted in seeming innocence that a man's "presence in a room" is "more cheering than the brightest fire," one almost immediately hears a "demoniac laugh" and sees "tongues of flame," no longer contained within the hearth, threatening to destroy him: "In the midst of blaze and vapour, Mr. Rochester lay stretched motionless."[34]

According to the line of tradition developed through cross-references such as these, whatever else fire may be, it is a dangerous woman tamed—but never with certainty. As Lady Macbeth sneers, the book of the hearth is "a woman's story at a winter's fire, / Authorized by her grandam" (3.4.63–64)—that is, so long as it is not the tale of her own unladylike exuberance. Or the book of the hearth is Jane Eyre, during the time when she is first encouraged to imagine herself domesticated with Edward Fairfax Rochester—which will be interrupted when she finds her story escaping its bounds to assume the form of pyromaniacal

Bertha Mason, the figure of both their improprieties. Or, from the masculine perspective and in the mode of comic resolution, it is Eugene Wrayburn after he is cured of his suspiciously irregular warmth of spirits and so led into marriage (and to the altar of the hearth) by the lesson of Bradley Headstone's assault upon him. "Better to Be Abel than Cain" is Dickens's cool heading for the chapter that follows the one telling of this murderous attack.

In all these versions of the story of fire, the qualities that in other contexts might figure in it as the transcendence of the ideal—its storied lightness, brightness, and mobility—are construed instead as being dangerous, and all the more so for offering the possibility of this difference in interpretation. No longer, as with John Foxe's account of the martyrdom of Lawrence, does one find a "fiery bed of iron" to be better described as a "soft bed of down"[35]—the situation is rather the reverse. One reads of the pains of burning, of the costs of pleasure, and of the necessities of suffering and sacrifice, with special reference to the case of women in their domestic emplotments as *genius loci* and *genius foci*— and so once again we come upon the dreariest of formulas in Dickens's fiction.

Once again, however, this formula is incomplete. For if fire is a woman—as it surely is, among other things—it may also be men such as the burnt Rochester and the beaten Wrayburn. It may even be Charles Dickens, who put himself in the place of the woman in figuring his work as a book of fire.

In itself this recognition may seem unremarkable enough, for criticism has long noted the role of the man who is "softened" (to use a Victorian term) or "feminized" (to use one more recent). Prominent examples include Hareton Earnshaw at the conclusion of *Wuthering Heights*, Major Dobbin in *Vanity Fair*, Rochester at the end of *Jane Eyre*, and Joe Gargery throughout *Great Expectations*. (As a blacksmith whose fire can create and renew, Joe also recalls a popular medieval image of Christ.) But this is precisely the point: that like others of his time, Dickens was aware that he was marking gendered types, and marketing them to consumers, in all the figures associated with the institution of the hearth. Therefore, in setting out to analyze the representation of gender in a case such as this one, we run the risk of obscuring what is most notable about it, which is precisely its obviousness: its unmistakably stereotypical nature, in which the figure of the woman seems to have no history but only a fate, which is to be, for all time, an offering to man of an emblem of sacrifice.[36]

Like fire and the hearth, woman, too, had a history, to say the least; and as with the fire and the hearth, we take only a cursory account of Dickens's writing if we fail to recognize that he was acutely aware of this. This awareness is shown even in his hostility to the issue of women's rights in his day, as in the portrait of Miss Wisk in *Bleak House*, since this hostility was presumably fired by a perception of possible changes in women.[37] It is important to distinguish between Dickens's fear of certain progressive historical changes, such as those sought through women's rights, labor, antislavery, and anticolonial movements, and the stereotypical formulas of his fiction, which may seem ahistorical not because they are or ever were, but because they were made to satisfy, polemically, a fearful and often ignorant consciousness of history that may lurk in even the most progressive among us.

Dickens did not believe in a Romantic conception of originality that could transport us entirely away from stereotypes. He was then concerned to argue that while there is no getting away from stereotypes, there is a crucial difference between their worthless reproduction (as in the rhetoric of Podsnappery) and their creative use in social life. So although the way he designed the types of value in his writing must certainly be challenged in many respects, we reveal nothing but our own simplicity if we think that Dickens's stereotypes, such as those epitomized in the book of fire, are simple things. For even as Dickens showed a sense of piety toward certain stereotypes, he also showed (as in the mockery of domesticity at the end of *Our Mutual Friend*) that there is really no end to pious frauds, including those that creative artists sincerely practice on themselves. If we fail to observe this recognition on his part, we reveal not his simplicity but our own, as in the stereotypes popularized in contemporary literary theory about "naive realism" and "the classic novel," which are straw figures that deserve nothing better than to be tossed onto the sort of fire to which they are so blind.

Though Dickens's works unquestionably traffic in all the most egregious Victorian clichés about woman's nature, place, role, and spiritual destiny, the effect of this fashioning of ahistorical values is then to call attention to their obvious unlikelihood, as in *The Cricket on the Hearth*. Simultaneously these novels propose the unobvious likelihood that the voice of Charles Dickens speaking to the reader out of a book, out of a fire, is the voice of a woman—in which case a woman is *not* a woman in that dreary formula we may have imagined ourselves to have understood in these novels. We must recognize, then, that we have read these novels only partially or too hastily, even if we have done so at the perverse urging of the author, who seems only intermittently to remember the more extended implications of these figurations.[38]

As configured within the scene of reading the fire in Dickens's novels, the reader, whether man or woman, is stereotypically male: isolated, independent, thoughtful, outwardly unemotional, deliberate, controlled. The book that offers itself to this reader is stereotypically feminine in its identification with the hearth and in its passive submissiveness before the reader, whom Dickens always describes as finding in it what he or she projects there, whether willingly and wittingly or not. This fireside scene then suggests a belief that if a story does not figure forth its sacrifice to the reader, to the blazing peculiarity and consuming abstraction of the reader, it cannot hope to be of any value; but in this way the fire that is the woman's symbol and consuming textual offering also comes to appear as her imagined author. So where do we, the readers, end up?

As in his frequent reconfigurations of sentimentality as affectation and manipulation, so in the lurchings of Dickens's characters between stereotype and idiosyncrasy, the sadomasochistic configurations of his plots, and the disfiguring of his own assigned gender within the book of fire: we are drawn within an all-pervasive sense of sacrifice. Within it, while the values of sentimentality are marked and marketed, they are also distanced from any fulfillment in the present, which is represented by the experience of reading, which in turn is made to emphasize a sense of unreality that must be painfully recognized within one's very self. In this way Dickens suggested a simultaneous necessity for and necessary abasement of art. In other words, the stereotypes in which his novels traffic are sold with the assurance that they will provide their consumers with all the anxiety and alienation they could possibly want. Fire, hearth, and woman appear as mutually redundant signifiers in search of an authorizing desire. With no one of them serving as center or base to the others, the story they tell is of their unrepresentativeness: of letters that turn to unreadable fire at the very moment when they make the most sense. It is as if reading at its most affecting is an experience of touching a flame that one cannot learn to stop touching, in which even the differences of male and female are consumed. To be sure, as David Hume had argued, the old adage "Once burned, twice shy" holds good as long as any sense of custom holds;[39] but Dickens's work is about nothing if it is not about how custom does *not* hold, cannot hold, in the devices, images, and rituals handed down through his books. These always serve as no more than holding actions which must expect to lose their ground in the fiery cross-referencing of social life.

So Dickens's book of fire is not a work of reference devoted to an already enshrined sense of fire, hearth, or woman. Instead, it is a book in which the very notion of reference must give way to the work of cross-referencing, which alone can begin to be adequate to the complexities and contradictions of Dickens's writing. This cross-referencing has a redemptive aspect, bearing witness to the spiritualizing cross of Christianity; a syncretic aspect, which articulates knowledge through symbolic connections across different images, stories, histories, and institutions; and an agonistic aspect, which is liable to double-cross these others, thus suggesting that the world they serve to establish in Dickens's fiction may be lost and proven unreadable in the very "characters," or printed types, by which it is illumined. In other words, these cross-referencings tell stories about the unquestionable appeal of universality, the unavoidable demands of symbolic articulation, and the all-consuming force of historical differences that are destined to unsettle this appeal and these demands—and so also to frustrate their imaginary resolution, within the crucible of the hearth, into the law and order of tradition within the form of the novel.

Cross-referencing in its redemptive aspect is probably the most obvious and in some ways the most simple of these aspects of Dickens's work.[40] On the evidence of his novels, Christianity for Dickens was little more than an enthusiasm, sometimes shrill and very often stupid, for the promise of redemption through suffering. This was taken in conjunction with his assumption that the Anglican church, conceived of as an institution more social than strenuously doctrinal or evangelically devotional, was the natural reference point for belief. Thus, even where Dickens's novels make specific reference to Christ or to the church, the suffering in question is always quite definitely a worldly issue of romantic love, family attachment, friendship, duty, or common humanity. (The closest Dickens comes to portraying the questing spirituality of a Dorothea Brooke is in the artsy selfishness of a Harold Skimpole.) In fact, his sense of faith is so broad as to function as the very grammar of humanity, as in Mark Tapley's syntactic characterization of himself: "A Werb is a word as signifies to be, to do, or to suffer (which is all the grammar, and enough too, as ever I was taught); and if there's a Werb alive, I'm it. For I'm always a bein', sometimes a doin', and continually a sufferin' " (MC, 7: 380–81).

Although Dickens took pains to emphasize his tolerance toward Catholics (in *Barnaby Rudge*) and toward Jews (in his repentant portrayal of Riah in *Our Mutual Friend*), the broadness of this understanding is always one granted, with marked generosity, from an assumed pinnacle of English life, which is inhabited, as a matter of course, by white, heterosexual, law-abiding, tender-hearted, tough-minded Protestants. This position cannot itself be assumed by others except in the character of presumptuousness, as exemplified, for instance, in the Americans met by Mark Tapley in *Martin Chuzzlewit*. In other words, this tolerant cross-referencing, which defines and unites humanity through the image of redemptive suffering, always overlooks certain limits from its position on high.[41] These are marked out in villains such as Uriah Heep—who, we may remember, is last seen assuming a Christian attitude that wins him much applause. At the same time, however, such limits are always so looked down upon as to be denied any recognition as such. Unlike the fire in the House of the Interpreter in *Pilgrim's Progress*, which is obscurely fed by Christ while the devil openly but ineffectually casts water upon it, Dickens's fire, no matter what trials it represents, demands an open and even universal celebration. That is why there is no persuasive evil in his novels, just as there is no figuring of sublime religious stirrings: because these novels assume that any dampening of their fires must be, in the last analysis, somehow inadvertent.

The most casual phrase in Dickens's novels may be very notable in this respect, as in Susan Nipper's confrontation with Mr. Dombey: "I may not be a Indian widow Sir and I am not and I would not so become but if I once made up my mind to burn myself alive, I'd do it!" (*DS*, 9: 217). The telling confusion in this assertion may remind us that the mingled fascination and horror with which Victorians typically represented the practice of suttee can be accounted for, at least in part, by the way this practice might seem to image the abominable ideal of their own book of fire. Having just allowed that she might not be "a Fox's [sic] Martyr" (*DS*, 9:215), Susan is at once asserting her universality and confessing the cultural and historical limits on her power to imagine this universality and the spiritual sacrifices proper to it.

In effect, Susan Nipper is thus making herself out to be a comic version of Jane Eyre, who also finds reason to insist that she will "not be hurried away in a suttee." And having rejected St. John Rivers's Calvinist desire for "a soul that revelled in the flame and excitement of sacrifice," Jane again takes Rochester to task when he still presumes to attribute to her a pleasure in sacrifice: "Sacrifice! What do I sacrifice? Famine for food, expectation for content ... Is that to make a sacri-

fice?"[42] Like *Middlemarch*'s Dorothea Brooke, who is seriously miffed
when her sister suggests that she "likes giving up,"[43] Jane seeks to ward
off the implications—at once psychological, ideological, linguistic, religious, and political—that she fears would spoil the supposed spirituality of her offering. Similarly, Susan Nipper's comment shows how
the redemptive cross of sacrifice in Dickens's novels must suffer itself
to be constructed of unconscious cultural defenses and of offensive historical differences.[44]

In contrast to the universality imagined by cross-referencing in this
redemptive aspect, its syncretic aspect offers the differentiated development of enlightened cultural organization. This allows one to distinguish the flame "that in its grosser composition has the taint of earth"
from "the sacred fire from heaven," which is "as gentle in the heart, as
when it rested on the heads of the assembled twelve, and showed each
man his brother, brightened and unhurt" (*DS*, 8:300).[45] Even if they are
written in fire, the powers of symbolic association, hierarchy, implica-
tion, inference, causality, and exclusion are made to appear stable
enough to allow for the establishment of identities—for instance, when
Lizzie Hexam discerns Bella Wilfer in a seemingly immemorial and yet
ostensibly individual metaphor. Bella is a "heart well worth winning,
and well won," Lizzie says with assurance, looking into the coals (*OMF*,
24:137).

Insofar as it can be imagined to prevail, this stability makes possible
comparison and analogy, such as a reader can see in the way Lizzie's
fate is the twin to Bella's, though reversed in attitude and social circumstances. Logically, then, it also brings forth various forms of repetition and so makes possible predictions of the future—even though
these must always be at least slightly displaced, never quite certain, lest
the implicit development of syncretic truth should seem to lapse into
the overt nonsense of sadistic manipulation. Like identities, predictions
are not made to appear as the manufactured goods of an author one
can identify, whether under the name of Dickens or the sacred name
of God. Instead, they must arise of themselves in "the rapture of these
words" in which cultural organization is syncretically cross-referenced.

Thus, when Jenny Wren urges Lizzie to look into the fire for the
identity she dare not claim on her own account—"I a lady!"—Lizzie
finds herself in just such a state of cultural ravishment. The "rapture of
these words" allows her to discover the equivoque within her exclamation, which need not be a disclaimer after all. In what turns out to
be an accurate précis of the relationship she is to have with Wrayburn,

she speaks again of the heart, which again can only be as individual as it is repeated, typical, formulaic, even as a cherished sentimental melody to the ear:

> Her heart—is given him, with all its love and truth. She would joyfully die with him, or, better than that, die for him. She knows he has failings, but she thinks they have grown up through his being like one cast away, for the want of something to trust in, and care for, and think well of. And she says, that lady rich and beautiful that I can never come near, "Only put me in that empty place, only try how little I mind myself, only prove what a world of things I will do and bear for you, and I hope that you might even come to be much better than you are, through me who am so much worse, and hardly worth the thinking of beside you." (OMF, 23:435).

Like the raptures Phillis Wheatley told of in her elegies, which were also bound up with the equivocal nature of predictions and aftereffects, Lizzie's rapture suggests the wild and violent overdetermination in the formulas of cherished cultural ideals, such as freedom. Compounded as it is of conflicting assumptions about the worth of women, the relations among class position and wealth and morality, and the spiritual functions of emotion, the stereotype cannot help but divide her from herself at the highest moment of her pleasure. Through Lizzie we see how the stereotype must simultaneously function as imitation and as travesty. As Homi Bhabha puts it, "The stereotype is in fact an 'impossible' object."[46]

Charley Hexam complains to his sister that the rapture of symbolic forms is, strictly speaking, "not justified." He tells her, "It was all very well when we sat before the fire—when we looked into the hollow down by the flare—but we are looking into the real world now" (OMF, 23:282). In this attitude he follows the lead of Bradley Headstone, who is his mentor, the would-be suitor of Lizzie, and the "smouldering" foil (OMF, 23:425) to Eugene Wrayburn. Briefly softened in his attitude, Charley tells Headstone, "I used to call the fire at home, her books, for she was always full of fancies—sometimes quite wise fancies, considering—when she sat looking at it"; but the schoolmaster is quite certain of the appropriate judgment. His curt response is to say, "I don't like that" (OMF, 23:286). For he recognizes what is, indeed, the case as Dickens puts it: that the story of fire in this aspect is not of the real world. Even Lizzie's quibble on this point ("Ah, we were looking into the real world then, Charley!") must remain equivocal, speaking of "then" rather than "now." To speak otherwise would be to accept Charley's selfishly manipulative character and thus to allow her own imaginary and symbolic identities to be extinguished in the real world. Her fiery sense of individuality would turn into that other kind of thing, the real thing, which is inarticulate and undifferentiated death, as with the loathsome corpses Gaffer Hexam made her help pull from the Thames—anonymous bodies whose only memorial was in the cold print, as the saying would have it, of the stereotyped bills posted on the walls of her childhood dwelling.

Thus, just as cross-referencing in its redemptive aspect must deny its limits, in its syncretic aspect it must sacrifice the real, reducing it to namelessness. In the real world, as Dickens portrays it, "a multitude of weak, imitative natures are always lying by, ready to go mad upon the next wrong idea that may be broached—in these times, generally some form of tribute to Somebody for something that never was done, or, if ever done, that was done by Somebody Else" (*OMF*, 23:425). That is why the identificatory and predictive logic of his novels requires counterexamples, such as Bradley Headstone, whose character is the occasion for the foregoing disquisition. They serve to stabilize the work of cross-referencing in its syncretic aspect not by signifying evil, which is itself a term at issue in the relation of type and anti-type, but by promising that the work of cross-referencing will have an end. It cannot be allowed forever to go on lest identity become random, disorganized, without logical positions or oppositions. Rather than taking offense at predictability in plot, character, or phrase, then, we are enjoined to recognize that predictability—as dreadful as it might always become—is to be treasured, as with the familiar fairy tales, folk stories, and popular novels, poems, and plays to which Dickens referred so fondly throughout his career. That is why Dickens's characters are always punished for identifying themselves with romances or fairy tales and yet always rewarded in proportion to their persistence in this stupidity.

As Dickens portrays it, the alternative to predictability is not sublime originality but mad imitation, which is the ignominious, nameless chaos of the godforsaken real world of social life, in which events bear no comprehensible relation to somebody or anybody. This is the real world to which Sir Leicester Dedlock so aptly refers when he speaks of the Court of Chancery "as a something, devised in conjunction with a variety of other somethings, by the perfection of human wisdom, for the eternal settlement (humanly speaking) of everything" (*BH*, 16:15). Those who fail to appreciate that they must suffer the real world to be burnt out of themselves are bound to be killed by it, as Richard Jarndyce learns too late, whereas those who make a propriety of refusing to acknowledge it, like Harold Skimpole or Mr. Podsnap, are likely to prosper. The real world must suffer itself to be burnt, to be tried and proven consumable, and thus to be made lovely (and readable) with scars, such as those that come to decorate the face of Esther Summerson.

It makes perfect sense, then, that this passage on Bradley Headstone's passion should have opened with an assured and unembarrassed reference to a banal feature of cultural tradition: "Love at first sight is a trite expression quite sufficiently discussed." And when Lizzie Hexam's foil turns up in another novel—"As the old woman . . . sat bending over the few loose bricks with which [the fire] was pent . . . she looked as if she were watching at some witch's altar for a favourable token" (DS, 9:59)—we can expect that Good Mrs. Brown, like Headstone, will not turn out to be unmitigatedly evil but instead will prove insufficiently stable. And again, as with the real world, anyone who fails to recognize the stereotypically divided condition of being of such characters is bound to suffer horribly, as Rogue Riderhood learns when he figures that he can get the upper hand over Headstone by counting on his predictability—an error that results in Riderhood's *second* death by drowning.

And yet, all cautions taken into account, "conventionalities" do appear also as fireworks or as "Furies" (OMF, 24:392), redemption as repression, and men and women alike as the "woman" of stereotype, because of the agonistic aspect to the cross-referencings in Dickens's book of fire. In this aspect, rather than signifying unifying redemption or symbolic totality, what is *cross* tells of unhappiness, dissatisfaction, or outright contradiction and hostility. ("I can stand any fire better than a fire of cross questions," says Mr. George, that upright representative of Christian penitence, military valor, and family love [BH, 16:461].) One might dwell here on the fact that the "family circle" around the institution of the hearth might, in fact, be more accurately described as a half-circle, a crossed circle. Or this aspect of cross-referencing might find an image in the correspondence of this period, in which one could economize on paper and postage by writing on the bias as well as horizontally—if we imagine this writing on the bias to be in a variant hand, on contradictory subjects, and to different ends than those otherwise marked out.

When revisions such as these become imaginable, the fire of sacrifice, in which all might be abstracted through redemptive tradition, and the fire of enlightenment, through which everyone is contracted to assume certain positions within ordered images, stories, histories, and institutions, appears as the fire of distraction, which takes people out of themselves. Neither a focus to imagination and culture nor their predictable destruction through reversal or inversion, this fire suggests a singular experience of reading that requires a language for which nothing of the past prepares us. It plays up the dissension of redemptive unity and the partiality of symbolic totality, calling attention to how the figurations of fire are also, always, disfigurations. Whereas cross-referencing in its redemptive aspect follows the law of denial and in its syncretic aspect the law of contradiction, in its agonistic aspect "the law is a ass" (OT, 489).

In *Great Expectations*, the resultant experience of reading is figured in a desire so unaccountable that fire itself, together with the hearth and the woman in question, must lose its coherence. Finding himself in love, Pip finds himself criss-crossed by all sorts of metonymic associations which he is pathetically unable or furiously unwilling (this difference, too, collapsing in flames) to resolve:

> Truly it was impossible to dissociate her presence from all those wretched hankerings after money and gentility that had disturbed my boyhood—from all those ill-regulated aspirations that had first made me ashamed of home and Joe—from all those visions that had raised her face in the glowing fire, struck it out of the iron on the anvil, extracted it from the darkness of the night to look in at the wooden window of the forge and flit away. In a word, it was impossible for me to separate her, in the past or in the present, from the innermost life of my life. (GE, 22:274)

To be sure, this representation has its traditional and stereotypical aspects, in which the unaccountability of love serves as its guarantee of spiritual authenticity. These aspects are crossed over, however, by an insistently reiterated emphasis on the undesirability of this desire—so much so that even by the end of the novel, Estella's attractiveness can scarcely be distinguished from a negativity that is punishing, mindlessly and unprogressively repetitive, and thoroughly disillusioned. Pip's desire appears as a sacrifice without intention and without any reliable prospects for a return of knowledge. In Pip's words: "Once for all; I knew to my sorrow, often and often, if not always, that I loved her against reason, against promise, against peace, against hope, against happiness, against all discouragement that could be. Once for all; I loved her none the less because I knew it, and it had no more influence in restraining me, than if I had devoutly believed her to be human perfection" (*GE*, 22:270).

Such a passage all but avows to the reader that "Estella," far from being "human perfection," is unhuman, even unrecognizable by any means, like a flame one can never learn to stop touching—thus giving the lie to the idiotically comforting and absurdly hallowed adage, "Once burnt, twice shy." In other words, "Estella" figures here as that which, "once for all," confounds all—which is, however, nothing without it. She marks that point at which one touches on reality, which is the point at which stereotypes burn most fiercely even as they are being completely consumed, destroyed, rendered meaningless. Similarly traversed by this sort of relentless cross-referencing, though in a more markedly comic mode—if this distinction can still survive—is the mourning of Tom Pinch, in *Martin Chuzzlewit*, after the Pecksniffian nature has finally been brought home to him: "Tom had so long been used to steep the Pecksniff of his fancy in his tea, and spread him out upon his toast, and take him as a relish with his beer, that he made but a poor breakfast on the first morning after his expulsion" (*MC*, 7:169).

As with the blithely homoerotic and cannibalistic pleasures of this passage, the agonistic aspect of Dickens's cross-referencing generally shows itself in what might be called the wickedness of his humor. For instance, there is the eulogy Sloppy offers for Betty Higden in *Our Mutual Friend*: "O Mrs. Higden, Mrs. Higden, you was a woman and a mother and a mangler in a million million!" (*OMF*, 24:120). Other instances are plentiful, of course, but an example especially relevant to a focus on hearth, fire, and woman may be found in the portrayal of Mr. Venus in *Our Mutual Friend*. For unlike the story of Eugene Wrayburn and Lizzie Hexam, that of Venus and his beloved does not parallel and repeat, with calculated variations, the story of John Harmon and Bella Wilfer. Instead, it crosses it on the bias in a fervently upsetting way that may be taken to epitomize this aspect of Dickens's cross-referencing.

First of all, there is the confounding of lines of gender and cultural tradition in the discordant name, "Mr. Venus," in relation to which one may also note the smirking contradictions lurking in "Pleasant Riderhood." Her "swivel eye" (*OMF*, 23:438) and freedom from any refinements of manner, mood, and behavior do not offer the slightest support for expectations of Venusian bliss, whether this be figured in a passive, active, or otherwise uncategorical mode of equestrian comportment on the part of her inamorato. No wonder, then, if one finds that the shop of Mr. Venus is "a muddle of objects," among which a visitor may chance to distinguish such *disjecta membra* as "two preserved frogs fighting a small-sword duel," bones both "miscellaneous" and "articulated," "a Hindoo baby in a bottle," "African ditto," "dried cuticle, warious"—'That's the general panoramic view," the proprietor impatiently concludes (*OMF*, 24:93–101). It makes a crazy kind of sense, too, that when his fire is put under a temporary curfew by Miss Riderhood, who "objects to the business"—" 'I do not wish,' she writes in her own hand-writing, 'to regard myself, nor yet to be regarded, in that bony light' " (*OMF*, 24:103)—Mr. Venus should prove no more capable of overcoming his passion than was Pip. "My very bones is rendered flabby by brooding over it," he says (*OMF*, 24:101), in what in other circumstances would have to be a counterintuitive testament to the influence of passionate love on a man. Mr. Wegg's toast—'Be it ever . . . so ghastly, all things considered there's no place like it" (*OMF*, 24: 100)—may then stand as the motto to this singular hearth and home.

Figuratively, thematically, and dramatically, the art of taxidermy by which Mr. Venus proudly makes dead things come alive recrosses Dickens's art in this novel, which is focused on reviving the figure of John Harmon, among other things. The art of Venus, however, crosses Dickens's art on a bias which makes redemption a risible and polymorphously obscure trade while showing symbolic articulation to be based on collections of fundamentally heterogeneous elements. (The situation is similar, and absurdly doubled, with that other artist figure, Jenny Wren.) In the shop of Mr. Venus, readers do not find the sentimental image of love suffering reversal or inversion, as with the mercenary plotting of Alfred and Sophronia Lammle within this novel; instead, this image is mocked, or at once imitated and travestied, as if Cupid had always been a Cock Robin that had ought to get stuffed—like this very figure in Venus's shop, which must further suffer the arrow in its heart to be borrowed, now and again, for service as a toasting fork.

It is thus that all the cross-referencings of Dickens's art come to bear on the notion of the stereotype. They all suggest how vital it is that we not consider the stereotype a simple thing, much less an emblem of simplicity itself. In the stereotypical scene in which Dickens's characters gaze into the fire, what they see is that the stereotype is most truly itself when it is most decidedly other than itself. As Dickens presents it, the fascination of the stereotype is the fascination of fire.[47]

In his fires Dickens makes the stereotype out to be an unreality that is a real part of our blood, flesh, and feelings. Like a flaming pain that we can never learn not to invite into our homes and our very selves, the stereotype possesses an irreducible power—and thus is still a stereotype and yet not much of a stereotype after all, since it takes the place of nothing less than everything.

Certainly it is true that in Dickens's novels stereotypes of fire, hearth, and woman were stamped out—but in both senses of that phrase. They were reproduced, repeated; but in that very repetition they were obliterated, or cross-stamped as signs of unimaginable desire, unmanageable oppression, and rebellious will. Thus, as Dickens portrays it, the stamping out of the stereotype stamps out its own stereotypical nature, finding new life within it. The stereotype is then the very image of the productivity of rules, laws, and writing in the most general sense, in which they are as necessary to cultural rebellions and transgressions as they are to the erection of dominant cultural formations.

For instance, in Wendell Phillips's "Letter" prefacing Frederick Douglass's 1845 *Narrative of the Life of Frederick Douglass, an American Slave*, we come upon this conjuration: "Go on, my dear friend, till you, and those who, like you, have been saved, so as by fire, from the dark prison-house, shall stereotype these free, illegal pulses into statutes."[48] As I trust is clear, I do not take the "free, illegal pulses" in Dickens's stereotypes to be particularly heroic (as I do Douglass's); but I do want to suggest that they can be of crucial importance if we wish to understand something of the complexity of history, desire, and gender in the Victorian era.

The general impression left by the cross-referencing in Dickens's fiction is that stereotypes are given their strength not by fixed forms but rather by the complex engine of tongues, swords, flames, and breath that is art in action. And in this action we see art not simply as the work of an individual writer but as the cultural operations with which all of Dickens's writings show him to have been preoccupied: the engines of war, capitalism, education, theatricality, domestication, and so on. Certainly there is something pointed to in Dickens's trinity of home, hearth, and femininity, but it is not these things in themselves—even assuming that we can know what these things simply are. One need only think of what an impossible object the domestic ideal is in Dickens's novels—traduced, parodied, delayed, mistaken, lost, and when found (if one can still speak of a finding after such tortures and deviations), found only, and most emphatically, through the machinery of art, as in the playacting that transforms Bella Wilfer into a wife in *Our Mutual Friend*.

To make this argument is in no way to suggest a neutral accounting of Dickens's work, as if finally all its ideological effects must cancel one another out in the mysterious sublimity of fire—a spiritual fire, a humanistic fire, a semiotic fire, call it what you will. On the contrary, this argument is designed to give full play to the stupid, cruel, and otherwise limited values to be found in the structuring of Dickens's world while just as fully respecting the desire that stamped them out by refusing to condescend to it, as one does if one defines the stereotype as a simple thing, overlooking all its ambivalent passions, many-faceted appeals, and complex historical turnings.

In effect, in this argument I am both drawing upon and writing against Jacques Derrida, who has seen fit to read Friedrich Nietzsche's animus against women as if feminism were solely a matter of positions assumed in books—thus overlooking almost entirely the implications of this historical movement in positions at home, in the economy, before the law, and elsewhere.[49] I am presenting an analysis of stereotypy for those truly dissatisfied with it, by which I mean those dissatisfied enough not to turn away from its challenge. For while fire does a lot of work in Dickens's novels—as in converting heavenly light into the forms of great factories, factories into the hearths of middle-class homes, and these hearths into books—what it does not do is stay where it is supposed to be. Precisely defined, the stereotype is that which proves not to be itself. As fire fails, strays, rebels, or attacks, depending on how one regards it, so does the stereotype. In fact, the only thing it can never do is be true to itself.

"We must now return, as the novelists say, and as we all wish they wouldn't . . ." (OMF, 23:18)—to what? Letters of fire that take on a character—feminine, sacred, suffering, and heartfelt—which, however, will not always stay at rest in the image of woman, the institution of the hearth, or the book of fire. As in the foregoing passages from *Our Mutual Friend*, *Martin Chuzzlewit*, and *Great Expectations*, Dickens's art is at its most provocative when its stereotypes show their fire: their tragic, misconceived, terrible attractiveness. In these moments the differing aspects of the cross-referencing in Dickens's art are simultaneously and, in effect, equally at work, showing up the immolations, amputations, and other sorts of disfigurations in the production of meaningful words, images, or types. It is then that his writing gives readers the chance to see history (as the suspiciously undisturbing stereotype would have it) in the making. Or in the words of another cliché, which really is so heterogeneous to our proper comportment that it ought to leave us, like Captain Cuttle, "in a state of unmitigated consciousness" (DS, 9:431), his art then makes the past "come alive." History turns to life in the contradictions of tradition and the sacrifices of understanding that lead us positively to desire the painful unreality of art.

Of course, at its worst Dickens's writing is simple enough to allow these differing cross-references to appear marvelously unified—in which case we must indeed return, as the novelists say, to the light of tradition and the warmth of understanding that makes each and every one of us (as untold numbers of popular songs have threatened) a heart of fire, a shining star, a blaze of glory, man or woman, and so on.

CHAPTER FIVE

The War of Tradition

Virginia Woolf and the Temper of Criticism

You will understand that as I write this a war is being fought, and as I write this the war is over. There is nothing to disturb you in these contradictory words. You, too, have confided ink to paper, finally beginning your letter to that friend kissed by distance and transformed into a promising abstraction . . . only to find that by the time you came to a close, the world you were addressing had changed once again. Revision was still possible, the margins left room for scribbled addenda, or you may have decided just to throw the damn thing away so you could start afresh; but whatever you did, you knew there was no way to get around this impossible time of writing, which is never so simple as even to let its beginning be named by the date when the first line is struck on a page. As Charles Lamb put it, "But what security can I have that what I now send you for truth shall not before you get it unaccountably turn into a lie?"[1]

I must trust that you know all this as well as I do. And so you must be aware that I cannot hope to direct your attention to this war without addressing others. If I can attribute the beginning of this chapter to the fall of 1990, when I began to make notes for it, I might just as well refer to other times, with any selection among them having no more significance than the outcome of a lottery—and certainly no less. You have read your Borges; or if you have not, I can refer you to a figure loitering in the grim lobby of a dormitory in East Lansing, Michigan, during another war, one the powerful enchantments of the media had yet to transform into a "syndrome," which in turn would be said to have been cured by the high-tech butchery of this impossible time, in which a war is now being fought and now is over. There may have been such an occasion, and this essay may have had its beginning at the time when this student of literature walked over to look at the list of randomly ranked birth dates just then posted on the wall so he could learn his chances of toiling on in school, serving a term in prison, seeking refuge in Canada, or heading into battle.

"An adverse drawing might mean mutilation, a varied infamy, death," says the narrator of "The Babylon Lottery."[2] Taking a cue from this story, I could go on to mention other events, this or that time, each having something of the lottery about it; but there is no getting over the suspicion that doing so would be pointless. One might as well ask Virginia Woolf actually to produce the images to which she called her readers' attention when she wrote in *Three Guineas*, "Also consider these photographs: they are pictures of dead bodies and ruined houses."[3] Woolf included other photographs in this book, and she did not think the destruction considered here was meaningful only as a symbol, negligible as a historical event. Taking these circumstances into account, I have to believe her omission of these photographs was an attempt to clarify something in them. Although it might seem perverse to say so, Woolf knew that what she was concerned to show us in these images of the Spanish civil war would only be muddled by their reproduction within her book. As if anticipating the critique of documentary photography in the photomontages Martha Rosler made between 1967 and 1972, which combined images of embattled Vietnam with pictures from *House Beautiful*, Woolf knew better than to let photographs of the Spanish civil war try to speak for themselves.[4]

"Great wars are strangely intermittent in their effects," Woolf noted elsewhere;[5] and certainly the time of other forms of art, such as photography, is no simpler than the time of writing. Woolf's decision was something of a gamble, then, something like a deliberate act of censorship, and just maybe a silent outburst of pure rage. One way or another, she figured the pictures would have said "this dead body" or "this ruined house" too simply, as I might have said "this war" or "this date"; and so the real battle would never have been joined.

In *Three Guineas* Woolf was concerned, inter alia, with the relation between anger and criticism, which is also the topic of this essay. War seems almost immediately to come to mind when this topic is raised, as does censorship, which is as closely associated with the art of warfare as it is with art in general. And censorship, too, may be identified too hastily if we think it sufficient to wag a finger at government office-holders, codes, and practices, all of which then appear to be related to warfare only by chance. Like Woolf, William Blake knew better. He could hear the chilling rage of Urizen in the voice of reason: "For we have Hirelings in the Camp, the Court, & the University: who would if they could, for ever depress Mental & prolong Corporeal War."[6] No wonder Woolf recalled his example in her late essay "Thoughts on Peace in an Air Raid" (1940), when she was contemplating the historical conditions that might lead women to suppress their own thinking on war in particular and politics in general.[7]

In its ordinary acceptance, in which it refers to the deliberate destruction or withholding of information, censorship does not begin adequately to represent the limits to "free speech," which is generally taken to be its opposite term. For instance, it cannot come anywhere close to grasping the phenomenon we witness when Henry Kissinger—a poisonous and unpardonable trafficker in power, under whose calamitous footsteps all of creation groans—is hailed by the media as an "elder statesman," a "distinguished diplomat," an "expert in foreign affairs." When these sorts of panegyrics are bestowed, the erasures necessary to produce such language could not be more obvious or odious; but how many in the media will be complaining about censorship?

The case is similar with war monuments, the works of art made to lend dignity to our frenzied butchery. As with the tomb of the Andronici in *Titus Andronicus* or Maya Lin's Vietnam Veterans Memorial (1982) in Washington, D.C., the only names they mention and the only figures they represent are "our own," and yet no one can hope to file suit under the Constitution to protest such practices. (This point was made by Chris Burden with his sculpture *The Other Vietnam Memorial* [1991], which is designed to remind us that the names of millions of Vietnamese killed in this war have been ritually suppressed.) In keeping company with the ordinary notion of censorship, the First Amendment proves as hapless in this instance as when it comes to defining the difference between violence and legitimate speech. Thus, we learn that Barbara Foley, then a professor of English at Northwestern University, had no right to be so angry in 1985 when she tried to stop a thug from spreading his lies about the Nicaraguan *contras* whom he had led (with the clandestine support of the Central Intelligence Agency and other government bodies);[8] meanwhile, the thug's record of stilling voices by killing the bodies whence they emerged was not viewed by Northwestern University as an infringement of free speech; and meanwhile, the Department of Defense would continue to sponsor research on our campuses as if the military engagements of the United States had never been known to trifle in the least with anyone's rights.

You have heard all this many times before—for instance, when June Jordan protested the appearance of William Shockley, the famous exponent of scientific racism, at Yale University in 1975.[9] You know all this as well as I do, and yet I must think there is something we are still overlooking here, something we are surveying and repressing, mapping and missing, all at once. For if we cannot get past the ordinary notion of censorship, it hardly matters that we can condescend to it, recognizing how inept it is at making the discriminations that would be necessary to lead us to truth. The grace of a lie, like the aesthetics of a monument to war, cannot be judged in isolation from its political duties. If Immanuel Kant's sense of aesthetics demands that we find war sublime, there are many curious reasons motivating it, but none into which we can enter through the traditional gateway between censorship and free speech.[10] And what I say of censorship I may say as well of wars and lotteries: that after we are sure we have all seen the same pictures, known the same words, and so shared the same experiences, there is still something we are overlooking, something that goes to the very heart of our conception of virtue.

Traditionally, temperance is accounted one of the four cardinal virtues. In thinking about criticism and critical tradition, what we tend to overlook (even as it stares us right in the face) is that where we see the cardinal virtues of temperance, courage, justice, and prudence, we must also orient ourselves to a compass in which temperance may figure as anger, courage as a brutal declaration of war, justice as the irrational outcome of a lottery, and prudence as the grace that seeks to render acts of censorship sublime. In short, in these cardinal virtues we must also see what Blake called "the four iron pillars of Satans Throne."[11]

To come to this recognition is to propose a different understanding of tradition—which is also, at the same time, a return to tradition. A consideration of the relation between anger and criticism may become an exemplary exercise in this respect. For from the time of Plato's *Republic* (in which lotteries, censorship, and warfare figure prominently) to the essay in which David Wojnarowicz happily envisioned the incineration of Senator Jesse Helms, thereby calling forth the panicked wrath of the National Endowment for the Arts,[12] the relation between anger and criticism has spelled out the polities we imagine for ourselves. However it is formulated, this relation appears fundamental to the chances we can expect of life, the battles we are led to fight, and the regulations through which we entertain experience. As they establish our sense of tradition, these issues of anger and criticism tell us what we can hope to arrive at through the impossible time of writing.

Of course, in what is most commonly pronounced in the name of Western critical tradition, anger is simply outlawed. As in Platonic discourse, it is said to show a lack of self-mastery, a groveling of the individual's higher self before his or her base passions, a failure of temperance or cultural tempering. So Kant noted that it must interfere with the freedom of the mind, without which one cannot hope to establish the vital possibility of a "censorship of taste."[13] This anger is then a solecism that marks the absence of a harmony one must desire— what Matthew Arnold, in *Culture and Anarchy*, called "sweetness and light."[14] Just as it can be counted on to sneer at dialectic or critical thought, so must anger mock the making of art, its cacophonous outbursts distracting us from what ought to be an imperative universality, as when William Wordsworth wrote of the "scorn and condemnation personal / That would profane the sanctity of verse."[15]

In this way of thinking, if art is not to run headlong toward its own destruction, its creators must either bridle themselves or, as Horace recommended in his *Art of Poetry*, look for a prudent critic to pull them back from the volcano's edge. Such anger is by no means the only danger artists and critics must avoid; but when they are possessed by anger, gripped by this madness, they are running wild and yet straight into the narrowest of cages. To those observing this spectacle, words such as *distorted* or *warped* will come to mind and tell of anger as anamorphosis, an all too familiar perversion that can be corrected only through an all too rare form of reflection, the very reflection anger would seek to smash. Or a self may have been so upset that it has disappeared or completely split off from the figure acting intemperately, as when we describe individuals "beside themselves" with anger. Therefore, in the contemporary United States we judge more severely crimes committed "in cold blood," and we construct an exception to the constitutional right to free speech based on the category of "fighting words." These are utterances considered to be such a provocation to anger as actually to constitute an act of violence in and of themselves— although the deathly palaver of Professor Henry Kissinger, the racist and homophobic rantings of Senator Jesse Helms, or the half-in-love-with-easeful-war eloquence of those dear to the CIA, such as Adolfo Calero or George Herbert Walker Bush, will not be judged to fall under this category, which is notorious in legal circles for its obscurity, as well it might be.[16]

In cases allowed to have extenuating circumstances, some pardon may await people in an angry condition, but precisely because these individuals are seen as pitiably disturbed. At the very least they will be considered troubling neighbors, difficult to have around, an embarrassing reminder of noisome and squalling infancy, wild animality, or ancient blundering chaos. More important, their anger is likely to associate them with stubbornness, fanaticism, unholy zeal, and violent menace. For according to the tradition we are following here, to be ill-tempered is to be dangerously narrow or limited, hopelessly enthralled by the moment, and so unable to rise above the song-and-dance of the passing show to reach the timeless realm of transcendence, which is the sole dwelling place of a truth forever young. Eternally in contrast to such failure will be the example of Socrates, whose jailer, in the act of handing him his poison, said he was certain the philosopher would not be mad at him.

This tradition would have it that those who are angry are unable to do justice to any subject. Insufficiently reserved, overrunning their own boundaries, they act with the warmth of a consuming fire. Like Bertha Mason in *Jane Eyre*, they must blacken and destroy whatever they touch. Their anger is indiscriminate, like the flailing about of someone tumbled into an alien element; or if we speak more in contempt than in sorrow, it is the moral equivalent of a riot, at once threatening to others and destructive to the individual suffering the anger, which will always have been misguided. This was a point appreciated by Matthew Arnold when he noted that Charlotte Brontë's mind contained "nothing but hunger, rebellion, and rage"; the more broad-minded critic was forced to conclude, "No fine writing can hide this thoroughly, and it will be fatal to her in the long run."[17] In fact, this critical tradition would have it that anger in general may be markedly feminine, temper more often than not a temptress, as when Cicero recommended against an unseemly tone in discourse: "Sharp exclamation injures the voice and likewise jars the hearer, for it has about it something ignoble, suited rather to feminine outcry than to manly dignity in speaking."[18] Instead of Socrates, large-browed and serenely seeking truth, we have Xanthippe, the scold.

To be sure, this critical tradition has always had its ironies, as when Arnold took his catchphrase "sweetness and light" from Jonathan Swift—hardly a model of dispassion either as poet or as critic, and a man who freely admitted as much. ("What I do," he wrote in a letter to Alexander Pope, "is owing to perfect rage and resentment."[19]) In the same century, Samuel Johnson was destined to become a critical model even though he proclaimed anger to have a devout role to play in criticism, and even Kant showed a sneaking sympathy with this emotion when he described the conditions under which he believed it would be *"aesthetically sublime."*[20] As such examples would indicate, the eighteenth century may have been an especially fine one for critical hostility; but Socrates had worked himself around to a comparable irony a couple of millennia earlier. In the *Phaedo* he was willing to allow that with the exception of the true philosopher, a type so rare as possibly to be without instantiation on this mortal earth, men called temperate may be so only "because they are intemperate." (So, too, many centuries later, Hegel would follow him in remarking on a moment when Reason, thinking itself enlightened, finds that "the function of 'measure' is immoderation.")[21] No wonder Socrates arrived at a point in *The Republic*, while reflecting on the dismaying historical fate of philosophy, when he could not help but lose his temper.[22]

A related case would be noted by authors such as Cicero and Quintilian, who insisted that anger had no proper role in public discourse— "An impudent, disorderly, or angry tone is always unseemly, no matter who it be that assumes it"[23]—even as they remarked that anger spontaneously aroused within an orator could lead to an especially effective speech, one that might seem divinely inspired. These and a host of similar passages throughout the centuries make it clear that we must speak of a familiar irony by the time we come to figures such as Swift and Johnson. We have no call to feel surprised when we stumble over expressions of anger from them or from other writers of their era, such as Pope, who urged critics to purge themselves of anger, spite, fury, and spleen and yet carved out an exception to this rule when he turned to those responsible for blasphemous writings: "These Monsters, Criticks! with your Darts engage, / Here point your Thunder, and exhaust your Rage!"[24] (As his editors inform us, these lines were written in seeming nostalgia for the Licensing Act of 1663, which was designed to censor Nonconformist and heretical works but which had been allowed to lapse after 1695.) Nor should we be surprised when writers of the nineteenth and twentieth centuries imitate their forebears by complaining of anger even as they out-Herod Herod in their own inflamed practice.

If any notice is taken of it within the history I have summarized here, this familiar irony is treated as just that: a bemusing aspect of criticism to which we have easily accommodated ourselves. It appears to be in but not of criticism, a violence that should be shunted aside by the same gesture that recognizes it (as in the old joke: "But aside from that, Mrs. Lincoln, how did you like the play?"). The irony of angry counsel against anger is then considered a mere figure of speech, as the saying would have it, and as such is dismissable from the terrific patriarchal

thrust of tradition. It is sublimated into something like Arnold's sweetness and light, as in Augustine's accommodating explanation that the
anger of God "is not a disturbing emotion of His mind, but a judgment
by which punishment is inflicted upon sin."[25] Those who fail to overlook this irony must be ill-educated, or worse, "political," and therefore
intellectually discreditable. The latter reproach can also be directed to
artists, as in John Lockhart's truly vicious and mythically killing review:
"We had almost forgot to mention, that Keats belongs to the Cockney
School of Politics, as well as the Cockney School of Poetry."[26]

Lockhart, it will be said, is a notoriously unrepresentative figure. We
will be assured that we need not concern ourselves with anger of this
sort since it arises only in uncommon or freakish circumstances, like
those addressed by Pope in his "Essay on Criticism" or by Arnold in
his 1873 preface to *Literature and Dogma*, in which he replied to the
cavilers who had presumed to observe that Christ and Saint Paul were
not above using harsh invective on occasion. In the tradition of Augustine, Arnold argued that these moments were exceptional: "Such
weapons can have no excuse at all except as employed against individuals who are past hope or institutions which are palpable monstrosi-
ties."[27] Following this logic, Arnold claimed he himself would never
reply "to any literary assailant" because "in such encounters tempers
are lost, the world laughs, and truth is not served."[28] When he nonetheless found himself accused of personally insulting F. W. Newman,
whose work he had critiqued in "On Translating Homer," he could
only profess dismay that his intentions had been so misunderstood.[29]
And with this posture of dismay, too, we are supposed to be familiar,
for it is a logical corollary to the irony of angry counsels against anger.
We hear it echoing and re-echoing down through the ages to the present day, as when bell hooks, than whom there can be no critic more
different from Arnold, professed a similar surprise at the fact that many
readers of her first book, *Ain't I a Woman: Black Women and Feminism*,
"would interpret the direct, blunt speech as signifying anger."[30]

But some, like bell hooks, will not let the matter rest there. In many
feminist writings since the 1960s, as in works by other politically identified critics, the relation between anger and criticism has been interpreted differently than Arnold would have had it. When Adrienne Rich
published an essay on Anne Bradstreet in 1966, raising a question about
her poetry—"Where are the stress-marks of anger, the strains of self-
division, in her work?"—she was looking not for flaws but for
something like transcendence in the name of anger.[31] Similarly, when
Sandra M. Gilbert and Susan Gubar sought to uncover the "covert au-

thorial anger" of women authors,[32] they were seeking something very like a universal truth. This is the direction epitomized by the title of Julia Lesage's essay "Women's Rage," in which she called for expressions of women's "own just rage"—expressions of an "authentic rage" that would no longer have to suffer the frustrating censorship of "displacement."[33]

Although writings such as these are often attacked on the grounds that they betray what other critics imagine tradition to have been, they do nothing of the kind. For even as they privilege what critical tradition had seemingly outlawed, they continue to share the conception of anger promoted within that tradition. For Lesage as for Plato, anger is a force of self-revelation. The self revealed by this means may be good or bad, and it may be more or less alert to its own condition, depending on one's argument; but there remains this assumption that the force of anger does reveal something of the self. If many would seek to ward off this force, seeing it as the enemy of propriety, harmony, and universality, others would woo it, believing that it is sure to convey a hungering sense of authenticity, revolt, or personal identity. In either case one maintains this psychological conception of anger, in which it erupts in truth by breaking through mechanisms of censorship. Thus, whether approvingly or disapprovingly, anger is described in terms of its supposed impatience toward its objects, contexts, and origins. This impatience then seems to guarantee a compelling revelation even in those cases where one wants to trump this with another statement presumed to be of greater consequence (as when Arnold is confident that their anger does tell us something about his opponents, albeit something not at all to their credit). Anger is a weakness or it is a strength; a loss of self-control or a righteous assertion of self; an incoherent cry or a pure surge of meaning—and so on. What persists through such differences is the basic premise of anger as a force that breaks through regulating forms to reveal a hidden, inward, disruptive truth.

Yet through their very fidelity to this tradition of criticism, hooks, Rich, Gilbert and Gubar, and Lesage have contributed to the making of a great difference in it. They have recognized that the anger generally assumed to be outlawed by critical tradition has never been so. They have been able to show that the familiar irony of angry counsels against anger was always constitutive rather than exceptional, marginal, and dismissible.[34] These latter characterizations are figures that now betray the tradition they served to invent. Recalling Socrates' dictum that children, women, servants, and inferior sorts of freemen are especially prone to intemperance—and perhaps remembering also that the state's prospective opponents in warfare are not even brought into this discussion—critics now may see those deemed philosophically competent as the truly outlandish cases, these outlawed figures as the censored reality.

In this realization they develop the example suggested by Woolf in *A Room of One's Own*: the case of Professor von X, who is the author of the "monumental work entitled *The Mental, Moral, and Physical Inferiority of the Female Sex*" (53).[35] Already angered at having been turned away from an Oxbridge library for reasons attributable to her sex, Woolf's protagonist ("call me Mary Beton, Mary Seton, Mary Carmichael, or by any name you please—it is not a matter of any importance" [6])[36] is further enraged when she encounters the writings of Professor von X, along with works by many others like him, in the British Museum. It does not take long for her to control her own feelings, but she is left with a question:

> How explain the anger of the professors? Why were they angry? For when it came to analysing the impression left by these books [about women] there was always an element of heat. This heat took many forms; it showed itself in satire, in sentiment, in curiosity, in reprobation. But there was another element which was often present and could not immediately be identified. Anger, I called it. But it was anger that had gone underground and mixed itself with all kinds of other emotions. To judge from its odd effects, it was anger disguised and complex, not anger simple and open. (54–55)

In this passage Woolf's protagonist rises above the anger for which her sex traditionally was faulted, and she turns the tables on the representatives of learning by finding—through a meditative, impressionistic, but quite definite analysis—that it is they who have been driven by this ignoble motive.

This is not the end of the matter. For if anger can be found underwriting the monuments of tradition, and this anger is not at all exceptional and dismissible, then something has happened to the very conception of this term. Traditionally—or in what had seemed to be tradition—it was assumed that anger showed itself in words, as in other kinds of behavior, through certain signs of disorder, disharmony, disfigurement, rebellion, or riotousness. Thus, in proceeding through this chapter, some readers will have rushed to the conclusion that anger is definitely visible in the language of certain passages whereas in others the author is more calm and objective. If anger now strikes us, however, in the very monuments that had been taken to represent the opposing qualities of order, harmony, and the like, then the psychological foundation of this term, its supposed basis in truth-telling and self-revelation, has been discredited. Consequently, anger becomes difficult to diagnose, perhaps even impossible to know. Oddly enough, as soon as one notices the anger of the professors ("or patriarchs, as it might be more accurate to call them"), one must wonder if it really makes any sense to call them angry. "Possibly they are not 'angry' at all" (58).

Woolf's protagonist is brought to realize that the issue of anger is the issue of what one will *call* anger. Anger has often been associated with calling names, as distinct from doing justice; but angry or not, we are always calling names, at once hurling them into and summoning them from out of the world—or what we call the world. So Woolf's protagonist makes fun of her own "sonorous phrases about 'elemental feelings,' the 'common stuff of humanity,' 'the depths of the human heart,' and all those other phrases which support us in our belief that, however clever we may be on top, we are very serious, very profound and very humane underneath" (159).

Anger does not declare itself, as critical tradition—or, more accurately, a traditional image of critical tradition—would have us assume. Nor does anger define and evaluate itself, as one might be led to believe by the form of Plato's dialogues, in which the philosopher is always so fortunate in getting those with whom he speaks to stipulate the premises he wants. (But then these dialogues make a very different impression if one recalls the crucial exception that haunts all these other exchanges: the failure of Socrates to obtain the premises he wants when he is put on trial and arguing for his life. In the *Apology*, Socrates suggests that the slim difference of thirty votes by which he was condemned would have turned out differently if he had had another day to make his case, as would have been true in other cities, or if the long-contemplated bringing of these charges against him had been delayed just a little longer, thus allowing him to die a natural death. "I have little time left to tell what I know," says the narrator of "The Babylon Lottery"; and we all know it is just a question of time . . .)[37]

Anger is a word over which people fight, or (if they hate the hostilities entertained by their governments) it is a word over which they may refuse to fight. In either case, issues commonly associated with the topic of anger and criticism—issues of war, censorship, and turns of fortune, as in the workings of a lottery—will be seen to dwell within the very conception of anger, which no longer can be viewed as exclusively, or even especially, a matter of individual psychology. That is why Woolf bothered to note that if Jane Austen "had lain as a child on the landing to prevent her father from thrashing her mother, her soul might have burnt with such a passion against tyranny that all her novels might have been consumed in one cry for justice."[38] What Woolf suggests is that even in matters of life and death, we cannot liberate the thesis of anger from its hypothesis; we cannot divide its premises from its always extravagant promises; we cannot think of it apart from the lottery, the warfare, and the censorship in which it has its only truth. As surely as language belongs to our social being, rather than being anyone's individual possession, so do our emotions; and lotteries, wars, and acts of censorship in various forms (including every recourse of style, such as contradiction, paradox, insult, and irony) are indissociable from all that we feel. As Catharine R. Stimpson, in writing about Woolf, has succinctly put this point about tradition, "A statement is often what the state has meant."[39]

Lotteries, wars, and censorship are not simply external to our emotions, acting on them from without, but intrinsic to any possible conception of emotion. Therefore, like any lottery you can name, anger is a matter of historical turnings and thus a question of rhetoric and politics, and it must be judged accordingly if we are to have any hope of knowing what we say we know. That is why many works of contemporary criticism have sought, in Brenda R. Silver's words, "to remove anger from the exclusive realm of the emotions and internal states: to move anger away from guilt, neurosis, or depression, and into the purview of cognition, external behavior, social relations, and politics."[40] As I write these words, which are not free of anger, I do not write off anger when I affirm the desirability of this movement.

Although Virginia Woolf is among those whom I follow in coming to this point, it might be objected that I show myself here to be more akin to Professor von X, a figure intent on disguising undeniable emotion. After all, Woolf herself might be seen as having partaken to some extent of the professor's disposition, despite her elaborate mockery of this character. We may remember that her protagonist in *A Room of One's Own*, like Arnold, criticized Brontë for writing "in a rage." She saw her predecessor's work as having been "deformed and twisted" as a consequence of this emotion: "Now, in the passages I have quoted from *Jane Eyre*, it is clear that anger was tampering with the integrity of Charlotte Brontë the novelist" (120, 121, 127). Woolf also failed miserably in her conclusion, in 1929, that the woman writer "is no longer angry."[41] Judging by these instances and others, in which her aesthetics could not tolerate what she took to be signs of an unredeemed personal urgency, some have viewed Woolf (and not without reason) as lamentably idealist in certain aspects of her art;[42] similar objections, or worse, might be made to my own reasoning here. If a war is now being fought, readers might say, bombs are not blossoming in this professor's backyard; while individuals and entire populations are being censored, he is writing as freely as he ever has; at a time when fortune's hostages are finding themselves consigned to battle, flight, jail, or the grave, he is unmolested; and so it is all very well for him calmly to discourse of anger as a question of rhetoric and politics. To such readers my playing with distinctions may seem a clever game (or perhaps I flatter myself, perhaps not even that); but however I work it out, what I have written may well be seen as entirely irrelevant to what I have supposed to be my topic. Say what I will, those who are angry will know what they feel. If not always, then often, there is no disputing about anger; in James Baldwin's words, "Rage can only with difficulty, and never entirely, be brought under the domination of the intelligence and is therefore not susceptible to any arguments whatever."[43]

Inevitably, in the scathing sense of the term that Audre Lorde called upon in "The Uses of Anger," my words will appear to some readers as nothing more than "academic rhetoric."[44] There is simply no getting around the fact that some will be angry with me, and they will not always be the ones I would love to enrage. For all my contention that anger is not a matter of truth-telling, self-revelation, and the overthrow of censorship, I may be told that I am being absurd, people know anger when they feel it, they have to fight against great odds to express it, and so anyone taking a position such as mine is denying the undeniable.

And this objection does make sense. As Kant said, critics must accept the fate of cooks, who cannot expect their work to please people just because an argument or theory says they ought not to turn up their noses at it.[45] Nevertheless, as I believe Woolf knew, the real question here is not whether anger is undeniable. There is no contradiction in saying that it is often so while maintaining that we can conclude nothing from this fact, if fact we would call it. Anger may be undeniable, but the point here is that what cannot be denied cannot be asserted. Hence the famous and profound stupidity of the comment about pornography that Justice Potter Stewart pronounced in the case of *Jacobellis v. Ohio* (1964): "I know it when I see it."[46] No matter how attached we feel to our perceptions, emotions, sensations, ideas—call them what you will—they are subject to communication and thus surrendered to our

experience over time, which lends itself only too generously to the conviction of certainty. ("Sluttish time," Shakespeare called it in his Sonnet
55 as he wrote about "wasteful war," thus criticizing the place of anger
in critical tradition even as he helped to reinforce its identification with
women.)[47] For all her impatience with academic rhetoric, Lorde was
well aware of these temporal considerations, as she made clear when
she recorded her response to the dim-witted sympathy a white listener
offered after Lorde gave a reading of her "Poems for Women in Rage":
"I do not exist to feel her anger for her."[48]

"Our lives are not debatable," said June Jordan,[49] and on this point
she was right and will always have been right. Like you, like Jordan, I
would dare anyone to tell me I am not furious when I know precisely
and undeniably what I feel. Yet in troubling myself to say as much, I
will have allowed uncertainty to be present, in the very possibility of
which I unsay what I believed myself to be saying. As so many popular
songwriters have noted in the name of love, anger demands more than
we can say. Its demands are beyond anyone's saying because one's own
anger will always have been at the mercy of its recognition by and
responsibility to others. Hence Peggy Kamuf's comment on *A Room of
One's Own*: "No 'one' figures there who is not already many and no
ownership guarantees there an undivided property."[50]

"Possibly they are not 'angry' at all," Woolf has her protagonist remark of the professors before going on to analyze the rhetorical shifts
by which "her own" art and anger are bound up with "other" people
both alive and dead, both real and imaginary, and with disparate and
changing phenomena such as literary theories, family traditions, economic structures, and educational institutions that she is not allowed
even to enter. She takes this course because she knows that what we
call anger is a fantastic, unpredictable historical construction from
which nothing can be predicated with anything like complete assurance. Because it is built of warring identifications, it is liable to disap-
pear and seem never to have existed at the very moment when we try
to address it. In this way Woolf's protagonist goes beyond the familiar
irony of angry counsel against anger to gesture toward the notably
slippery truth—"the pure fluid, the essential oil"—that she had hoped
would emerge after "what was personal and accidental" in her im-
pressions had been strained off (42). When imagining how her audience
must be criticizing her narrative, picking it apart and adding to it, even
as I am doing here, she comes to the conclusion that truth "is only to
be had by laying together many varieties of error" (183). And despite
her insistence on what is undeniably true, Jordan showed the same

conviction when she troubled herself to explain what should never have needed any explanation, what should have been forever known as soon as it was seen: the obscenity of William Shockley and of anyone who would claim that his views deserve even the slightest respect.

Those who would outlaw anger from criticism and those who would privilege it share the same fantasy that anger might be *uncalled for*, without reason or calculation, as if it somehow might appear in advance of its objects, contexts, and origins, like the hands of an angry God thrashing our submissive souls. Within this fantasy, the only frustration of anger—the angriness of anger, as it were—is that its precedence goes unnoticed. It wants to have been first: not a response, not a movement already subject to equivocation, not the eternally provoking belatedness built into the shuttling assertion and denial of tradition, but truly *uncalled for*, like the divine sign of Socrates' daimon. In contrast, the hell of this anger must resemble the *Monty Python* routine in which a man strides into a firm that specializes in arguments, pays a fee for its services, and then finds himself embroiled in contradictions before he can even get started on what he had to say ("You're not arguing, you're just contradicting me!" "No I'm not!" "Yes you are!" "No I'm not!"). The merciless humor relies on our recognition that rhetorical impasses are an irreducible aspect of communication, which leads us in our every utterance toward the possibility of such a farcical contretemps, which in its turn may result, lo and behold, in dead bodies and ruined houses.

Thus, to imagine anger as a breaching of censorship, as a speaking of the unspeakable, is not to imagine communication but an apocalyptic release from the violent conditions of communication. The desire is then to forget the demands by which we know history—to repress or censor them through the immediacy of one's anger—even though these demands are bound to disturb this desired immediacy as surely as they will shatter the fantastic continuity desired in the ravishing name of tradition. As Wojnarowicz has said in recounting fantasies in which he would murder cops, politicians, religious leaders, and others whose existence promised violence to his own, such as certain lovers of art ("I remember times getting picked up by some gentle and repressed fag living in a high-rise apartment filled with priceless north american indian artifacts and twentieth-century art who was paying me ten bucks to suck on my dick"), one wants a gesture that will completely erase any offense against our being, expunge it, so that it will never have been; but "no one gesture can erase it *all* that easily."[51]

Its long and complex history shows that we gain a lot through the fantasy of an apocalyptic release from the violent conditions of communication—perhaps most notably a capacity for disavowal that may be crucial in strengthening people to imagine and fight their way out of oppression. In such gains, however, we too often forget that God is pleased to dine with those on both sides of any war one may care to name. As Nancy Armstrong and Leonard Tennenhouse have noted, "Violent events are not simply so but are called violent because they bring together different concepts of social order."[52] The fantasy of apocalyptic release from the violent conditions of communication, then, finally asks less of our imagination than we ought to ask and so allows us to get off too easily. It is then that we end up seeing, always with such dismally predictable surprise, the Old Priest writ large in the New Presbyter, or the object of anger in anger's very own self-representation. With the predictable irony that struck Karl Marx in the provision for liberty in the French Constitution of 1848, the word shows itself to be other than itself.[53]

So you have heard all this before. John Milton recognized the complex rhetoric and politics of anger when he made his reply to the *Eikon Basilike*, which was supposedly written by Charles I, the deposed and soon-to-be headless monarch, in the aftermath of England's Civil War. Replying to the argument that Charles had not wanted to convene a parliament because he judged its prospective members to be unreliable, Milton said that although these men "were indeed not tempered to his temper," they were not unreasonable on that account. Milton could come to this conclusion because he construed the king's "temper" as "his will"—a will that in its "glozing words and illusions" actually consisted of "rage and . . . violence";[54] and even though we need not necessarily agree with Milton's interpretation, it cannot be denied save through political calculations such as those involved in the organization of states, wars, lotteries, and critical texts such as his own. For no matter how often we go beyond it, the familiar irony is always lying in wait, even in the case of the famous proponent of free speech whose *Eikonoklastes* and *Defensio Populi Anglicani* were to be ceremonially burned by the decree of Charles II in 1660. We may remember that Milton spent some time licensing books for his government and so allowed himself an "exception" to his ideals, one that might have been surprising had it not been dismally predicted by the "exceptions" to free speech written into his *Areopagitica*.

Having read Milton intensely if idiosyncratically, Blake dealt with the irony of angry counsels against anger when he scribbled in the margins of the bishop of Llandaff's *Apology for the Bible* (1797). Bishop Watson's *Apology* was a reply to the second part of *The Age of Reason*, which Thomas Paine, Blake's friend, had written in the wake of the revolutionary wars recently fought in America and France. Bishop Watson had previously published, among other works, a sermon meant to justify God's wisdom in having made men both rich and poor; and in commenting on the beginning of this good shepherd's latest work, Blake wrote:

> If this first Letter is written without Railing & Illiberality I have never read one that is. To me it is all Daggers & Poison. The sting of the serpent is in every Sentence as well as the glittering Dissimulation Achilles' wrath is blunt abuse Thersites' Sly insinuation Such is the Bishops If such is the characteristic of a modern polite gentleman we may hope to see Christs discourses Expung'd.[55]

Like Milton before him and Woolf, Lorde, Jordan, and Wojnarowicz after him, Blake argued that anger could be identified only in the context of differing desires, conflicting wills, and words expunging one another—in short, in the contested dimensions of politics through which our cultures take shape and our histories are written and rewritten. He himself was once tried for sedition on account of words he was alleged to have uttered; and he knew that whatever else we may be and whatever else we do, we are fighting words. That is, we are fighting words as we are living history, in the doubled sense of these phrases, which divides and multiplies and ravishes us and so impassions us to go on. Blake was able to draw this lesson from classical and biblical literature, from contemporary theology, and, of course, from his ongoing attempts to figure out good strategems for communication. ("At a Friends Errors Anger Shew / Mirth at the Errors of a Foe."[56]) He could not know that post–World War II U.S. constitutional law would argue otherwise, enforcing upon us the theory that anger is psychologically localized and localizable; but the preoccupations of his writings suggest that an angry vision of the histories of law and war contributed to his recognition that we are always fighting words, despite what institutionalized legal and military practices would claim to be undeniable.

Through their very insistence on a pure and uncompromising anger, this is the recognition at which writers such as Rich and Lesage have also arrived. Proclaiming their anger, they establish that there is no formal way of measuring the presence, influence, or value of anger in a text. More generally, by representing anger as a compelling eruption of truth, they establish that it is no such thing.

Rich's notion of anger might have seemed simple enough when she characterized Woolf's tone in *A Room of One's Own*: "It is the tone of a woman almost in touch with her anger, who is determined not to appear angry, who is *willing* herself to be calm, detached, and even charming in a roomful of men where things have been said which are attacks on her very integrity." Rich wrote this essay in 1971, at a time when she judged much contemporary writing by women, despite Woolf's prediction, to be "charged with anger." In this passage Rich values the anger of which she writes, and thus far she is revisionary while yet seeming quite traditional in her treatment of anger as a revelatory emotional outburst that a reader can confidently identify in someone's words. Her next sentence, however, may be even more revisionary: "I think we need to go through that anger, and we will betray our own reality if we try, as Virginia Woolf was trying, for an objectivity, a detachment, that would make us sound more like Jane Austen or Shakespeare."[57]

The interesting suggestion is that women "need to go through that anger," for it is here that Rich's historical and political judgment fights against the traditional inheritance—the ancestral voices prophesying war—that she, like the Woolf of whom she wrote, could not hope entirely to distinguish from the voice she called "her own." A "need" that is in opposition to a "betrayal" is a need given at least as much by calculated political aspiration as by spontaneous psychological essence; an anger one is recommended "to go through" cannot be an anger that carries within itself its own truth or revelation of the self; and an anger addressed as "that anger," in implicit contradistinction to others, not only does not pretend to universality but effectively insists on its polemical difference. It is thus that the name of anger in Rich's criticism turns into an utterly changed word even as it is being written: it is thus that it goes to war.

We should not be surprised, then, to find that Rich brought up the relation between rhetoric and politics when she returned to the topic of anger in a later essay, "Disloyal to Civilization: Feminism, Racism, Gynephobia" (1978). Declaring herself angry at the "abstractly 'correct' language wielded by self-described political feminists," she added, parenthetically, that she too had pronounced the word "racism" in this stultifying way. Her conclusion about racism might also apply to the name of anger: "We have to go on using the word, however."[58] Once in possession of this recognition, we may remember that the author of *A Room of One's Own* had already raised the disturbing historical question, in "Professions for Women," "Ah, but what is 'herself'?" We would then find that in the same essay she anticipated Rich's comments about the relation between criticism and "her own" feelings. The problem of "telling the truth about my own experiences as a body," Woolf says, "I do not think I solved."[59]

A similar drama is played out in Lesage's essay "Women's Rage," in which the author's seeming attachment to anger as an authentic, self-possessed, and immediate force is belied by other elements in her argument, as when she declares a "need to promote self-conscious, collectively supported, and politically clear articulations of our anger and rage." This passage and others related to it take note of undeniably urgent emotion while simultaneously demanding our attention to "theory."[60] The effect might seem to be an appeal to contradictory conceptions of anger, but it is more accurate to speak of differing gestures through which Lesage, like others I have named, was trying to come to terms with the divisive political implications, identifications, and possibilities historically bound up in the name of anger. Lorde, for instance, ended her address on anger by calling on "our power to examine and redefine the terms upon which we will live and work,"[61] effectively insisting that the opposite of anger should be seen not as self-possession but as cowering submission.

When these critics addressed anger, they lost track of the very term, but not because of some form of censorship imposed by themselves or others. They lost track of it because it was bound to turn into other issues involving the relations between aesthetics and politics, war and consciousness, and fortune and subjectivity, among other things, in which the name of anger was no longer able to bear the complexity of the historical differences through which human destinies have been defined. "Possibly they are not 'angry' at all," says Woolf's protagonist, because the critical thinking with which she dismantles what had seemed to be tradition cannot leave the name of anger intact. Indeed, the very words that I have had to treat here as if they might be synonymous—anger, rage, spleen, intemperance, hate, and all the others, including words translated from foreign tongues and diverse cultures—actually testify to wildly incompatible conceptions of art, science, nature, anatomy, and destiny.

An influential tradition would have it that where historical differences such as these become apparent, we must speak of competing conceptualizations addressing the same object. If Aristotle thinks revenge the defining motive of anger whereas Samuel Johnson would speak of piety, we have conflicting opinions and thus a better and worse judgment; but we are supposed to rest assured that the boundaries of tradition can accommodate these differences until time has enough time to sort out the truth of the matter. It is of the essence of tradition, however, not to have been what it is imagined to have been—it is only by this means that it can subsume historical differences under the ultimate reasoning of time—and the same holds for anger. Friedrich Nietzsche made this point when he described the Christian whose conception of God's wrath, like Augustine's, may be transformed into an impression of beneficence in scarcely the blink of an eye: "If he previously thought he saw warnings, threats, punishment, and every kind of sign of divine anger in all occurrences, so now he *reads* divine goodness *into* his experience."[62]

When we address anger, we point to and establish its place in the same gesture. Despite David Hume's claim that a man "in a fit of anger, is actuated in a very different manner from one who only thinks of that emotion," we cannot cut our distinctions so finely—unless, like Hume, we support them by way of assumptions about rigid hierarchical distinctions between philosophers and plebians, men and women, and white Europeans and other races.[63] Angry or not, we call names, at once hurling them into and summoning them from out of the historical conflicts in which we are fighting words. One's anger is never in a room of one's own. So the "young airman up in the sky," writes Woolf, "is driven not only by the voices of loudspeakers; he is driven by voices in himself—ancient instincts, instincts fostered and cherished by education and tradition."[64] And so the protagonist of *A Room of One's Own* insists that the name by which she is called "is not a matter of any importance." She knows that although they go by formally indistinguishable names and even bear some of the same characteristics, her Brontë is no more Arnold's than Blake's Jesus is Milton's; and so she knows that it would be a mistake to place too much emphasis on the name supposed to be "her own."

Why, then, does there remain this issue of anger and criticism? What draws these words together, establishing what must seem a continuing historical problem in their relation, despite all the differences (in texts, bodies, sexualities, histories, cosmogonies) forcing them apart? This is a question of ravishing tradition: a question of the understanding we have trusted to be at work in the impossible time of writing even as we have had to expect all that we address to suffer unpredictable metamorphoses. Woolf commented on this question in relation to the problem of artistic evaluation when she wrote:

> Are not reviews of current literature a perpetual illustration of the difficulty of judgment? "This great book," "this worthless book," the same

book is called by both names. Praise and blame alike mean nothing. No, delightful as the pastime of measuring may be, it is the most futile of all occupations, and to submit to the decrees of the measurers the most servile of attitudes. So long as you write what you wish to write, that is all that matters; and whether it matters for ages or only for hours, nobody can say. (184)

Open even the slightest space between artist and critic and it is as if we glimpse, as on a dimly remembered stage, forms terribly dividing and proliferating, weapons forged in a storm of fire, helpless leaf and vine shrieking in witness to the fall of a lark's song into a gaping human mouth, which swallows it and promptly spews forth ungrateful and vengeful children, squabbling lovers, lying and impious philosophers, an endless horde of interchangeable figures writhing in the blood-streaked vomitus of history. In the English language this sense of things is embodied in the very name of criticism, which suggests that we cannot dream of distinguishing thoughtful analysis from disparagement. It is as if criticism of its very nature must be censorious and censoring, not merely fault-finding with Momus but perversely inventing flaws—as if all critics were the "hypercritics" of whom John Dryden complained.[65] The seemingly immemorial animus between critics and the figures of whom they write—what does this tell us if not that any response to art other than the encomium of stunned silence must be a malediction, a grievous offense, even a theft of the artist's soul? Hence the traditional accusation that if we scratch a critic, we will find an artist manqué: "Thus the corruption of a poet is the generation of a critic."[66] A historical suspicion, and yet one's own, is that any act of criticism is an intolerable and profoundly self-lacerating periphrasis. As John Ashbery puts it, "To praise this, blame that, / Leads one subtly away from the beginning, where / We must stay, in motion."[67] It is as if there is something fundamentally repulsive in the act of criticism, in the absence of which we could all be such great friends, with the contretemps of time never coming between us—time, that infernal creation of critics, who surely are the ones who invented before and after, the artwork and the commentary, the besieged integrity of the artist and the terribly cutting demands of art. Some such image of time appears to have been worked into the very structure of human emotions.

This will never do. (Or "Here let me pause a moment, for the sake of making somebody angry," as Thomas De Quincey would have it.)[68] Whether we like it or not, measuring will go on; and in the contemporary United States, as I have been concerned to suggest, the political dimensions of the critical imagination have been marked out most compellingly by the history of the civil rights, antiwar, feminist, and gay and lesbian rights movements. When Wojnarowicz, for example, expresses a fear that our current rituals of death lead people away from "a relatively simple ritual of life such as screaming in the streets,"[69] a professorial reader may hear an echo of James Joyce's *Ulysses*, in which one of the names of anger is God, who in turn is identified as a "shout in the street";[70] but this echo will be almost indistinguishable within the clamoring memories of all the public demonstrations carried out over the last four decades, right up to the recent ones organized by ACT UP, in which individuals have gathered into crowds in order to define their integrity against the forces of society and state murderously arrayed against them. "I have always viewed my friends," writes Wojnarowicz, "as checkpoints in a series of motions of resistance to the flood of hyenas in state or religious drag";[71] and one may recall the photographs of distinguished male leaders in outlandish costumes of power that Woolf included in *Three Guineas*.

Currently the anger of those who claim not to be political in their criticism and art, the anger that defines this claim for them, has arisen in response to public movements of protest, resistance, and rebellion. For instance, it is an injury to their absurd pride that infuriates the members of the National Association of Scholars and those who sympathize with them, such as Donald Kagan, the Yale dean who was appalled that people might want to prevent Shockley from speaking at his university. They cannot bear how these movements have shown that the determining locus of aesthetics is not the room of anyone, whether artist or critic. It is maddening to the likes of Kagan that crowds marching in the streets may know perfectly well something that his mind in its imagined isolation cannot bring itself to admit, that neither art nor criticism has ever dwelt in a room of its own. There may still be a future in imagining a tradition that says otherwise, because figures like Kagan certainly seem to be thriving in and out of academe, despite their whining about a supposed persecution at the hands of enemies; but for as long as it has been around, this imaginary tradition of theirs has functioned as the power of censorship for the very people who claim to represent the principles of free inquiry. It censors the way well over a hundred thousand Iraquis were slaughtered in the Persian Gulf war as a result of what is called objective scholarly research, much of it carried out in universities; it censors exploited human flesh under an image of universal human spirit, as if it were discreditable that art and criticism will never be able to transcend the example of those who put their bodies on the line in Selma or rioted in Chicago or filled the streets of Washington, D.C., because they dared to revise the reigning definitions of temperance, courage, justice, and prudence; it censors the way art and criticism have been historically made, communicated, institutionalized, taught, and employed; it censors the truth of how people come to enter universities, ludicrously picturing their environment of choice as a God-like lottery that shows no special favor toward any kinds of persons—but really, there is a limit to the patience I can be expected to show in addressing these matters.

But if I may try your patience just a bit longer: like wars and acts of censorship, lotteries are never simple things. Thus, in referring to the "Company" said to be responsible for the Babylon lottery, Borges's story concludes with the narrator mentioning the "vile" conjecture "that it is indifferently inconsequential to affirm or deny the reality of the shadowy corporation, because Babylon is nothing but an infinite game of chance."[72] Earlier the narrator had made reference to Platonic tradition, but here he seems to have been attending more to a passage in Kant's *Critique of Judgment* describing games of chance:

> But the affections of hope, fear, joy, wrath, scorn are put in play by them, changing their roles at every moment [indem sie jeden Augenblick ihre Rolle wechseln]; and they are so vivid that by them, as by a kind of internal motion, the entire activity of life in the body [das ganze Lebengeschäft im Körper] seems to be promoted, as is shown by the mental vivacity excited by them, although nothing is gained or learnt thereby. But since the game of chance is not a beautiful game [Aber da das Glückspiel kein schönes Spiel ist], we will here set it aside.[73]

Whether or not Borges was actually aware of this passage when he was bringing his story to a conclusion, it is as if his tale is predicated on this moment in Kant's text, in which games of chance are said to be unbeautiful because they stimulate sensation without attending to reason. (Schopenhauer similarly found card playing to be "quite peculiarly the expression of the miserable side of humanity."[74]) Borges raised the stakes from "unbeautiful" to "vile" by extending the image of the game from the evening parties of which Kant wrote ("hardly any of them can be carried on without a game") to the whole of a state's existence; but in doing so he was still following Kant, since the crucial distinction between taste and sensation in the *Critique of Judgment* is based on the need to dispense with the general possibility that beauty might be heteronomous, answerable to no design except that of chance, as in the lottery of pleasures to which Plato's "democratic man" submits himself.[75] In other respects Borges's vertiginous fiction might seem as different as different can be from Kant's deliberate exposition of a compelling rule of subjective universality in aesthetic judgments; but the appeal of both texts derives from the way they subsume the undeniable urgencies of political differences under the all-encompassing name of chance, which is utterly indifferent to them. Like Kant's *Critique of Judgment*, "The Babylon Lottery" comes to a conclusion in which this all-encompassing image of chance is nominally rejected, but not before this image has served its purpose, which is to carry the question of political demands away with it when it goes. The enchantment of his tale lies in the way Borges imagined a carnivalesque state of political abandon; and however unlikely it may seem, this is also the enchantment of Kant's work. The fictional and the critical text both impress us with a sense that nothing is to be gained or learned by any political feelings, among which the exemplary case is anger. In both works the concept of chance unites what this anger would divide and censors what it would demand.

Like Kant's *Critique*, the tale that Borges wrote makes room for feelings such as disgust, which are presented as a matter of personal idiosyncrasy, but not for feelings involved in political commitments. "Like all men in Babylon," the story begins, "I have been a proconsul; like all, a slave; I have also known omnipotence, opprobrium, jail":[76] given such changes in roles from moment to moment, there can be no question of anger. In making this criticism, however, I assume I do not need to tell you that this is a brilliant story, one well-nigh perfect in suggesting the impossible, which is a moment of peace long enough to give us time fully to appreciate the farcical vileness that our history would have to appear to be from a divine standpoint (or from the infinite point of the Aleph in Borges's story of that title). It is as if I could bring us to an assured understanding by identifying the time when I came to this conclusion (9:10 A.M. on June 21, 1991), now that a war is over and the war goes on, as you read this, here in Babylon.

CHAPTER SIX

Getting It

John Ashbery and Colloquial Tradition

COLLOQUIAL LANGUAGE would have it that anomia is a common condition, so common in fact as to be almost unremarkable, as when we observe of someone's heartfelt desire, "I hope you find it, whatever it is." "It" could be practically anything, but we seem undismayed by our failure to put a name to it. (More wearily, we may suppose that this failure of comprehension actually contributes to our composure.) Or take the expression "I lost it," as used in circumstances that make it clear we are not referring to any fungible thing. A popular catchphrase in the United States at least since the early 1980s, "I lost it" is said of an extremely upsetting event and the response occasioned by it. But what is it that one claims to have lost? Although it may have been derived from expressions such as "I lost my temper" and "I lost control," "I lost it" is more than a reformulation of them; "it" in this instance does not simply refer to one's own being, possessions, or circumstances. Although it partakes of all these, "loosely referring" to them, as we might say, it insists on turning beyond them. It is something else: a coherence as precisely unnameable as it is presumptively familiar and vital to whatever it is we call communication. It is like the transport of being caught up in a conversation, as the saying goes, or of being lost in a book. The "slab of business rising behind the stars" in John Ashbery's "Couple in the Next Room" (*HD*, 13),[1] that is what it is like. Or "that *invisible light* which spatters the silence / Of our everyday festivities" ("French Poems: 3," *DD*, 38), maybe that is it.

Referentially indeterminate and yet demonstrably meaningful, the "it" in "I lost it" embodies this transporting coherence crucially involved in communication. It is less like a word than like a patchy cloud of scribbling in a painting by Cy Twombly. If it says anything, all it offers is the decidedly unenlightening slogan, "Wherever it is, there we may be." It is closer to being a demonstrative than an anaphoric pronoun, and yet its function is not to point to anything identifiable. Neither naming anything nor "standing for" the name of anything, it leads us to conclude that it must be agrammatical, strictly speaking; and yet it establishes its propriety in our discourse despite its refusal to suffer categories to be applied to it with formal rigor. It happens every day that we find ourselves lost in it. Reason nods, syntax suffers a syncope, and nothing could be more ordinary—it is simply not a problem at all. As Donald Davidson says, "We all get away with it all the time; understanding the speech of others depends on it."[2] There is nothing major or supreme about it. Doing this or that, one way or another, we hear ourselves speaking from a lexicon that turns out to be like that of Gertrude Stein's *Tender Buttons*, and we yawn and go about our business.[3]

Not in itself communication, understanding, or culture, the coherence thus exemplified falls just *this* short of anything that might be brought within the form of a statement. What we recognize in the way we call upon it is that our language must offer more coherence than it can suffer because it lives beyond its means, promising too much to too many in its desperate bid for our attention. The premises of language prove to be promises established prior to (and thus way beyond) any possible conception of their fulfillment.

Therefore, as against the stuff of assertions and propositions, this transporting coherence can be given voice only in the shadow of violence. That is why, as a colloquialism, "getting it" is more closely related to "getting by" than to "having it." The coherence at issue here must suffer its promise also to be a warning and thus an incitement to turn against the fetishized integrity of all names, no matter how generous they may appear. As all of us seem to know even when we are not at one another's throats, it will not come out right if we try to say it; that is all there is to it. "*It* is *it*, probably," as Ashbery wryly allows ("Litany," *AWK*, 38). Or as Ian Hacking says in a reply to Davidson, offering an image he evidently regards as absurd—and I must confess myself astonished that he takes it to be counterintuitive in any respect— "It is as if every time that I enter into a conversation with another, I have to hold before me the possibility that he is an alien."[4]

So people speak of "getting it," as in Werner Erhard's est seminars of the 1970s, or point out those who "just don't get it," as in the debates over the 1991 confirmation hearings on the nomination of Clarence

Thomas to the Supreme Court. "I've still got it!" an exuberant someone might exclaim—with "it," of course, meaning "what it takes"—so that we all know this is testifying to a transporting experience, not a state of self-possession, and so not anything reliable at all, really. Or "You know how it is," a neighbor might say to you, confidingly, while telling of someone who is "out of it" or (more quaintly) of others who are "with it" and who know "where it's at." And then "I've got it!" I might exclaim while dashing out a line in this essay, having grabbed hold of . . . *something*; perhaps shortly thereafter, "You've got it all wrong," I might whine to a quarrelsome lover, not referring to anything in particular . . . but never mind, just forget it, you know how it goes. It happens, shit happens, as our sayings would have it, as in the impatient fiat of "Let's get on with it."

In cases such as these, "it" will not tolerate so much as a question, no matter how polite. If you say much more than the closest thing to nothing at all, which is "it", you'll lose it. "Who cares, anyway, about / What it is or what it was like?" ("Litany," *AWK*, 59). If you have to ask, you might as well give it up, it's clearly beyond you. It's as if "a god has bungled it again" (*FC*, 5)—we might as well leave it at that. You have to go for it, or else you might as well forget about it.

That's just the way it is as it embodies what we have to go through in trying to make it in this world; no wonder "making it" does double service in the United States as a colloquialism for sex and for the achievement of success. We rest on what we wrest from "it," making it up as we go along—and has it not ever been so? In the eighteenth century, Jorge Luis Borges noted, Georg Christoph Lichtenberg "proposed that in place of 'I think' we should say, impersonally, 'it thinks,' just as one would say 'it thunders' or 'it rains.' "[5] But then again, in considering this very substitution, Friedrich Nietzsche had suggested that "one has even gone too far with this 'it thinks'—even the 'it' contains an *interpretation* of the process, and does not belong to the process itself."[6] No wonder Kurt Cobain was brought to find himself writing, "I found it hard / It's hard to find / Oh well, whatever, / Nevermind."[7]

It is not vagueness, generality, ambiguity, paranomasia, or anomaly that is at issue here. What is at issue is what we go on in drawing such distinctions. For instance, as opposed to deixis as conventionally understood, the usage with which I am concerned here does not point to what people intend to communicate. If this is deixis, it is Karl Bühler's *Deixis am Phantasma* with a vengeance.[8] As in an irreducible equivocation, it points out what people know that they do not know—how it tells on us—or as the Derrida of *Glas* might put it, how it tolls (on) us.[9]

We are threaded through these "it"'s as if tracked down through the marks of a secret society, such as Borges's Sect of the Phoenix. What is at issue is how social life may be an experience of slipping through a colloquialism, an inconsequential exchange, a passing moment, a gust of air—even, and especially, in the moments that count most in our lives.

That is why this "it" is given voice only in the shadow of violence: because it bodies forth the sense that what allows us to hit it off with one another is perfectly familiar, to be sure, and yet terrifically volatile. It shows popular recognition that the most ordinary word in the small talk of Smallville, USA, may turn out to be a superhuman neologism, even as we deal with it on a daily basis, like an appealing landscape that we casually decide to explore and only then discover to be the stirring lineaments of an alien's flesh. So it may be "that it, / Not we, are the change; that we are in fact it / If we could get back to it" ("Self-Portrait in a Convex Mirror," *SP*, 76); and so we might well ask, "What is it now with me/ And is it as I have become?" ("Fear of Death," *SP*, 49). No wonder this presumed coherence may appear to do violence to our language—that is, when it is not appearing in its reversed role as the very antithesis of violence, as an empty or purely conventional usage, as when it shows up in relation to the artist in Virginia Woolf's *To the Lighthouse*: "What does it mean then, what can it all mean? Lily Briscoe asked herself.... What does it mean?—a catchword that was, caught up from some book, fitting her thought loosely."[10]

This usage of "it" resembles the role played by tautologies in everyday language. As Maurice Blanchot has said in writing of everyday speech, by way of an allusion to the work of Henri Lefebvre, "In the end there is no event other than this movement of universal transmission: 'the reign of an enormous tautology.' "[11] Like the volatile "it," tautologies are the very pulse of society, the percussive singsong that tells of the ongoing conceivability of "our social something" (*FW*, 107),[12] as James Joyce called it in his mocking turn on the classical term *res publica*. Thus, "The law's the law" was the conclusion of one of the jurors who acquitted the defendants of police brutality in the 1992 case involving Rodney King, in a decision that touched off riots in Los Angeles and elsewhere; with a different attitude but to a similar effect, the only juror who had tried to hold out for a conviction said of the others that they "wanted to see what they wanted to see" on the videotape that was the basis of the charges.[13] "What's done is done," we say, following Lady Macbeth (*Macbeth*, 3.2.12),[14] or "A deal's a deal," "Past is past," "Rules are rules"—the list goes on and on. "No means no," we may say; or "Boys will be boys," we may be told, no doubt with the expectation that we will also remember Robert Burns's admonition that "a Man's a Man for a' that."[15] "Whither I must, I must," says Hotspur to Lady Percy (1 *Henry IV*, 2.3.108); "A man's gotta do what a man's gotta do," some comedian says, imitating John Wayne; "He is what he is," someone else will comment off to the side, ruefully shaking his head and adding, "You need to learn what's what."

"To speak is to fall into tautologies," says Borges's narrator in "The Library of Babel."[16] Demotic (and demonic) counterparts to the axioms that serve as the foundation of traditional logic, idioms such as these are "tootoological," as Joyce said (*FW*, 468). They are always at hand to remind us that if we ask too much of language, we will lose it— "lose it *big time*," in the current Americanism. They remind us that communication is bound to return us to the condition of tautologies, to the "same old same old," which—if we know what is good for us— we are to recognize as an articulation with necessity but without name. It is as in the famous story of Samuel Johnson, when Boswell asked how he would refute Bishop Berkeley's philosophical idealism and the distinguished lexicographer responded by dramatically kicking a large stone: "I refute him *thus*."[17] The emphatic "*thus*" says that it is not any dreary *word* that decides this matter, even though this demonstration relies on our lexical associations of "rock" with solidity, impermeability, reality, and analogous terms. (Boswell would have been baffled if Johnson had kicked a butterfly, say, or the "empty air.") If Johnson's gesture works, it does so because it appeals beyond these connotations to something like a resounding tautology, to the demonic materiality of *the rock of the rock*, which is found at precisely the point where demonstrations succeed and names fail us—as through the emphatic italics I employ here. For all the differences between irrefragable stone and blank nothingness, our perception is then like that at the conclusion of Wallace Stevens's poem "The Snow Man," which in this context appears as a particularly brilliant elaboration of a tautology, telling as it does of "nothing that is not there and the nothing that is" (*CP*, 10).[18]

On a more pedestrian level, this way with words resembles a shrug, which does not say yes or no, this or that, but something like "Let's get on with it," thus conceding the premise that "it is what it is." There are innumerable gestures and colloquialisms that work similarly, as in the classic exchange between child and parent: "Why?" "Because." Or consider the popular formula for explaining why one is taking an important step, such as getting married or tattooed: "It just feels right." Moreover, the most sophisticated contemporary philosophers may show the same alacrity as the rabble (or as Doctor Johnson) in relying on an emphasis that turns us toward namelessness, as when Saul Kripke grapples with the hoary metaphysical problem of identifying a table: "If I am talking about it," he insists, "I am talking about *it*."[19]

But we all know we cannot always have it our way—don't we?—and so there is certainly some reason for caution here. Once they are remarked upon, these tautologies may turn out to be foreboding statements (as in the concluding line to the first part of Ashbery's *Turandot*: "It is late to be late"). Skirting the violence shadowed in such utterances, we may yet be fortunate enough to correct ourselves (as Ashbery does in the first line of the next section: "Let us ascend the hearts in our hearts"), but no guarantees are to be had. Tautologies such as those I have described are what we might call "throwaway remarks"; but if in fact they are thrown away on us, if we are unimpressed by the anomia with which they are supposed to strike us, then we may learn that we are also not we, it not it, as at the end of Paul Celan's "Where I," in which "you / come not / to / you."[20] One need only glance at the news: a reporter writes, "Witnesses described the mob as a single unit, an 'it,' as though 15 or 20 people fused to become one multi-headed, many-fisted beast."[21] Through the itineraries of "it" we may even be seen by those supposed to be our fellows as having called violence down on our own heads, much as Rodney King was seen by the jurors in Simi Valley. (And yes, you are right, I must return to my titular concern with Ashbery's poetry—but then it is what I have been concerned with in all this—I must hope against hope, as we are given to say, that you will stay with it.) This popular understanding offered to us in colloquial language perhaps was summarized best in the jingle of a Miller Lite beer commercial: "It's it, and that's that."

To be sure, those semimythical creatures colloquially termed "traditionalists" may believe that an advertising slogan such as this one must represent a horrible descent from, say, the advertisement for love in the conclusion to Shakespeare's Sonnet 74 (13–14), in which the beloved's body is evaluated as follows: "The worth of that is that which it contains, / And that is this, and this with thee remains." The brutal elegance of the beer slogan, however, is entirely in keeping with Shakespearean uses of language, such as Richard III's "I am I" (*Richard III*, 5.3.183). If we pay attention to "it," I do not know that we can prefer one advertisement to the other as being more valuable in its power of suggestion.

Other idioms may seem to run counter to the aforementioned tautologies, as when we make statements such as "There are poets and then there are poets." In this regard, John Bunyan was about as succinct as one can get in one of his marginal glosses to *The Pilgrim's Progress*: "A way and a way."[22] Or one could cite expressions that turn away from exact tautology, such as "All's well that ends well"; that come right out and deny it, as when Ashbery says, "The soul is not a soul" ("Self-Portrait in a Convex Mirror," *SP*, 69); that offer contradictions, as in the Fluxus motto, "Anti-art is art," in Ben Vautier's *Ben's Window* (1962; reconstructed 1993); or that evoke irony, such as the lyrics of "As Time Goes By": "A kiss is still a kiss, / A sigh is just a sigh."[23] Yet these expressions—ironically, archly, whatever the case may be—still confess to this necessary failure in naming or in recognizing the names of things. Colloquial tautologies always allow for qualifications, as when Thomas Hardy's Susan Henchard tells her drunken husband, "A joke is a joke, but you may make it once too often, mind!"[24] But these qualifications do not challenge the function of tautologies in recalling us to a sense of the unnameable coherence of language. On the contrary, the emphatic particularity of these qualifications makes their formulaic nature all the more evident, so that we can hardly fail to see that the ostensible topic of the discussion—"poets," "a way," and so on—is not really what it is about at all. Instead of articulation as conventionally understood, we are left with a kind of spluttering as the image of communication, something like the "glubbal glub" in Stevens's "Chocorua to Its Neighbor" (*CP*, 301).[25] Thus struck by the force of tautologies, we are like W. C. Fields in the vertiginous moment of his discovery that his cocktail shaker is actually filled with what it had been said to contain—"*Somebody's been putting pineapple juice in my pineapple juice*"[26]— or like the Prince in Ashbery's *Turandot*, melodically spluttering, "Lovely Stradivarius / It it follows / In. In no way / Lord it in known way follows" (n.p.). If I may borrow another term from Joyce, it appears, then, that our names may turn out to be so much "nomanclatter" (*FW*, 147).

Other colloquialisms that may convey much the same effect as these tautologies include the common usage (erroneously thought of as an error) in which people switch the terms *literally* and *figuratively*. "I was literally tongue-tied," one might say, or "He was literally jumping out of his skin." What some grammarians find to be a confusion in these cases is better described as a recognition that the logical distinction between these terms is finally either an empty or a violent distinction, resting as it must on an invocation of coherence wrested from tautology. In other words, if this is a confusion, it is a confusion that recalls us to a consideration of the material, institutional, political forces that determine what kinds of things figures of speech will be—including the forces that determine whether they will be classified as figures or as literal realities.

To much the same effect, Black English may have one say "bad" or "stupid" to mean "good," much as the history of British English has allowed "I doubt that it is so" to mean "I believe it"; this is also why people can say "That's history" to suggest "That's not of any historical significance." Similarly, expressions such as "I wasn't myself" snatch Arthur Rimbaud back from the grave, at once acknowledging and denying a fracturing of identity, making it logically impossible to describe their component words as being either literal or figurative in their usage. Or one might instance the role of certain bromides in everyday speech, such as "Life is hard," "Time will tell," or "You've got to get a grip." Like the volatile "it," each of these expressions can be glossed and yet does not really serve to convey any specific meaning (as one can see by considering how these three examples may be used interchangeably in all sorts of conversations). Instead, these expressions witness to the pulsing of the system, the erratic plashing and pounding of communication, by which we are transported. They may be throwaway remarks, they may be foreboding, or they may remain clichés and yet somehow be possessed of a mantic mantric power, of as much truth as can ever be told in truth, in this or that moment of passing conversation. Whatever the case may be, they bring forth the coherence from which they absolve us, calling us back to the condition of anomia with which we are always supposed to be on the most familiar terms.

The situation is like that in Yip Harburg's lyrics to the Depression-era song "Brother, Can You Spare a Dime?": "Say don't you remember, they called me 'Al,' / It was 'Al' all the time."[27] Rather than being a "rigid designator," as Kripke has argued that all proper names are,[28] "Al" in this instance is dramatized as being so flexible that the idea of its ever having had any application is actually amazing, haunting, and perhaps finally unbelievable in any possible world. The sense of names conveyed by this lyric is one in which no baptism can be good enough to bring coherence to them; not to show the effects of anomia is a wondrous achievement on which nothing can be predicated. "It was 'Al' all the time," the singer marvels, failing to heed what he must find to be an unmeaning philosophical distinction between use and mention. It seems that in the name that names an individual, one cannot help but hear the name that names itself, as we may find also in the use Stevens made of allusions to Popeye, Shakespeare, and Yahweh, among others, through the self-reflexive homophony of his line "I have not but

I am and as I am, I am" ("Notes toward a Supreme Fiction," *CP*, 405). In Harburg's lyrics as in Stevens's poem, we can hear the name tautologically striking out an assurance of coherence that is necessary but from which there can be no guarantee of grace extended to our everyday discourse, no matter how melodic or melancholy its pulsations may be.

Even to have remembered Harburg's words in this way, ever since I first heard them and after having encountered the song only once or twice in the years since then—simply to have become so attached to this lyric, as I have been—is to illustrate what I am addressing here. It is notable that I do not remember the song as a whole, in fact recall only a few other scraps of it, and those with much less certainty than these lines. (Otherwise the sense of it I have just mentioned would need be very different.) In and of itself, the way such passages can stick with us, whether they derive from songs, poems, conversations, or some other source, suggests that the *striking utterance* may be the basic unit of signification in our everyday lives.

As opposed to elements such as the word, line, sentence, strophe, individual act of performance, or whatever it is we designate as a complete text, the striking utterance is distinguished by its cavalier attitude toward the niceties of form. In "No Way of Knowing," Ashbery dramatizes just this point with an equivocal verb phrase that can mean both "beginning" and "disappearing": "As when the songs start to go / Not much can be done about it" (*SP*, 56). The striking utterance is then not so much a saying as it is a linguistic event. It is a stroke of genius, if you will, that bears no relation either to an individual source or to a universal logos. Whether its content is grammatical and reasonable, or even decipherable and reproducible (for it may be no kind of communication at all in a conventional sense but rather a fugitive sign, less identifiable even than a moan or a bird's cry), this striking utterance mocks the reverence for reference evident in our institutions if not in our speech.

In other words, in our colloquial behavior every day we show our awareness that we share not a vernacular but at most what Adrienne Rich has termed the dream of a common language.[29] (The general absence of this awareness in scientific and professionalized discourse is one of the many good reasons why intellectuals appear in the popular imagination as hopelessly naive characters.) It simply does not make sense to wonder if a striking utterance is meaningful; it does not care about that. One certainly may mull over the passage in question, as I have over this one from Harburg's lyrics, but in doing so one neglects

the nature of its insistence, which is not concerned with soliciting jus-
tifications from any quarter. One might as well ask whether the breath
that goes into our speech is *appropriate* breath (as it happens, a query
anticipated by Ashbery when he breaks off, in the midst of a long poem,
to remark on an inescapable but absurdly unpoetical afflatus: "Excuse
me while I fart" [FC, 201]). The reason why certain passages strike us
at certain times and places is intimately related to the reason why tautologies are not always empty statements when we utter them in our
everyday confabulations, why they may be something else entirely, like
an ad libbing of reality in which we venture upon the wild surmise
that the parts of our speech might one day make sense—and upon an
even more breathtaking conjecture that that day might be this.

The volatile "it," in fact, may be viewed as a compressed or syncopic
tautology. This "it" says "So be it," and in doing so it appears as a
vital spot one can touch to feel the risky and improvisatory pulse, the
striking tautological rhythms, of communication. It might be called a
fiaticum to implore salvation for threatened communication and to
speed it on its way. As in the German locution *es gibt*, colloquially
translated as "there is" or "there are" but "literally" as "it gives," this
"it" gives us to know what gives, what's what.

Along with the potential for generalization suggested by the it of
natural circumstance (as in "It is raining"), the factors that make it
especially suitable for this role include the common use of cleft and
extrapositional constructions in English (as in sentences such as "It had
to be you" and "It's as easy to fall in love with a rich girl as with a
poor girl"). As Lewis Carroll once observed with a related construction,
"it" has a dummy role in such sentences and so seems naturally fitted
to its telling service in signifying nothing in particular in locutions such
as "I lost it."[30] It equally seems to lend itself to radically equivocal
expressions, as in Mary Chapin Carpenter's song, "You never had it so
good, / I never had it so bad,"[31] or as in the title of Peter Medak's 1991
film *Let Him Have It*, in which the words are alternatively an encouragement to or a dissuasion from murder.[32] Moreover, we demonstrate
that we recognize it in this equivocal and ultimately agrammatical role
by the way we play up its associations with sex (which is sometimes
called "doing it") and with horror (as in Stephen King's *It*).[33] Through
associations like these we recognize the tendency of "it" to take on a
life of its own, becoming a character in its own right, like Nemo in the
medieval *Historia de Nemine* or like Cousin Itt in *The Addams Family*.[34]
(That is why "It's alive!" is the quintessential horror-movie scream.) In
statements such as "So it goes," "It never gets easy," or "I can't take it

anymore," "it" is always ready to put itself forward, to become remarkable in its idiomatic conventionality, and thus to make us lose our grasp on the names of things in the same way fear or ecstatic sex may cause us to lose it. (Voices murmur: "You feel it? That—that right there—that's it.") We have to try to make it better, to get it while we can, to make it all right, when it has gotten out of hand or when we have lost it by *becoming* it, losing our own names in this shadowy process, as in a game of tag played for keeps.[35] It only makes sense that Freud, always the provocative theorist of colloquialisms, found his name for the ego's repressed origin in "das Es," the it, of which he noted, "It cannot say what it wants."[36]

Other colloquialisms comparable to this usage of "it" include the indeterminate "they," which appears in statements such as "They say that too much TV isn't good for you."[37] In this usage "they" may mean something like "authorities," "informed sources," or the vox populi, depending on what is at issue and the seriousness with which it is being said; but it is not simply a substitute for some more definite expression. Thus, when asked to identify this "they," a character in a story by Charles Dickens and Wilkie Collins exclaims impatiently, "Them! Them as says pretty well everything, you know."[38]

The distinctiveness of this "they" is that it shows our readiness to take note of the unnameable coherence on which our discourse depends. (An attitude taken to its logical conclusion in the 1960s psychedelic motto "Death is the greatest trip of all—that's why they save it for last.") If they are a bit less excitable than Joey Ladle, the character in the story by Dickens and Collins, those who employ this idiom and then find themselves challenged—"Who are 'they'?"—are likely to respond very simply, smiling or shrugging, "You know—*they.*" And this "you know" is also relevant to this discussion, especially in its hypertrophic usage among some speakers, for whom it becomes a refrain to stitch together words that might otherwise do things dreadful to contemplate. One might also note in this regard the habit, often recorded as being more frequent in the speech of women, of ending sentences with a questioning intonation, as if seeking assurance that the conversation (which we all have good reason to suspect might always turn into who knows what?) can still be conceived to be intact, mutual, coherent.

The foregoing examples involve different aspects of language, including diction, syntax, intonation, and gender. All of them, however, suggest a popular recognition that our linguistic orientation cannot come close to being pinned down in terms of formal parameters of time, space, perspective, or native competence. (This is a point addressed by the title of one of Ashbery's poems in *April Galleons*, "Never To Get It Really Right.") Our most common ways of speaking suggest that we know full well that we are better off in not trusting to our ability to name what we are talking about and in not attributing too much to the names we do in fact use. ("It could be anything, you say," is Ashbery's beginning to the last section of "The System" [TP, 105].) They suggest that if we approach something in language, get at something, as we say, then the orientation thus established is only nominal, as we also say. It is finally a question of having a feel for it, of being "plugged in," as when we think ourselves in or out of touch with things—with certain tender buttons—and so as in the difference (famously difficult to formalize) between "good sex" and "bad sex."

In effect, as we speak of "getting it" or "losing it," voices fly out of "it," voices equally oblivious to standards of identity, reference, and topicality, yet not without their own finely nuanced demands to carry us away. Thus, we may speak of being "gone on" somebody with whom we are in love, just as we may speak of being "blown away" by an image, poem, experience, or striking utterance that really gets to us, or that we really get. This transporting coherence of our anomia might be described in terms of the way we feel "close to" certain people or things—close to them in a sense that is liable to be as disorienting as it is demanding because it proves so resistant to the conventional grammar of space and time through which we are obliged to parse ourselves. For instance, if we were trying to deal with the loss of someone close to us, struggling to "get over it," as the saying goes, no doubt it would be difficult for us, and maybe even an insult and torture to our sensibilities, if we were pressed to say exactly what that "it" is—or was—for even tenses abandon us here (*here*, that is, where "it's all over or soon will be or just was, in any / other language sufficient to tell it in—just like it was" [FC, 19]).

Thus, in Ashbery's "Riddle Me" (AG, 2–3), the poet-as-lover asks, "O in all your life were you ever teased / Like this, and it became your mind?" In this line we cannot be sure how to take the word "became" (does it mean "turned into" or "proved fitting to"?) or the word "it" (does it refer to teasing, the desire that teases, the past of which the poem speaks, or something else entirely?). Nonetheless, in the experiences of love and interpretation, the poet and the reader are identified with each other insofar as they share this riddling representation of a riddle. Ashbery is even willing to go so far as to consider the prospect of "some permanence" for his desire, but he explains that carefully measured quantifier in terms of desire overreaching itself, expecting joy but also a kind of puzzling alienation in time: "we catch up / To ourselves, but they are the selves of others." Therefore, one becomes (or it becomes one to be) "afraid to retrace steps." We are teased with the riddle of what could possibly be the fitting measures, quantities, and transformations in this situation, teased even with the question of appropriate breath, as the poem concludes, "We mix / Breathless greetings and tears and lately taste / The precious supplies."

Here, as in the mock-Romantic "Too Happy, Happy Tree" in the same collection (*AG*, 44–5), our "transports" through time and space finally defeat us, and in fact are even called on to do so. "In the end your narrative lost us," the poet says, and so he asks, "How does it add up?" "It" here is the apostrophized tree equivocally present to experience and recalled from the poetic tradition represented by Wordsworth, Shelley, and Emerson, among others; it is also its "branching out" into virtually everything, into a wide range of contingencies, "inevitable voyages to be accomplished or not." This tree (and we might glance here also at "trees" used to chart syntax) returns along with the poet from their various transports to an "it" that remains unnameable, beyond any fixed logic of transformations: "And one lopes along the path / Thinking, forcibly, and by evening we have become the eye, / Blind, because it does the seeing. / It kind of makes it stand out from the rest." Casual and colloquial ("kind of"), difficult to measure and put into poetic numbers (in relation to "the rest"), both the agent and the object of transformations ("It kind of makes it stand out"), the "it" of the last line does the work of revelation, in proper Romantic fashion, but reveals—what? Certainly itself least of all. We could gloss the last line as "The eye kind of makes the tree stand out from the rest"— perhaps that is the reading to which we feel most close. But then again, it could be "the seeing" that the eye causes to "stand out," especially considering the emphasis throughout the poem on perception as an experience that transports us beyond the presumed tautological givenness of things, so that it is only logical to find Ashbery paying homage to Shelley even as he revises him, addressing his titular subject as "tree / That you are." Or again, the "it" in both instances could be the eye, in its paradoxical characterization here as visionary and blind; in this respect it is not itself and in fact is the "we" of the poem, which we may remember represents a defeated, lost, and hence appropriately modest (albeit energetic) number. (And here we might want to turn as well to the opening lines of another poem in this collection, "Dreams of Adulthood" [*AG*, 6]: "Why does he do it like that say it like that you might ask / Dream it like that.") All in all, the "it" of this poem's conclusion certainly can be said to communicate (in terms of perception, poetic tradition, revelation, and so on), but it is impossible to add it up.

Take it as you will, we can at least agree that saying "the it" sounds funny here, much as "the the" must strike us oddly in Stevens's poem "The Man on the Dump" (CP, 203). Saying "the it" simply does not sound right—surely the reason why Freud's translators chose to render *das Es* with a pronoun from a foreign, classical, now medico-scientific "dead language."[39] Yet in this translation a certain resonance is lost: the spluttering percussion of "it" in colloquial discourse, in which it regularly jumps out of its anonymous and wholly servile role to take on a volatile identity of its own. It becomes the argot of the metaphysics of everyday life. ("It's all so important yet so excruciatingly / banal, isn't it, darling?"—thus Ashbery commenting on the statements, "You fuck me, I'll / fix you. You give me that, and I'll give you this" [FC, 202].) For in its transporting coherence we find the articulation of social drives, which in our daily lives render history in terms of unavoidable demands for idiomatic choices: How would *you* put it? Do you identify yourself with this, that, or the other? Are you with us on this, or are you out of it? Has it been brought home to you? Will you stand for it? Well, *do you get it*?

Precisely because it is unalterable and irrecoverable, fixed in that sense, the past on which such questions must depend is radically flexible. It is right here and right there, in the dynamic materiality of everyday social life, and yet is knowable only through its questionings, as in those ambient "it"'s blown about by the gusts of all the exorbitant identifications with which we must contend in establishing any imaginable communication. ("I have this thing / I must do without knowing what it is or whether anyone/ will be helped or offended by it. Should I do it? And there, it was gone. / It will never be printed on a banner in a political demonstration / or fed to rabbits first to see whether they die" [FC, 114].) Observed in this way, the volatile "it" tells of the pastness of the present, of all that is bound to escape us in it but that nevertheless will refuse to let us rest easy, even in phenomena as precisely identifiable as a tap on the shoulder, a sudden gust of air, a cough, a wave of your hand, a shuffling of warm bars of sunlight on your face, or a voice calling your name. This word *it*, what could be more trivial and common? And so it is—as trivial and common as (let's say) that scene you check out through your bedroom window each night before going to bed, its scattering of laughs and silhouettes in humid blue-black darkness, which you know perfectly well and have no need to observe, and yet do; or as those occasions when you are sitting at a table during a meeting, knowing better than to say anything about it while you watch flames boiling over the stolid countenance of that waste of space squatting across from you; or as the hole in the world left by a hot love gone bad, which allows you an exquisite sense of what things will look like if you should ever not see anything—until, over time, you come to look elsewhere, and it is no longer what it was, and so you are over it (in the sense in which we may speak of a story being over because we have read it to the end and so imagine it is no longer being told); or as . . . you know. (But what has happened to it right here, in all this? Well, sometimes you just let it go, right? Because you can do that, sometimes it just is not worth it, you gotta do what you gotta do, or if you prefer you can scrabble at some bunch of stony something so as to ask it not to fling you off; you just let it go, or maybe you are talking with someone and you both understand, no need to say it, what a bore it would be even to try to say it, you might as well relax for a while and do something else, it doesn't matter what, maybe browse through a newspaper just to get a sense of what's going on these days . . .)

And here it is, here and there, in this environment of colloquial discourse, in which anomia is an unremarkable condition of being, in which communication must suffer itself—no matter how eloquently— to splutter forth, that John Ashbery's poetry takes its bearings.

This is not to say that his language is notably colloquial in the usual, colloquial sense of that word—far from it. Although colloquialisms regularly turn up in his work, they never take it over; and when Ashbery turns to them most emphatically, they are likely to seem almost fussy, not casual and informal, in their utterance. In this respect he is closer to Henry James than to Frank O'Hara, and one would never confuse his style or interests with those David Antin tries to work out in his "talk poems," for instance, or with slangy Ezra Pound's.[40] His language overall is sumptuous, leisurely, balanced in an offbeat way, sophisticated, and even classic in the devotion of its resources to perceptions of nature, emotions, memories, pleasures, and uncertainties. One need only think of the titles of his volumes, with their references to rivers and trees, shadows and waves, dreams and artworks.

And yet the characteristic unit of Ashbery's poetry is the striking utterance, the linguistic event, without distinction as to compositional elements, forms, or themes, and thus his poetry must be said to be demotic even where his style might seem to say otherwise. That is why the ravishing scraps of language across his pages, which I love and do not care to memorize, are in fact quite difficult to remember, even as one is reading them, beyond the last line or two: because his language aspires to the condition of colloquial happenstance. Though always carefully wrought, even ornately and obsessively so, his is a poetry that dwells on words at the point of their volatility. It is more concerned with capturing captivating effects than with establishing meanings for itself; at its best it is made of linguistic usages that do not add up and yet prove uncannily more than sufficient to get our recognition. Something is always happening in it but never anything dramatic, and in this sense it is a poetry of linguistic routine, as perverse as it may seem to say so. It lacks dramatic events—for instance, one would not know from his work if anyone close to him had ever murdered, died, or committed suicide—and this reticence, which will not allow an individual identity to seem isolated in his words, is a way of paying attention to the anomia characteristic of the linguistic routines of colloquial discourse. Rather than elevating, redeeming, or triumphing over ordinary language, in the tired formula that many critics persist in applying to his poems, his idiolect follows the avant-garde of everyday language even as it flaunts itself as needless luxury in contrast to the orientations of everyday business, work, or productivity, which are almost never evident in his poems and when mentioned at all appear only as that with which the fashioning of his art can have nothing to do. For Ashbery's model of language is not the mythically identifiable speaker of productively intended communications in a context that can be theoretically corrected to a null state; his model (if this term still fits) is the quotidian scattering of meaning in a lived environment, in which one must expect language to be diverse in its orientations, initiated and broken off at odd points, smeared with noise, serenely unobservant of dogmatic laws and moralities, and yet capable of all at once flashing into a sense of coherence, as when several conversations overheard at a party may jostle one another into a drunkenly resplendent harmony. As Ashbery put it with characteristic casualness in a 1980 interview with Peter Stitt, "Suddenly something fixes itself in the flow that is going on around one and seems to have a significance."[41]

Fittingly, then, Ashbery's words often seem barely to hang together as a coherent poetic production. "Too many armies, too many dreams, and that's / It" ("All and Some," SP, 65). His words seem as if they had not really expected to meet together on the page, like people in a crowd who are all off on purposes of their own even though they obey a certain order, one that can even be measured and plotted if there are those plodding enough to turn their hands to it. It is as if his words are uttered just a heartbeat in advance of reflection, thrown out into the thick of things without overcoats or cab fare to get them where they want to go, and yet impelled by a curious sense of promise that keeps them from panicking. His writing practically invites the familiar accusation that a great deal of art in the twentieth century has turned into an arcane, elitist, and historically moribund activity, cut off from common language and social commitments, precisely so that it may turn this accusation into a challenging account of the transports involved in whatever we are able to imagine as the language with which we are familiar. He is concerned with recording its striking effects and the consequences that ensue when we irritably cling to these effects, in the name of commonality or of commitment or of love or of anything else, thus believing not badly but too well. In this way Ashbery comes to terms with the traditional notion of poetry as elevated language, thought, and emotion in an era in which any such claim for art is likely to appear not only delusional but also quite vulgar, ironically enough, as in a kind of *bovarysme*. (And yet still, today, and in spite of work such as Ashbery's, how many of those who frequent poetry readings would not be insulted if one were to compare them to sixteen-year-olds who fall head over heels for Pearl Jam or Ayn Rand?) The skeins of consciousness tangled on Ashbery's pages form recognizable knots, figuring desire in the difficulty and frequent opacity of the linguistic effects of which they are composed; it is thus that he refers to traditional art, as characterized by rarefaction, exclusivity, and mysterious mastery, even as he treats the very idea of reference as a curious kind of beast, perhaps something like a unicorn, in which people are said once to have put their faith even though now its possible existence is largely of interest only to philosophers of semantics, for whom it is a favorite example in discussions of linguistic reference.

Ashbery, however, does not come off as one who mounts theses about language. His is an antithetical art, as colloquial language is antithetical, returning always to points (such as tautologies, shrugs, grunts, or the phatic, haptic, gnostic "it") that are profoundly unsettling to our very names. In Ashbery's case, what this antithetical orientation entails is that his attachment to all the resonance that may strike us in the name of poetry, now, in the second half of the twentieth century, is pursued by way of an elaborately calculated diminishment of poetic voice as this was traditionally articulated in terms of one's supposed vocation, emotions, responsibilities, and destiny. His discipline involves an intense dispersal of attention, not a concentration that sooner or later would have to settle on the name as its normative object. Where his poetry is obscure, as it frequently is if one tries to interpret it word for word or line by line, it is so not in the way of hermeticism but rather in the way phrases flown out of a riotous mob or stuttered out when one is twirling a radio dial may be funny, suggestive, moving in all sorts of ways—which is to say, impressively meaningful—even though their sources are not only beyond one's reach but also of no conceivable interest if they were miraculously to be made available.

This antithetical orientation of Ashbery's poetry is notable especially in its refusal of ideas. His works pack more intelligence per page than most writers do in their entire career, but his intelligence spends itself not in ideas but in linguistic occurrences, striking effects, shrugs from one good patch to another, as if his poems were written to chart the possibilities of fragments for an audience entirely attuned to incompletion as the normal state of affairs. It would seem as if all of human life were destined not to become a book, but to become quotable. In this context ideas are seen not as odious (one would not bestir oneself thus to dignify them) but as otiose, or really rather tactless when you come down to it. ("You must have said *it* a long way back without knowing it. . . . It is best then that the buried word remain buried . . ." ["The System," *TP*, 95].) To be sure, his poems are strewn with what seem like editorial comments, attractive little summary abstractions: "All things are palpable, none are known" ("Poem in Three Parts," *SP*, 22), or "Each of us circles / Around some simple but vital missing piece of information" ("Fantasia on 'The Nut-Brown Maid,' " *HD*, 85). Such passages are like attractive hooks to catch readers (*ah, this is what it is all about!*), especially those academic readers (*ah, that could work as an epigraph!*) who compose so much of the audience for poetry these days; but they are just that, the hooks of letters promising themselves absurdly, against all our experience, as if anything but heedless hellbent greed could account for our willingness to see in the chaste formula an embrace of spluttering life. Obiter dicta such as these are tokens of a type of discourse which squirm their way out of this very distinction, placing an emphasis instead on the ordinary but unpredictably pulsing idiom. In this respect, for all his self-professed ambition, it is as if Ashbery is devoted to writing in a sublimely *un*monumental tradition. Therefore, when he entertains the question of what writing is, he begins diffidently ("it's getting down on paper / Not thoughts, exactly, but ideas, maybe"), then remarks that he does not have the name for it ("Ideas is better, though not precisely what I mean"), and concludes with a shrug, "Someday I'll explain. Not today though" ("Ode to Bill," *SP*, 50).

In this respect Ashbery's poetry borders on a kind of neurotic stul-
tification, in which every statement one might conceive is immediately
accompanied, if not in fact forestalled, by a series of more or less implicit disclaimers—as if he were forever saying, *Of course I could be
wrong. There are other viewpoints. It doesn't really matter.* The consistent
resistance to ideas in his writing may suggest that whatever it is that
we are talking about, we cannot ever really get over it; we might as
well sink back, let things wash over us, since we are feeling too punk
to rouse ourselves to any effort of thought, or since we are feeling too
deliciously impressionable in our languor; and so we may make a virtue of our passivity. Yet Ashbery's poetry is not merely undogmatic
but decidedly so. Its intellectuality shows a yearning for experience, as
if to say with an ironic flourish, ah, yes, would that it *were* of a nature
to which one could simply submit oneself! The transports of his poetry
may be cheap, the stuff of everyday discourse, but to say this is not to
say that they come easy.

In fact, through its antithetical, colloquial orientation, which resists
ideas and always recalls us to our ultimately familiar condition of anomia, Ashbery's poetry offers a precise definition of thought as nothing
more or less than needless difficulty. His poetry is always very intent
on displaying this difficulty, as we see in the way it is so overwhelmingly saturated with intelligence. (This explains its droll history
of inspiring extremes of dislike and adoration, which always turn on
this question of "difficulty.") It is equally intent on displaying this difficulty just long enough to point out its needlessness, which seemingly
can give rise only to endless labors. Whatever it is with which we are
concerned, we will not come to terms with it today, not yet, in this
discursive turbulence in which we must only live. It is as much as to
say, *You were expecting something else? C'mon, get real.* That is why this
intelligence has such a dreamily antithetical quality, shrugging off ideas
as distractions from whatever point is at hand, as in the line Kenneth
Koch is supposed to have offered to epitomize Ashbery's style: "It
wants to go to bed with us."[42] Ashbery himself has been quoted as
saying, in a 1965 conversation with Koch, "I would not put a statement
in a poem."[43]

The poetry that issues from an intelligence thus conceived, a poetry
deliberately restrained from vaunting any relations to history, productive conditions, ideology, and artistic privilege, is bound to be a kind
of unsaying. As readily as it offers itelf to quotation, it strictly refuses
itself as established knowledge or as wisdom likely to be anthologized.
Modestly but firmly, it turns away from whatever it might be taken

definitively to be so as to become a poetry of fugitive linguistic events, as I have said, or what might be called a poetry of asides. It effectively proposes that the aside is not a peculiar form of theatrical speech but the mortal form of all utterances, which are bound to speak in the same impossible breath to divided and radically heterogenous universes. Communication is then characterized in terms of obliquities, indirections, and side effects, or in terms of a constant shimmying edginess. No matter how trivial it may be, every linguistic turn is a tour de force, shadowed in the instant of its utterance by a potential for discord that might conceivably extend to an apocalyptic disruption of the entire community presumed in the name of human life. "I don't see how we are expected to live with it, but the fact of the matter / is we do" (FC, 116), he observes; or in a more jaunty mood, "I didn't mean for it to be this way / But since it has happened I'm glad" ("By the Flooded Canal," AG, 88).

All this does not quite add up to an unflinching observance of the unaccountability of death. As far as Ashbery's poetry is concerned, we are always addressing and addressed by death, transported by it especially in our most coherent moments. We are like those elements of Hans Holbein's painting The Ambassadors (1533) gathered around its anamorphic skull, which acts as an aside that turns all the world into a stage without clear distinctions among actors, settings, and audiences. Ashbery writes, "Our daily imaginings are swiftly tilted down to / Death in its various forms" ("Fragments," DD, 80); and his poetry seems always possessed by the spin death so offhandedly puts on things, by its warning promise of unwilled transformations and relentless trivialization. Like Parmigianino's hand in "Self-Portrait in a Convex Mirror," death is "shield or greeting, / The shield of a greeting" (SP, 82). Yet though it is written from the prospect of death, with its unsettling effect on all values, this poetry does not convey a predictable anxiety but rather a kind of nonchalance, an elegiac patience, which lingers without fretting on whatever it is that it happens to contemplate. In a sense it does not matter what it is—there is no typical occasion for an Ashbery poem—for whatever else it is, in this poetry, it points to death, which is taken to be unnameable even when we pretend otherwise for the sake of convenience. As one of Dickens's characters has it, it is "that what's-his-name from which no thingumbob comes back."[44] This it about which we talk so much is the deictic sign of death anamorphically caught up in the pulsing coherence of our social something. This is the logic we see worked out when Ashbery is brought to write of how "it / Always keeps getting sorted out / And there is still the same amount to do" ("Litany," *AWK*, 4). Without addressing this event or anything like it, Ashbery's poetry thus explains how strikingly appropriate it is that Gary Gilmore's last utterance, before he was executed on January 17, 1977, should have been "Let's do it." This is why the it can take the place that might otherwise be assigned to the hapless name or the dreadful idea: because it is always referring to death in a world in which the construction of reality through names and ideas, in fact all the deferred gratification bound up in ideation, must deny it.

Traditionally, deixis is supposed to be the most direct form of reference, by which we demonstratively point out what we intend to communicate. Although deixis is generally considered more difficult to theorize in writing, which lacks the extralinguistic or pragmatic cues ordinarily taken to determine deictic reference, linguists generally find that the problems peculiar to such reference can be understood in terms of a textual organization that takes the place of the experiential organization around any act of ostension. After all, even at its simplest—a pointing finger—any act of "direct reference" must depend on an implicitly structured environment of conventions, spatial and temporal perspectives, and assumptions of various sorts about these conventions and perspectives. Such is the usual scholarly understanding, which Ashbery's poetry rejects in favor of the popular understanding evinced in colloquial language. Thus, his poetry either dramatizes an impression of immediacy in the absence of a supporting environment or portrays an environment suitable for and yet lacking any sense of immediacy. As a result, when his poetry does not seem positively dreamy or hallucinatory in its images, it is likely to seem burdened by its own casualness and leisure, as if waiting for an ultimatum that would at long last install an uninterpretable language. Ignorance of the law, he writes, "far from being no excuse, is the law, and we'll see who rakes in / the chips come Judgment Day" (*FC*, 123). We patiently observe our world, and "it is finally as though that thing of monstrous interest / were happening in the sky / but the sun is setting and prevents you from seeing it" ("As You Came from the Holy Land," *SP*, 7).

Yet it would be silly to overplay this aspect of his poetry. After all, Ashbery does not make a big deal of death; he is more like the boy whom Freud was astonished to hear saying, "I know Father's dead, but what I can't understand is why he doesn't come home to supper."[45] Death is not a matter of ideas or professed values in Ashbery's writing; as I have noted, it is never significant as a *name*; it is simply what courses through the dimensions of consciousness represented by his poetry, continually disturbing the work of idealization that is our language, not only in its service to the supposed transcendence of particular cultural values but also in the fixity and rationality of things seemingly promised by grammar. Ashbery's view of things gives us to understand that the immediate gratification we may be said to defer in any exercise of consciousness appears also, always, as the coherence on which we depend and as the death we obscurely desire. For better or worse, this is the view on which Ashbery chooses to dwell in his poetry, as when he writes of "the end that is past truth, / The being of our sentences, in the climate that fostered them, / Not ours to own, like a book, but to be with, and sometimes / To be without, alone and desperate" ("Soonest Mended," *DD*, 18). His is a vernacular metaphysics because his poetry struggles *not* to rise above the anomia that is our condition in everyday speech, not to flatter itself by engaging in "dwarf speculations / About the insane, invigorating whole they don't represent" ("Fragment," *DD*, 93), but rather to see what can be made of it, whatever it may be, always keeping in mind that the it thus figured finally is a finger of speech pointing us to death. His poetry is interesting not for anything it has to say of death, then, but for what it shows of the brilliant vagaries of colloquial language in its unsaying of its own unavoidable forms, which often are so strikingly beautiful and yet finally seem to come out of nowhere, like refugees from scorned perfection.[46]

In other words, this is a poetry of small talk, inasmuch as it constructs its beauty through a resolute resistance to statement, idea, and theory. Like colloquial language, conceived of as founded on idiom rather than rule, Ashbery's poetry chooses transporting coherence over nomothetic form and the intriguing shadow of violence over the blinding light of idea. It prefers the vitality of the striking utterance, which takes note of the prospect of death, over the memorialized language of reference. In this way Ashbery has been trying to work out the possibility of a discipline that may be valuable without desiring to be authoritative or monumental. It is significant in this respect that in addition to not giving themselves as autobiographical revelation, his poems also pay almost no attention to widely recognized authorities, institutions, codes of values, and historical events of the sort that I mentioned at the outset of this chapter. (One would scarcely know that there are such things as races and riots and cases of sexual harassment, much less a judicial system and a Supreme Court, on the evidence of Ashbery's poetry.) The personal and the public alike are swept away in favor of an insistence on the necessary and necessarily unnameable coherence of their communication. Ashbery's is a poetry that stays news (in both senses of "stays") by eliminating the private and the public in favor of the popular, which then appears as the endlessly disturbing realm of experience below or above (here the distinction must fail us) the notice of ideas. The indulgence it begs is that we may let the avant-garde of everyday language lead the way for us: that we may ritually, poetically, submit the dream of a common language to the powers of popular understanding.

Of course, it could be that we do not want to grant him this indulgence; and even if we grant it, we may want to challenge him on this very basis, inquiring about ways in which he may be dawdling behind or falling away from everyday language. After all, there are tautologies and then there are tautologies. Precisely because they are so famously difficult "to get," so preoccupied with getting and losing a volatile "it," Ashbery's poems seem freely to offer themselves to our judgment on a colloquial basis; but one might well ask whether the fatalism that characterizes the realm of popular understanding as it is worked out by his poetry is the most we can say of this subject. It could be that this fatalism is less distinctive of colloquial language than of a professional attitude, among poets speaking of matters poetic, which serves to distract us from more challenging colloquialisms. One need not adopt Sam Spade's skepticism in The Maltese Falcon (1941) ("The cheaper the crook, the gaudier the patter") to remember that vernaculars are various, and to feel that the striking utterance may not be all there is to colloquial discourse—or again, to know that there are striking utterances and then there are striking utterances.

I think, for instance, of the T-shirts that were popular in the late 1980s, emblazoned with "IT'S A BLACK THING—YOU WOULDN'T UNDERSTAND."[47] The "it" in this slogan is exactly the kind of usage of which Ashbery makes so much, so brilliantly, and yet it would be asking too much to suggest that his poetry should capture more than the idiomatic appeal of this kind of uncommunicative communication—that it should also touch upon the social, historical, and political complexities of the smart-ass defiance it conveys. Similarly, it would be asking too much to expect that Ashbery's work should show him to be struck not only by Wallace Stevens's verdant tautologies and marvelous way with names but also, for instance, by Stevens's miserable casual racism. As Ashbery never ceases to remind us, it is dangerous to assume that intelligence will be convenient. To note that his poetry cannot satisfy us in this respect, then, is in no way to diminish his accomplishments, without which I would never have come to dwell on this question of the idiomatic specificity of T-shirts. I would observe only how Ashbery's works all suggest that we still must be seeking a poetry worthy of our language, one finally able to catch up to the avant-garde of our everyday chatter and thus to make our names make sense, so that the stuff dreams are made of (as we may say in our drastic vernacular, quoting Sam Spade, who was quoting Prospero) no longer would be that. Because that would be pretty much it, right?

Notes

CHAPTER ONE   *Conspiring with Tradition*

1. Quotations from David Hume, *An Enquiry Concerning Human Understanding*, ed. Eric Steinberg (Indianapolis: Hackett Publishing, 1977), pp. 76–90.

2. Quotations from Friedrich Nietzsche, "History in the Service and Disservice of Life," trans. Gary Brown, in *Unmodern Observations*, ed. William Arrowsmith (New Haven: Yale University Press, 1990), pp. 91, 100.

3. On this subject, see R. M. Burns, *The Great Debate on Miracles: From Joseph Glanvill to David Hume* (Lewisburg, Pa.: Bucknell University Press and Associated University Presses, 1981).

4. Hume, *Enquiry*, p. 19.

5. Page references to the writings of Jorge Luis Borges are given in the text, as quoted from the following works: "Three Versions of Judas" (trans. Anthony Kerrigan), "The Garden of Forking Paths" (trans. Helen Temple and Ruthven Todd), "The Sect of the Phoenix" (trans. Anthony Kerrigan), "Tlön, Uqbar, Orbis Tertius" (trans. Alastair Reid), "Pierre Menard, Author of Don Quixote" (trans. Anthony Bonner), "An Examination of the Work of Herbert Quain" (trans. Anthony Kerrigan), "Theme of the Traitor and the Hero" (trans. Anthony Kerrigan), and "The Babylon Lottery" (trans. Anthony Kerrigan), from *Ficciones*, ed. Anthony Kerrigan (New York: Grove Press, 1962); "The Wall and the Books" (trans. James E. Irby), "The Theologians" (trans. James E. Irby), "A New Refutation of Time" (trans. James E. Irby), "Story of the Warrior and the Captive" (trans. James E. Irby), and "The God's Script" (trans. L. A. Murillo), from *Labyrinths: Selected Stories and Other Writings*, ed. Donald A. Yates and James E. Irby (New York: New Directions, 1964); "Luke 23" (trans. Irving Feldman) and "Matthew 25:30" (trans. Alastair Reid), from *A Personal Anthology*, ed. Anthony Kerrigan (New York: Grove Press, 1967); "Preface to the 1957 Edition," from *The Book of Imaginary Beings* [with Margarita Guerrero], rev. and ed. Norman Thomas

di Giovanni (New York: E. P. Dutton, 1969); "The Meeting," "The Other Death," "The Challenge," and "The Maker," from *The Aleph and Other Stories: 1933–1969*, ed. and trans. Norman Thomas de Giovanni in collaboration with the author (New York: E. P. Dutton, 1970); "The End of the Duel," "The Gospel According to Mark," and "Dr. Brodie's Report," from *Doctor Brodie's Report*, trans. Norman Thomas di Giovanni in collaboration with the author (New York: E. P. Dutton, 1972); "Preface," from *In Praise of Darkness*, trans. Norman Thomas di Giovanni (New York: E. P. Dutton, 1974); "The Book of Sand," "The Other," "The Congress," "Ulrike," "There Are More Things," and "Afterword," from *The Book of Sand*, trans. Norman Thomas di Giovanni (New York: E. P. Dutton, 1977); "Avatars of the Tortoise" (trans. Karen Stolley), "Borges and I" (trans. Norman Thomas di Giovanni), and "The Circular Ruins" (trans. Anthony Bonner), from *Borges: A Reader*, ed. Emir Rodriguez Monegal and Alastair Reid (New York: E. P. Dutton, 1981).

Throughout this book, with quotations from Borges and others, I have given the original language where I have modified translations; translations not otherwise credited are my own.

6. See Brian Stock's argument that defining tradition by opposition to the modern is "definition by default," in *Listening to the Text: On the Uses of the Past* (Baltimore: Johns Hopkins University Press, 1990), p. 163.

7. Quoted in Hugh Trevor-Roper, "The Invention of Tradition: The Highland Tradition of Scotland," in *The Invention of Tradition*, ed. Eric Hobsbawm and Terence Ranger (Cambridge: Cambridge University Press, 1983), p. 31.

8. See Jorge Luis Borges, "The Challenge," in *The Aleph and Other Stories*, p. 139: "All over the Argentine runs a story that may belong to legend or to history or (which may be just another way of saying it belongs to legend) to both things at once." In terms of my argument here, it is notable that this legend or history involves the relation between community and culture through "the cult of courage," which modern Argentinian literature and popular culture have often portrayed as definitive of national identity.

9. Edward Shils, *Tradition* (Chicago: University of Chicago Press, 1981), p. 22.

A similar point is emphasized in Karl R. Popper, "Towards a Rational Theory of Tradition," in *Conjectures and Refutations: The Growth of Scientific Knowledge* (London: Routledge and Kegan Paul, 1963), pp. 120–35. In relation to my concerns here, it is notable that Popper's argument touches on the role of conspiracy theories in social life.

10. Antonin Artaud, "Le rite des rois de l'Atlantide," in *Oeuvres complètes*, 14 vols. (Paris: Gallimard, 1956–), 9:89.

11. An instructive comparison is furnished by the way Romantic historicism, as analyzed by Gadamer, can be seen to share the premises of the Enlightenment attitudes it purported to reject. See Hans-Georg Gadamer, *Truth and Method*, 2d ed. rev., rev. trans. Joel Weinsheimer and Donald G. Marshall (New York: Crossroad, 1991), pp. 265–77.

12. See Sir Thomas Browne, *Pseudodoxia Epidemica*, in *The Works of Sir Thom-*

as *Browne*, ed. Geoffrey Keynes, 4 vols. (Chicago: University of Chicago Press, 1964), 2:5.

Also, on the topology of Borges's fictions, with special reference to the figure of the labyrinth, see Jean-Pierre Mourey, *Jorge Luis Borges: Vérité et univers fictionnels* (Liège: Pierre Mardaga, 1989).

13. See Catherine Clément, *La syncope: Philosophie du ravissement* (Paris: Bernard Grasset, 1990).

14. For an analysis of this emphasis on immanence in relation to issues of memory and the past, see Nicolás Rosa, "Texto-palimpsesto: Memoria y olvido textual," in *Jorge Luis Borges: Variaciones interpretatives sobre sus procedimientos literarios y bases epistemológicas*, ed. Karl Alfred Blüher and Alfonso de Toro (Frankfurt am Main: Vervuert, 1992), pp. 185–92.

15. J. C. Heesterman, "India and the Inner Conflict of Tradition," in *Post-Traditional Societies*, ed. S. N. Eisenstadt (New York: W. W. Norton, 1972), p. 97.

16. Chinua Achebe, "An Image of Africa: Racism in Conrad's *Heart of Darkness*," in Joseph Conrad, *Heart of Darkness*, ed. Robert Kimbrough, 3d ed. (New York: W. W. Norton, 1988), p. 259.

17. Friedrich Nietzsche, *The Gay Science*, trans. Walter Kaufmann (New York: Random House, 1974), p. 183.

18. Friedrich Nietzsche, *Human, All Too Human: A Book for Free Spirits*, trans. Marion Faber with Stephen Lehmann (Lincoln: University of Nebraska Press, 1984), p. 67. C.f. Eric Hobsbawm's description of the use of history "as a legitimator of action and cement of group cohesion" in "Introduction: Inventing Tradition," in Hobsbawm and Ranger, *The Invention of Tradition*, p. 12.

19. Franz Kafka, "A Report to an Academy," trans. Tania Stern and James Stern, in *The Complete Stories*, ed. Nahum N. Glatzer (New York: Schocken Books, 1946), p. 255.

20. Terence Ranger, "The Invention of Tradition in Colonial Africa," in Hobsbawm and Ranger, *The Invention of Tradition*, p. 250. On this point, see also Elizabeth Colson's discussion of J. A. Barnes's writings on innovative tradition in colonial Africa in *Tradition and Contract: The Problem of Order* (Chicago: Aldine, 1974), pp. 77–80.

21. G. K. Chesterton, "English Literature and the Latin Tradition," in *Chesterton on Shakespeare*, ed. Dorothy Collins (Henley-on-Thames: Darwen Finlayson, 1971), p. 13.

22. Stephen Orgel, "Shakespeare and the Cannibals," in *Cannibals, Witches, and Divorce: Estranging the Renaissance*, ed. Marjorie Garber (Baltimore: Johns Hopkins University Press, 1987), p. 55.

23. Quoted and trans. in Hugh Trevor-Roper, *The Plunder of the Arts in the Seventeenth Century* (London: Thames and Hudson, 1970), p. 26.

24. Walter Benjamin, "Theses on the Philosophy of History," in *Illuminations*, ed. Hannah Arendt, trans. Harry Zohn (New York: Schocken Books, 1969), p. 256.

25. On this point, with special reference to Benjamin's interest in the Kabbala, see Susan Buck-Morss, *The Dialectics of Seeing: Walter Benjamin and the Arcades Project* (Cambridge: MIT Press, 1989), esp. pp. 228–52.

26. Walter Benjamin, "Theses on the Philosophy of History" and "Some Reflections on Kafka," in *Illuminations*, pp. 255, 142–43.

27. See the essays usefully collected by Juan Fló, *Contra Borges* (Buenos Aires: Editorial Galerna, 1978); also valuable in this regard is Maria Luisa Bastos, *Borges ante la crítica Argentina: 1923–1960* (Buenos Aires: Hispamerica, 1974). For a recent argument against the tradition that identifies Borges as an aesthete detached from social, historical, and political concerns, see Daniel Balderston, *Out of Context: Historical Reference and the Representation of Reality in Borges* (Durham: Duke University Press, 1993).

28. Wole Soyinka, "Neo-Tarzanism: The Poetics of Pseudo-Tradition," in *Art, Dialogue and Outrage: Essays on Literature and Culture* (Ibadan: New Horn Press, 1988), p. 329.

29. Raphaël Lellouche, *Borges ou l'hypothèse de l'auteur* (Paris: Balland, 1989), p. 167; also, on the topic of the uselessness of erudition, see pp. 116–25.

30. Kwame Anthony Appiah, *In My Father's House: Africa in the Philosophy of Culture* (New York: Oxford University Press, 1992), p. 32.

31. Arthur Schopenhauer, *The World as Will and Idea*, trans. R. B. Haldane and John Kemp, 3 vols. (London: Routledge and Kegan Paul, 1964), 3:313.

32. Gerardo Mario Goloboff addresses this topic, comparing Borges's fiction to alchemy and citing Gaston Bachelard's emphasis on the specifically masculine nature of alchemical tradition, in *Leer Borges* (Buenos Aires: Editorial Huemul, 1978), pp. 206–23.

33. Momcilo Krajisnik, quoted in the Associated Press story "Serbs Are Cornered but Defiant," *Gainesville Sun*, October 9, 1994, 12A.

34. The patriotic criticism was produced by various hands, but see, for instance, Juan Carlos Portantiero, " 'Borges y la nueva generacion' de Adolfo Prieto," in Fló, *Contra Borges*, pp. 83–88; for the characterization of Borges as a eunuch—an extreme version of the more common insinuation of decadence or irrelevance in relation to manly concerns—see Blas Matamoro, "El juego trascendente," in Fló, *Contra Borges*, p. 163.

35. On the subject of Borges's writings in the context of issues of nationalism and immigration, see Rafael Olea Franco, *El otro Borges: El primer Borges* (Buenos Aires: Fondo de Cultura Económica de Argentina, 1993).

36. Nietzsche, *Human, All Too Human*, p. 15.

37. See Luce Irigaray, "Women on the Market," in *This Sex Which Is Not One*, trans. Catherine Porter with Carolyn Burke (Ithaca: Cornell University Press, 1985), pp. 170–91.

38. Compare the description of the home of the narrator's uncle in "There Are More Things," in *The Book of Sand*, p. 52: "As a boy, I used to accept all this ugliness, just as one accepts those incompatible things which, only because they coexist, are called the world."

39. Heesterman, "India and the Inner Conflict of Tradition," p. 102.

40. Schopenhauer, *The World as Will and Idea*, 1:28.

41. In *La prosa narrativa de Jorge Luis Borges: Temas-estilo*, 2d ed. rev. (Madrid: Editorial Gredos, 1974), Jaime Alazraki notes another possible pretext to "The Other Death" in a reference to Damiani in Bertrand Russell's *History of Western Philosophy*.

42. Schopenhauer, *The World as Will and Idea*, 1:249.

43. Sylvia Molloy, *Signs of Borges*, trans. Oscar Montero in collaboration with the author (Durham: Duke University Press, 1994), p. 56.

44. Browne, *Pseudodoxia Epidemica*, 2:3.

45. Nietzsche, *Human, All Too Human*, p. 75.

46. Nietzsche, *The Gay Science*, pp. 136–37.

47. Walter Benjamin, "The Task of the Translator," in *Illuminations*, p. 75.

48. Nietzsche, *The Gay Science*, p. 137.

49. Nietzsche, *Human, All Too Human*, p. 243.

50. Friedrich Nietzsche, *Daybreak: Thoughts on the Prejudices of Morality*, trans. R. J. Hollingdale (Cambridge: Cambridge University Press, 1982), pp. 2, 10–11.

51. For a thoughtful study of Borges's politics in their relation to his critical reception, especially in France, see Eric Flamand, *Le nom et le savoir: Abrégé de culture borgesienne*, 2d ed. rev. (Paris: Sillages, 1987).

52. See the questioning of the tradition/modernity contrast in Eisenstadt, *Post-Traditional Societies*, especially in Eisenstadt's introductory essay, pp. 1–28.

53. Benedict de Spinoza, *Theologico-Political Treatise*, in *The Chief Works of Benedict de Spinoza*, trans. R. H. M. Elwes, 2 vols. (New York: Cover, 1951), 1:85.

54. Friedrich Nietzsche, "On Truth and Lying in an Extra-Moral Sense," in *Friedrich Nietzsche on Rhetoric and Language*, ed. Sander L. Gilman et al. (New York: Oxford University Press, 1989), p. 247. Compare Georges Bataille's assertion that *"the sexual act is in time what the tiger is in space,"* in *The Accursed Share: An Essay on General Economy*, trans. Robert Hurley, 3 vols. (New York: Zone Books, 1988), 1:12.

55. Nietzsche, *Human, All Too Human*, p. 238.

56. Nietzsche, "On Truth and Lying," p. 252.

57. Sigmund Freud, "A Difficulty in the Path of Psycho-Analysis," in *The Standard Edition of the Complete Psychological Works of Sigmund Freud*, ed. James Strachey et al., 24 vols. (London: Hogarth Press and the Institute of Psycho-Analysis, 1955), 17: 40.

58. Sigmund Freud, *The Interpretation of Dreams*, in *Standard Edition*, 4:131.

59. See my *Abyss of Reason: Cultural Movements, Revelations, and Betrayals* (New York: Oxford University Press, 1991), chaps. 6–9.

60. Friedrich Nietzsche, *On the Genealogy of Morals*, trans. Walter Kaufmann and R. J. Hollingdale, in *On the Genealogy of Morals and Ecce Homo*, ed. Walter Kaufmann (New York: Vintage Books, 1967), p. 103.

61. Sigmund Freud, *Jokes and Their Relation to the Unconscious*, in *Standard Edition*, 8:59.

62. On this point compare Michael Taussig's meditation on the significance of the RCA Victor "talking dog" logo in Cuna and North American culture, in *Mimesis and Alterity: A Particular History of the Senses* (New York: Routledge, 1993), pp. 212–35; Donna Haraway's studies of the interrelationship of animality and textuality in *Simians, Cyborgs, Women: The Reinvention of Nature* (New York: Routledge, 1991); and Jacques Derrida's criticism of the opposition

drawn between animals and humans on the basis of language, in "Afterword," trans. Samuel Weber, in *Limited Inc*, ed. Gerald Graff (Evanston: Northwestern University Press, 1988), pp. 134–36.

63. Franz Kafka, "The Metamorphosis," trans. Willa and Edwin Muir, in *The Complete Stories*, p. 91.

64. Antonin Artaud, "Théatre Alfred Jarry," in *Oeuvres complètes*, 2:25.

65. Franz Kafka, "A Report to an Academy" and "Investigations of a Dog," in *Complete Stories*, pp. 258, 289–90.

66. Kafka, "A Report to an Academy" and "Investigations of a Dog," pp. 253, 292.

67. Laurence Sterne, *The Life and Opinions of Tristram Shandy, Gentleman*, ed. Graham Petrie (London: Penguin, 1967), p. 498; Charlotte Brontë, *Jane Eyre*, ed. Richard J. Dunn, 2d ed. (New York: W. W. Norton, 1987), p. 210; Italo Calvino, *Mr. Palomar*, trans. William Weaver (New York: Harcourt Brace Jovanovich, 1985), p. 27.

68. See George Berkeley, *The Principles of Human Knowledge*, in *The Works of George Berkeley*, ed. A. A. Luce and T. E. Jessop, 9 vols. (London: Thomas Nelson and Sons, 1949), 2:48: "I say it is granted on all hands (and what happens in dreams, phrensies, and the like, puts it beyond dispute) that it is possible we might be affected with all the ideas we have now, though no bodies existed without, resembling them."

69. Gottfried Wilhelm von Leibniz, "Introduction," in *New Essays on the Human Understanding, The Monadology, and Other Philosophical Writings*, trans. Robert Latta (London: Oxford University Press, 1925), p. 373. In the same volume, see also *The Monadology*, p. 251, where the same quotation from Hippocrates is cited to the same effect.

70. Leibniz, *The Monadology*, pp. 237–38.

CHAPTER TWO   *Unpardoning Tradition*

1. See Jacques Derrida's comment, in the course of his analysis of J. L. Austin's work, " 'Ritual' is not a possible occurrence [éventualité], but rather, as iterability, a structural characteristic of every mark," in "Signature Event Context," trans. Samuel Weber and Jeffrey Mehlman, in *Limited Inc*, ed. Gerald Graff (Evanston: Northwestern University Press, 1988), p. 15.

2. Emily Brontë, *Wuthering Heights*, ed. William M. Sale, Jr., 3d ed. (New York: W. W. Norton, 1990). Page references are given in the text.

3. All quotations from the works of William Shakespeare are taken from *The Riverside Shakespeare*, ed. G. Blakemore Evans (Boston: Houghton Mifflin, 1974). References are given in the text; I have omitted the editor's brackets for questionable readings.

4. On this point, see Peter Stallybrass and Allon White, *The Politics and Poetics of Transgression* (Ithaca: Cornell University Press, 1986), esp. pp. 21–22.

5. See Albert H. Tricomi's analysis of "the oddly alluring relation between language and event" in this play, in "The Aesthetics of Mutilation in 'Titus

Andronicus,'" *Shakespeare Survey* 27 (1974): 12; Lawrence Danson, "Introduction: *Titus Andronicus*," in *Tragic Alphabet: Shakespeare's Drama of Language* (New Haven: Yale University Press, 1974), pp. 1–22; S. Clark Hulse's argument that *Titus* "calls on a dramatic medium in which Shakespeare can create a stage space both personal and emblematic, stripped of precise geographical identity and capable of breaking down entirely the barriers between the inner and outer worlds," in "Wresting the Alphabet: Oratory and Action in *Titus Andronicus*," *Criticism* 21 (Spring 1979): 113; and Gillian Murray Kendall, "'Lend me thy hand': Metaphor and Mayhem in *Titus Andronicus*," *Shakespeare Quarterly* 40 (Fall 1989): 299–316.

6. For a particularly striking example of this approach, see Cynthia Marshall's suggestion that "we are secretly glad . . . all of us, not to hear what Lavinia would say, and grateful that the story of the rape is channelled into mythological allusion—distant, bookish, unreal" in "'I can interpret all her martyr'd signs': *Titus Andronicus*, Feminism, and the Limits of Interpretation," *Sexuality and Politics in Renaissance Drama*, ed. Carole Levin and Karen Robertson (Lewiston, N.Y.: Edwin Mellen Press, 1991), p. 201.

See also the characterization of the use of Ovidian allusion in this play in Charles Martindale and Michelle Martindale, *Shakespeare and the Uses of Antiquity: An Introductory Essay* (London: Routledge, 1990), p. 54.

7. See, for instance, Antonin Artaud, "Le théâtre que je vais fonder," in *Oeuvres complètes*, 14 vols. (Paris: Gallimard, 1956–), 5:35–37; and "Théâtre Alfred Jarry," in *Oeuvres*, 2:37. Volume and page references for quotations from these works are given in the text. See also Artaud's repeated references to Elizabethan drama in "Dossier de Van Gogh le suicidé de la société," in *Oeuvres*, 13:149–228.

8. W. Jackson Bate, *The Burden of the Past and the English Poet* (Cambridge: Harvard University Press, 1970), p. 35. (Bate was writing of "the neoclassic dilemma" in a later period, but his comment is still apposite here.)

9. William Hazlitt, "On the Doctrine of Philosophical Necessity," in *The Complete Works of William Hazlitt*, 21 vols. (London: J. M. Dent and Sons, 1934), 20:61.

10. Charlotte Brontë, *Jane Eyre*, ed. Richard J. Dunn, 2nd ed. (New York: W. W. Norton, 1987), p. 106.

11. On this point and others related to this essay, see Gilles Deleuze, *Différence et répétition* (Paris: Presses Universitaires de France, 1968).

12. John Webster, *The White Devil*, ed. John Russell Brown (Manchester: Manchester University Press, 1960). In relation to my argument here, Vittoria's words to the Cardinal presiding over the court are also notable: "Yes you have ravish'd justice, / Forc'd her to do your pleasure" (3.2.274–75).

13. Or is that *wives*, given the more than two dozen children?

14. Sandra R. Joshel, "The Body Female and the Body Politic: Livy's Lucretia and Verginia," in *Pornography and Representation in Greece and Rome*, ed. Amy Richlin (New York: Oxford University Press, 1992), p. 125.

See also the discussions of gender and patriarchy in David Willbern, "Rape and Revenge in *Titus Andronicus*," *English Literary Renaissance* 8 (Spring 1978): 159–82; Douglas E. Green, "Interpreting 'her martyr'd signs': Gender and

Tragedy in *Titus Andronicus*," *Shakespeare Quarterly* 40 (Fall 1989): 317–26; and Marshall, " 'I can interpret all her martyr'd signs,' " pp. 193–213.

15. On this point see Leonard Tennenhouse's analysis of the "Elizabethan use of the female body" that "identifies the power of the state with the state of the female body," in *Power on Display: The Politics of Shakespeare's Genres* (New York: Methuen, 1986), p. 111.

16. Compare Stanley Cavell's comments, of great relevance to *Titus Andronicus*, "To feed means both to give and to take nourishment, as to suckle means both to give and take the breast," in " 'Who does the wolf love?': Reading *Coriolanus*," in *Representing the English Renaissance*, ed. Stephen Greenblatt (Berkeley: University of California Press, 1988), p. 202.

17. See Artaud's complaint about Mossé in a letter to Jacqueline Breton (*Oeuvres*, 7:239) and his editors' brief note identifying Mossé and her fate (7: 450).

18. A study relevant to this point and to others in this chapter is James E. Young, *The Texture of Memory: Holocaust Memorials and Meaning* (New Haven: Yale University Press, 1993).

19. On this point, see Robert Miola, *Shakespeare's Rome* (Cambridge: Cambridge University Press, 1983), p. 55; see also Andrew V. Ettin's argument that "with what almost seems to be deliberate perverseness Shakespeare has evoked from Virgil the moments of sorrow, of anger, of futility, of danger," in "Shakespeare's First Roman Tragedy," *ELH* 37 (September 1970): 328.

20. On this point, see Amy Richlin, "Reading Ovid's Rapes," in Richlin, *Pornography and Representation in Greece and Rome*, pp. 158–79.

21. See Grace Starry West's suggestion that Shakespeare calls into question "the wisdom of relying on the past, not only on the Roman literary past but on Roman tradition as models for speech and deed," in "Going by the Book: Classical Allusions in Shakespeare's *Titus Andronicus*," *Studies in Philology* 79 (Winter 1982): 74.

22. See D. J. Palmer's argument that this play unfolds, in effect, within the Renaissance iconography of Saturn, in "The Unspeakable in Pursuit of the Uneatable: Language and Action in *Titus Andronicus*," *Critical Quarterly* 14 (Winter 1972): 326. See also Palmer's suggestion that "the action of the play as a whole seem to turn upon the dual nature of the mouth that utters and devours" (335).

23. See Sigmund Freud, "Mourning and Melancholia," in *The Standard Edition of the Complete Psychological Works of Sigmund Freud*, ed. James Strachey et al., 24 vols. (London: Hogarth Press and the Institute of Psycho-Analysis, 1953–74), 14:237–58.

24. On this point, see T. J. B. Spencer's argument that the portrayal of Rome in this play is representative of the Elizabethan sense of Roman history, in "Shakespeare and the Elizabethan Romans," in *Discussions of Shakespeare's Roman Plays*, ed. Maurice Charney (Boston: D. C. Heath, 1964), esp. pp. 8–9.

25. H. Rap Brown (ca. 1966), quoted in *Familiar Quotations*, ed. Emily Morison Beck, 15th ed. (Boston: Little, Brown, 1980), p. 915.

26. Jonathan Goldberg, *James I and the Politics of Literature: Jonson, Shake-

speare, Donne, and Their Contemporaries (Baltimore: Johns Hopkins University Press, 1983), p. 149.

27. See Eugene M. Waith's description of Titus as "a personified emotion" in which "character in the usual sense of the word disintegrates completely," in *Patterns and Perspectives in English Renaissance Drama* (London: Associated University Presses, 1988), p. 51.

28. Relevant to this point are Reuben A. Brower's comments on the Senecan "sweetness" of death in the opening of *Titus Andronicus*, in *Hero and Saint: Shakespeare and the Graeco-Roman Heroic Tradition* (New York: Oxford University Press, 1971), pp. 178–80.

29. See Norman Bryson's reading of this story in *Tradition and Desire: From David to Delacroix* (Cambridge: Cambridge University Press, 1984), p. 8.

30. See Mary Laughlin Fawcett's analysis of the "alliance between body and writing" in this play, in "Arms/Words/Tears: Language and the Body in *Titus Andronicus*," *ELH* 50 (Summer 1983): 261–77.

31. As Brower points out (*Hero and Saint*, p. 194), it is also notable that Lucius is the namesake of the king traditionally seen, as in Foxe's *Book of Martyrs*, as the first of the British monarchs, "descended from their 'ancestor' Aeneas, or from his brother Brute."

32. Garry Pierre-Pierre, "In a Tiny Haitian Port, Even Grief Is Political," *New York Times*, July 8, 1994, p. A6.

CHAPTER THREE *Captioning the Image of Tradition*

1. See Kathryn Gravdal, *Ravishing Maidens: Writing Rape in Medieval French Literature and Law* (Philadelphia: University of Pennsylvania Press, 1991), p. 5. Gravdal's book in its entirety is relevant to my argument here.

2. See Richard Whelan, *Robert Capa: A Biography* (New York: Knopf, 1985).

3. Jorge Luis Borges, "Pierre Menard, Author of Don Quixote," trans. Anthony Bonner, in *Ficciones*, ed. Anthony Kerrigan (New York: Grove Press, 1962), pp. 54, 55.

4. In relation to the preceding examples, I might also note the 1994 exhibition at the Boston Museum of Fine Arts, curated by Trevor Fairbrother, "The Label Show: Contemporary Art and the Museum."

5. See G. W. F. Hegel, *The Phenomenology of Mind*, trans. J. B. Baillie (New York: Macmillan, 1931), p. 166.

6. See Virgil, *Aeneid*, 9.184–87.

7. See Jacques Derrida, *Limited Inc*, ed. Gerald Graff (Evanston: Northwestern University Press, 1988).

8. Quotations from Shakespeare are taken from *The Riverside Shakespeare*, ed. G. Blakemore Evans (Boston: Houghton Mifflin, 1974). Citations are given in the text.

9. John Donne, "Batter my heart, three person'd God," in *The Complete English Poems of John Donne*, ed. C. A. Patrides (London: J. M. Dent and Sons, 1985), p. 443.

10. See the discussion in J. Bruyn et al., *A Corpus of Rembrandt Paintings*, 3

vols. (Dordrecht: Martinus Nijhoff, 1989), 3:166; Margarita Russell, "The Iconography of Rembrandt's *Rape of Ganymede*," *Simiolus* 9 (1977): 5–18; and, for a more extensive discussion of the representation of Ganymede, James M. Saslow, *Ganymede in the Renaissance: Homosexuality in Art and Society* (New Haven: Yale University Press, 1986).

11. Friedrich Nietzsche, *Daybreak: Thoughts on the Prejudices of Morality*, trans. R. J. Hollingdale (Cambridge: Cambridge University Press, 1982), p. 204.

12. John Keats, "Ode on a Grecian Urn," in *Complete Poems*, ed. Jack Stillinger (Cambridge: Harvard University Press, 1982), p. 283.

13. All references are to the facsimile text in *The Collected Works of Phillis Wheatley*, ed. John C. Shields (New York: Oxford University Press, 1988). References to other writings by Wheatley are also to this edition; page numbers are given in the text.

14. In *Phillis Wheatley and Her Writings* (New York: Garland Publishing, 1984), pp. 119–21, William H. Robinson notes that Wheatley had this letter printed in ten New England newspapers in March and April 1774.

15. There is some question about the accuracy of these dates; see Robinson, *Phillis Wheatley and Her Writings*, p. 31.

16. Henry Louis Gates, Jr., *Figures in Black: Words, Signs, and the "Racial" Self* (New York: Oxford University Press, 1987), p. 28.

17. Benjamin Bussey Thatcher, *Memoir of Phillis Wheatley, a native African and a slave* (Boston: George W. Light, 1834), p. 6.

18. See Robinson, *Phillis Wheatley and Her Writings*, p. 48. Robinson notes that subsequent advertisements did identify her as a servant.

19. Robinson, *Phillis Wheatley and Her Writings*, p. 108.

20. Quoted in M. A. Richmond, *Bid the Vassal Soar* (Washington, D.C.: Howard University Press, 1974), p. 6.

21. See Barbara E. Johnson's argument that "Wheatley in a sense wrote her way to freedom simply by letting the contradictions in her master's position speak for themselves," in "Euphemism, Understatement, and the Passive Voice: A Genealogy of Afro-American Poetry," in *Reading Black, Reading Feminist: A Critical Anthology*, ed. Henry Louis Gates, Jr. (New York: Meridian, 1990), p. 210.

22. Sondra O'Neale, "A Slave's Subtle War: Phillis Wheatley's Use of Biblical Myth and Symbol," *Early American Literature* 21 (Fall 1986): 145–65. O'Neale provides important readings of many of the passages in Wheatley's verse that I touch on here.

23. See, for example, Charles W. Akers, " 'Our Modern Egyptians': Phillis Wheatley and the Whig Campaign against Slavery in Revolutionary Boston," *Journal of Negro History* 60 (July 1975): 405, where the author quotes the remarkable epitaph of John Jack, originally published in the *Boston Gazette* of October 9, 1775. It reads, in part: "Tho' born in a land of slaves / He was born free. / Tho' he lived in a land of liberty / He lived a slave, / 'Till by his honest tho' stolen labour / He acquired the source of slavery / Which gave him his freedom."

24. See Arthur P. Davis's analysis of how "Wheatley realizes the advantage of the race label and inserts it" in her poetry, in "The Personal Elements in

the Poetry of Phillis Wheatley," in *Critical Essays on Phillis Wheatley*, ed. William H. Robinson (Boston: G. K. Hall, 1982), pp. 93–101.

25. William Blake, "The Divine Image" and "The Human Abstract," in *The Complete Poetry and Prose of William Blake*, ed. David V. Erdman (New York: Doubleday, 1988), pp. 13, 27.

26. June Jordan, "The Difficult Miracle of Black Poetry in America, or Something Like a Sonnet for Phillis Wheatley," in *On Call: Political Essays* (Boston: South End Press, 1985), p. 91.

27. J. J. Winckelmann, *Gedanken über die nachahmung der griechischen werke in der malerei und bildhauerkunst* (Neudeln: Kraus Reprints, 1968), p. 39.

28. Margaretta Matilda Oddell, "Memoir," in Robinson, *Phillis Wheatley and Her Writings*, p. 438. (Robinson reprints the entirety of this work, which was first published in an 1834 reprinting of Wheatley's *Poems*.)

29. See J. Saunders Redding, *To Make a Poet Black* (1939; rpt. Ithaca: Cornell University Press, 1988), pp. 10–11.

30. Quoted in Kwame Anthony Appiah, *In My Father's House: Africa in the Philosophy of Culture* (New York: Oxford University Press, 1992), p. 173. (Achebe is discussing what being "from Africa" means to "some people" in Cambridge.)

31. John Milton, "Lycidas," in *Complete Poems and Major Prose*, ed. Merritt Y. Hughes (New York: Odyssey Press, 1957), p. 120.

32. William Blake, *Milton*, in *Complete Poetry and Prose*, p. 106.

33. See Gates's discussion of the eighteenth-century philosophical debates over "kinds" (or species) in *Figures in Black*, esp. pp. 62–64.

34. See Houston A. Baker, Jr.'s, remarks about how Wheatley "comes to us . . . an African successor to Terence's precursorial spirit," in *Workings of the Spirit: The Poetics of Afro-American Women's Writing* (Chicago: University of Chicago Press, 1991), p. 39.

Alice Walker notes another aspect of this paradox in the title essay of *In Search of Our Mothers' Gardens* (New York: Harcourt Brace Jovanovich, 1983), p. 236, where she describes Wheatley as "a slave of wealthy, doting whites who instilled in her the 'savagery' of the Africa they 'rescued' her from."

35. But see the criticism of this emphasis on the issue of imitation in William H. Robinson, *Phillis Wheatley in the Black American Beginnings* (Detroit: Broadside Press, 1974); and in Gates, *Figures in Black*, pp. 43–44.

36. Cynthia J. Smith, " 'To Maecenas': Phillis Wheatley's Invocation of an Idealized Reader," *Black American Literature Forum* 23 (Fall 1989): 590.

37. Phillip M. Richards, "Phillis Wheatley and Literary Americanization," *American Quarterly* 44 (June 1992): 187; Thomas Jefferson, *Notes on the State of Virginia*, ed. William Peden (Chapel Hill: University of North Carolina Press, 1954), p. 140; Margaretta Matilda Oddell, "Memoir," in Robinson, *Phillis Wheatley and Her Writings*, pp. 435–36; Addison Gayle, *The Black Aesthetic* (New York: Doubleday, 1971), p. 409.

In his essay as a whole (163–91), Richards offers an interesting analysis of Wheatley's personae; see also the multiple characterizations suggested by June Jordan, "The Difficult Miracle of Black Poetry in America," in *On Call*, pp. 87–98.

38. Blyden Jackson, *A History of Afro-American Literature*, vol. 1: *The Long Beginning, 1746–1895* (Baton Rouge: Louisiana State University Press, 1989), p. 46.

In terms of this issue of acculturation, a suggestive comparison to Wheatley's life is furnished by the case of Eunice Williams, as studied by John Demos in *The Unredeemed Captive: A Family Story from Early America* (New York: Knopf, 1994). Another apposite text for many of the issues with which I am concerned here is *Clarissa*, as studied by Terry Eagleton in *The Rape of Clarissa: Writings, Sexuality, and Class Struggle in Samuel Richardson* (Minneapolis: University of Minnesota Press, 1982).

39. Frederick Douglass, *Narrative of the Life of Frederick Douglas* (1845), in *The Classic Slave Narratives*, ed. Henry Louis Gates, Jr. (New York: New American Library, 1987), p. 262.

40. Robinson notes (*Phillis Wheatley in the Black American Beginnings*, p. 49) that this work originally was titled "A Poem on the Death of Charles Eliot aged 12 Months"; the changes Wheatley made for the 1773 volume (like similar changes in other poems) show her engagement with the wrenching relation between genre and occasion and, more generally, with the nature of language and literary tradition, as I argue later on.

41. See Celeste Margarite Schenck, *Mourning and Panegyric: The Poetics of Pastoral Ceremony* (University Park: Pennsylvania State University Press, 1988). See also Gregory Rigsby, "Form and Content in Phillis Wheatley's Elegies," *CLA Journal* 19 (December 1975): 248–57.

42. Erwin Panofsky, *Studies in Iconology: Humanistic Themes in the Art of the Renaissance* (New York: Oxford University Press, 1939), p. 223.

43. Russell, "The Iconography of Rembrandt's *Rape of Ganymede*," 8–9.

44. Walter Friedlaender, *Nicolas Poussin* (Paris: Editions Cercle d'Art, 1965), p. 138.

45. Stephanie H. Jed, *Chaste Thinking: The Rape of Lucretia and the Birth of Humanism* (Bloomington: Indiana University Press, 1989), p. 57. See also Ian Donaldson, *The Rapes of Lucretia: A Myth and Its Transformations* (Oxford: Oxford University Press, 1982).

46. Victor Shklovsky, "Sterne's *Tristram Shandy*: Stylistic Commentary," in *Russian Formalist Criticism*, trans. Lee T. Lemon and Marion J. Reis (Lincoln: University of Nebraska Press, 1965), p. 57.

CHAPTER FOUR *Sterotyping Tradition*

1. See Satan's parenthetical reference to God (3.220) in John Milton, *Paradise Regained*, in *Complete Poems and Major Prose*, ed. Merritt Y. Hughes (New York: Odyssey Press, 1957), p. 510: "'(Whose ire I dread more than the fire of hell)'"; and see William Shakespeare, Sonnet 45, in *The Riverside Shakespeare*, ed. G. Blakemore Evans (Boston: Houghton Mifflin, 1974). All further references to Milton and Shakespeare are to these editions, with line numbers given in the text.

2. Guillaume de Lorris and Jean de Meun, *The Romance of the Rose*, trans. Charles Dahlberg (Princeton: Princeton University Press, 1971), p. 221.

NOTES TO CHAPTER FOUR 201

3. Plato, *Timaeus* (79c–d), trans. Benjamin Jowett, in *The Collected Dialogues of Plato*, ed. Edith Hamilton and Huntington Cairns (Princeton: Princeton University Press, 1973), p. 1201.

4. [G. W. F. Hegel], *Hegel's Philosophy of Nature*, ed. and trans. M. J. Petry, 3 vols. (London: George Allen and Unwin, 1970), 2:39.

5. All quotations from Dickens's works are taken from *The Works of Charles Dickens*, ed. Andrew Lang, 34 vols. (London: Chapman and Hall, 1897–99). Page references are given in the text according to the following abbreviations: *Oliver Twist*, OT; *The Old Curiosity Shop*, OCS; *Barnaby Rudge*, BR; *Martin Chuzzlewit*, MC; *The Cricket on the Hearth*, CH; *The Haunted Man*, HM; *David Copperfield*, DC; *Dombey and Son*, DS; *Bleak House*, BH; *Great Expectations*, GE; *Our Mutual Friend*, OMF; *The Battle of Life*, BL.

6. Dickens also brought this scene into one of his nonfictional pieces, "The Long Voyage" (*Works*, 34:3–14), which tells of a fire in which books appear and may be reread. This scene was, of course, a popular topos in nineteenth-century literature in general, not just in Dickens's writings. See also, for instance, the poems "Pictures in the Fire," *Household Words* 181, September 10, 1853, pp. 36–37; "Faces in the Fire," *All the Year Round* 2, February 11, 1860, pp. 369–70; and "Shadows on the Wall," *All the Year Round* 2, February 18, 1860, p. 392.

7. Compare the scene in *Oliver Twist* (3:429) in which Nancy, at her midnight meeting on London Bridge with Rose Maylie and Mr. Brownlow, tells of the fear that has been oppressing her: "Horrible thoughts of death, and shrouds with blood upon them, and a fear that has made me burn as if I was on fire have been upon me all day. I was reading a book to-night, to wile the time away, and the same things came into the print."

8. Plato, *Laws*, in *Collected Dialogues*, pp. 1500–1501.

9. It may be relevant to note that in the *Paradiso* (18.100–103), Dante makes reference to those who base auguries on the sparks of a fire. See Dante Alighieri, *The Divine Comedy*, trans. John D. Sinclair, 3 vols. (New York: Oxford University Press, 1939), 3:261.

10. "On the Chimney-Piece," *All the Year Round* 6, October 12, 1861, p. 67.

11. George Eliot, *The Mill on the Floss*, in *The Personal Edition of George Eliot's Works*, 12 vols. (New York: Doubleday, Page and Company, 1901), 2:161–62.

12. In *The City of Dickens* (Oxford: Oxford University Press, 1971), p. 160, Alexander Welsh notes the curious—I would say "telling"—anachronism in the fact that one "of the signatures of Victorian literature . . . is the frequent reference to 'household gods.'"

13. "Fire," *All the Year Round* 6, January 18, 1862, p. 393.

14. See Benjamin Rumford, *The Complete Works of Count Rumford* (Boston: American Academy of Arts and Sciences, 1870–75).

15. "Our Eye-Witness and a Salamander," *All the Year Round* 3, May 19, 1860, p. 14. See also "Dragons, Griffins, and Salamanders," *Household Words* 371, May 2, 1857, pp. 427–32; and for an essay similarly ironic toward ancient legends of fire, see "Eternal Lamps," *Household Words* 87, October 22, 1853, pp. 185–88. In terms of the relation between fire and the sword discussed later in this chapter, it is relevant to note that in the nineteenth century, fire-eaters were known as "salamanders."

16. "The Genii of the Lamps," *All the Year Round* 6, October 12, 1861, p. 56.

17. See, e.g., Mark Spilka, *Dickens and Kafka: A Mutual Interpretation* (Bloomington: Indiana University Press, 1963). See also *Keepers of the Flame: The Role of Fire in American Culture, 1775–1925* (Princeton: Princeton University Press, 1992), p. 61, where Margaret Hindle Hazen and Robert M. Hazen refer to nineteenth-century novels in which andirons or firescreens figure as storytellers.

18. Compare the scene at the end of "The Poor Relation's Story" (Dickens, *Works*, 31:45), in which looking into the fire is associated with telling a story that turns out to be a "Castle . . . in the Air."

19. Dante, *The Divine Comedy*, 3:182.

20. See Henri Stierlin, *Le livre de feu: L'Apocalypse et l'art mozarabe* (Paris: Bibliothèque des Arts, 1978).

21. Compare Mikhail Bakhtin's comments on the carnival fire that "simultaneously destroys and renews the world," in *Problems of Dostoyevsky's Poetics*, ed. and trans. Caryl Emerson (Minneapolis: University of Minnesota Press, 1984), p. 126.

22. When John Harmon is almost drowned, he experiences this event, in terms that foreshadow Wrayburn's experience, as involving "a great noise and a sparkling and a crackling as of fire" (*OMF*, 23:461). Compare Thomas Carlyle's portrayal of the "Baphometic Fire-baptism" in *Sartor Resartus*, in *The Complete Works of Thomas Carlyle*, 22 vols. (Boston: Colonial Press, n.d.), 1:129. See also the analysis of the "pyrotechnics" of *Great Expectations* in Robert M. Polhemus, *Erotic Faith: Being in Love from Jane Austen to D. H. Lawrence* (Chicago: University of Chicago Press, 1990), pp. 157–64.

23. Virgil, *Aeneid*, trans. H. Rushton Fairclough, 2 vols. (Cambridge: Harvard University Press, 1935), 1:559.

24. Charlotte Brontë, *Jane Eyre*, 2 vols. (Oxford: Shakespeare Head Press, 1931), 2:30, 2:223–24.

25. See Sonnet 1, ll. 5–6: "But thou, contracted to thine own bright eyes, / Feed'st thy light's flame with self-substantial fuel."

26. Aristotle, *De Anima*, trans. J. A. Smith, *The Works of Aristotle*, ed. W. D. Ross, 12 vols. (Oxford: Oxford University Press, 1931), 3:405a. On this point, see also Helena Michie, " 'Who is this in Pain?': Scarring, Disfigurement, and Female Identity in *Bleak House* and *Our Mutual Friend*," *Novel* 22 (Winter 1989): 199–212.

27. Augustine, *The City of God*, trans. Marcus Dods (New York: Modern Library, 1950), p. 384.

28. See *Barnaby Rudge*, 13:111, where one of his characters quotes this adage; see also "The Fire Brigade of London," *Household Words* 7, May 11, 1850, p. 145, where it is quoted and elaborately glossed.

29. William Blake, *The Marriage of Heaven and Hell*, in *The Complete Poetry and Prose of William Blake*, ed. David V. Erdman, rev. ed. (New York: Doubleday, 1988), p. 35; Antonin Artaud, *Nouvelles révélations de l'être*, in *Oeuvres complètes*, 14 vols. (Paris: Gallimard, 1956–), 7:166.

30. In relation to this point, see the connection drawn between pagan and

Christian fires in "British Fire-Worship," *Household Words* 475, April 30, 1859, pp. 526–28.

31. One might compare this scene to chapter 48 in *Oliver Twist*, in which Bill Sykes labors to lose himself in fire.

32. *Beowulf*, trans. John R. Clark Hall, rev. C. L. Wrenn (London: George Allen and Unwin, 1950), p. 77.

33. Augustine, *The City of God*, p. 233.

34. Brontë, *Jane Eyre*, 1:188, 190.

35. John Foxe, *The Acts and Monuments of John Foxe*, ed. Josiah Pratt, 4th ed., 8 vols (London: Religious Tract Society, n.d.), 1:208.

36. For a study of the stereotypes in which Dickens was trafficking, see Patricia Ingham, *Dickens, Women, and Language* (Toronto: University of Toronto Press, 1992). For an analysis of Dickens as a self-conscious merchandiser of his fictional wares, see Mary Poovey, "The Man-of-Letters Hero: *David Copperfield* and the Professional Writer," in *Uneven Developments: The Ideological Work of Gender in Mid-Victorian England* (Chicago: University of Chicago Press, 1988), pp. 89–125. See also David Simpson's argument that Dickens "presents consciousness itself as historical" or involved in "fetished representations" related to "modes of commerce and exchange," in *Fetishism and Imagination: Dickens, Melville, Conrad* (Baltimore: Johns Hopkins University Press, 1982), pp. 39–68.

Also, for a discussion of the clichés of the hearth, see Welsh, *The City of Dickens*, pp. 141–63. For a description of how the image of the hearth was used as an advertising gimmick during the second half of the nineteenth century, see Hazen and Hazen, *Keepers of the Flame*, p. 56.

37. See, e.g., "Rights and Wrongs of Women," *Household Words* 210, April 1, 1854, pp. 158–61.

38. In relation to this issue and others in this essay, see the fine analysis by Sonia Hofkosh, "The Writer's Ravishment: Women and the Romantic Author—The Example of Byron," in *Romanticism and Feminism*, ed. Anne K. Mellor (Bloomington: Indiana University Press, 1988), pp. 93–114. See also Jean Ferguson Carr, "Writing as a Woman: Dickens, *Hard Times*, and Feminine Discourses," *Dickens Studies Annual* 18 (1989): 161–78; and Audrey Jaffe's questioning of the putative masculinity of omniscient narration in *Vanishing Points: Dickens, Narrative, and the Subject of Omniscience* (Berkeley: University of California Press, 1991), pp. 169–70.

In relation to this issue of gendered identities, it may also be relevant to note that although the hearth fire was stereotypically female, fire as such could be gendered male. Thus, according to Campanella, as cited by John Horne Tooke, the Pythagoreans held fire to be masculine (because active) in gender. (Horne Tooke, it is further to be noted, associated such gendering with diverse and conflicting "mythologies.") See *The Diversions of Purley*, 2 vols. (Menston, Eng.: Scolar Press, 1968), 1:53n.

39. See David Hume, *An Enquiry Concerning Human Understanding*, ed. Erik Steinberg (Indianapolis: Hackett Publishing, 1977), pp. 25–30.

40. On this point, see, e.g., Dennis Walder, *Dickens and Religion* (London: George Allen and Unwin, 1981); and Janet L. Larson, *Dickens and the Broken*

Scripture (Athens: University of Georgia Press, 1985). In *The Reader in Dickensian Mirrors: Some New Language* (London: Macmillan Academic, 1992), pp. 176–81, John Schad writes of the cross in Dickens's work.

41. See Susan R. Horton's comments on the restrictiveness of "the huddle around the hearth" in *The Reader in the Dickens World: Style and Response* (Pittsburgh: University of Pittsburgh Press, 1981), p. 9.

42. Brontë, *Jane Eyre*, 2:44, 2:218, 2:274.

43. George Eliot, *Middlemarch*, in *Personal Edition*, 1:17.

44. On this point and others related to the exclusions in Dickens's sense of universality, see Gayatri C. Spivak, "Three Women's Texts and a Critique of Imperialism," *Critical Inquiry* 12 (Autumn 1985): 243–61; and Joyce Zanona, "The Sultan and the Slave: Feminist Orientalism and the Structure of *Jane Eyre*," in *Revising the Word and the World: Essays in Feminist Literary Criticism*, ed. Vèvè A. Clark, Ruth-Ellen B. Joeres, and Madelon Sprengnether (Chicago: University of Chicago Press, 1993), pp. 165–90.

45. Compare the quasi-Pentecostal flame that lights upon the head of the Ghost of Christmas Past in *A Christmas Carol*.

46. Homi K. Bhabha, "The Other Question—the Stereotype and Colonial Discourse," *Screen* 24 (November–December 1983): 33.

47. On this point and others related to this essay, see Jacques Derrida, *Cinders*, ed. and trans. Ned Lukacher (Lincoln: University of Nebraska Press, 1991). Also relevant is Gaston Bachelard, *La psychanalyse du feu* (Paris: Gallimard, 1938), and *Fragments d'une poétique du feu*, ed. Suzanne Bachelard (Paris: Presses Universitaires de France, 1988).

48. Wendell Phillips, "Letter," in Frederick Douglass, *Narrative of the Life of Frederick Douglass, an American Slave*, ed. Houston A. Baker, Jr. (New York: Penguin, 1986), p. 46.

49. See Teresa de Lauretis's criticism on this score in "The Violence of Rhetoric: Considerations on Representation and Gender," in *The Violence of Representation: Literature and the History of Violence*, ed. Nancy Armstrong and Leonard Tennenhouse (London: Routledge, 1989), pp. 239–58.

CHAPTER FIVE   *The War of Tradition*

1. Charles Lamb, "Distant Correspondents," in *Elia, The Works of Charles and Mary Lamb*, ed. E. V. Lucas, 7 vols. (London: Methuen, 1903), 2:104.

2. Jorge Luis Borges, "The Babylon Lottery," trans. Anthony Kerrigan, in *Ficciones*, ed. Anthony Kerrigan (New York: Grove Press, 1962), p. 68.

3. Virginia Woolf, *Three Guineas* (London: Hogarth Press, 1943), p. 60.

4. For an account of Martha Rosler's series, which was titled "Bringing the War Back Home: House Beautiful," see Brian Wallis, "Living Room War," *Art in America* 80 (February 1992): 105–7. In " 'No More Horses': Virginia Woolf on Art and Propaganda," in *Critical Essays on Virginia Woolf*, ed. Morris Beja (Boston: G. K. Hall, 1985), p. 159, Jane Marcus has argued that in the light of the photographs Woolf did include in *Three Guineas*, the omission of the Spanish civil war photographs signifies that "we are meant to put the

patriarchal horse before the Fascist cart." (Marcus's entire essay is an important context to my argument here.) Diane Gillespie continues this line of analysis in " 'Her kodak pointed at his head': Virginia Woolf and Photography,"
in *Virginia Woolf: Themes and Variations*, ed. Vara Neverow-Turk and Mark
Hussey (New York: Pace University Press, 1993), pp. 33–40, in relating Woolf's
omission of these photographs to John Tagg's argument about the way documentary photography may feminize its supposed objects of knowledge.

5. Virginia Woolf, "Four Figures," in *Collected Essays*, 4 vols. (New York:
Harcourt, Brace and World, 1967), 3:193.

6. William Blake, "Preface" to *Milton*, in *The Complete Poetry and Prose of
William Blake*, ed. David V. Erdman, rev. ed. (New York: Doubleday, 1988),
p. 95.

7. See Virginia Woolf, "Thoughts on Peace in an Air Raid," in *Collected
Essays*, 4:174: " 'I will not cease from mental fight', Blake wrote. Mental fight
means thinking against the current, not with it."

8. The incident in question occurred on April 13, 1985. Adolfo Calero, then
leader of the Nicaraguan Democratic Forces, as they called themselves, had
been invited to give a talk at Northwestern University. Because she took the
stage before Calero arrived and urged the audience not to let him speak—a
plea that some in the crowd were to succeed in fulfilling—Barbara Foley was
formally reprimanded by Northwestern University and ultimately was denied
tenure.

9. See June Jordan, "On the Occasion of a Clear and Present Danger at
Yale," in *Civil Wars* (Boston: Beacon Press, 1981), pp. 90–95.

10. See Immanuel Kant, *Critique of Judgment*, trans. J. H. Bernard (London:
Macmillan, 1931), p. 127 (1.1.28).

11. Blake, *Milton*, p. 128.

12. David Wojnarowicz, "Post Cards from America: X-Rays from Hell," in
Tongues of Flame (Normal: University Galleries/Illinois State University, 1990),
p. 106.

Tongues of Flame is the catalogue for an exhibition of Wojnarowicz's art
organized by Barry Blinderman; "Post Cards" was originally published in the
catalogue for *Witnesses: Against Our Vanishing*, a show by various artists concerned with the AIDS epidemic. This exhibition was held in 1989 at Artists
Space in New York City, with the accompanying catalogue having been partially funded by the National Endowment for the Arts. Ostensibly, the furor
resulting from the show was caused by Wojnarowicz's invective against
Helms, Cardinal O'Connor, and others (such as the loathsome Congressman
William Dannemeyer, whose death by a push from the Empire State Building
Wojnarowicz took pleasure in imagining). Comments made by Helms and
others (such as the chuckleheaded and craven John Frohnmayer, the head of
the NEA), however, made it clear that homophobia, sexual prudery, and a
reactionary aesthetics were among the more important motivations.

Wojnarowicz was also involved in a battle over censorship when he sued
the Reverend Donald Wildmon, who headed something called the American Family Association, after Wildmon blew up details from his artworks
(depicting naked bodies and sexual activity) and included them in his

publications. Wojnarowicz won a court order enjoining Wildmon from any further appropriations of his work.

See also David Wojnarowicz, *Close to the Knives: A Memoir of Disintegration* (New York: Vintage Books, 1991), in which "Post Cards" is reprinted along with other writings.

13. Kant, *Critique of Judgment*, pp. 140n, 149 (1.1.29).

14. Matthew Arnold, in *Culture and Anarchy, The Complete Prose Works of Matthew Arnold*, ed. R. H. Super, 11 vols. (Ann Arbor: University of Michigan Press, 1965), 5:90. In this quotation Arnold was referring specifically to Charlotte Brontë's *Villette*.

15. William Wordsworth, *The Prelude* (1850), in *The Prelude: A Parallel Text*, ed. J. C. Maxwell (New York: Penguin Books, 1972), p. 439 (11.60–61).

16. This obscurity has not been alleviated by recent attempts in some universities to institute rules against "hate speech," which often depend on the notion of "fighting words."

17. *The Letters of Matthew Arnold to Arthur Hugh Clough*, ed. Howard Foster Lowry (London: Oxford University Press, 1932), p. 134.

18. Cicero, *Rhetorica ad Herennium*, trans. Harry Caplan (Cambridge: Harvard University Press, 1954), p. 195.

19. Jonathan Swift to Alexander Pope, June 1, 1728, in *The Correspondence of Jonathan Swift, D.D.*, ed. F. Elrington Ball, 6 vols. (London: G. Bell and Sons, 1911), 4:34.

Arnold took the phrase "sweetness and light" from Swift's *Battle of the Books*; on this point, see the discussion by Sandra M. Gilbert and Susan Gubar of Swift's splenetic figure "Goddess Criticism" in *The Madwoman in the Attic: The Woman Writer and the Nineteenth-Century Literary Imagination* (New Haven: Yale University Press, 1979), p. 33.

20. See, for instance, the remark quoted in James Boswell, *The Life of Samuel Johnson* (New York: Random House, 1952), p. 618: "Being angry with one who controverts an opinion which you value, is a necessary consequence of the uneasiness which you feel"; and Kant, *Critique of Judgment*, p. 141 (1.1.29).

21. G. W. F. Hegel, *The Phenomenology of Mind*, trans. J. B. Baillie (New York: Macmillan, 1931), p. 579.

22. Plato, *Phaedo*, in *The Dialogues of Plato*, trans. B. Jowett, 2 vols. (New York: Random House, 1937), 1:452 (69a); and *The Republic*, in *Dialogues*, 1:796 (7:536).

23. Quintilian, *Institutio oratoria*, trans. H. E. Butler, 4 vols. (Cambridge: Harvard University Press, 1961), 4:171.

24. Alexander Pope, "An Essay on Criticism," in *The Poems of Alexander Pope*, ed. E. Audra and Aubrey Williams, 6 vols. (New Haven: Yale University Press, 1961), 1:304.

Of course, the reader who hesitates over the first line quoted here—"These Monsters, Criticks! with your darts engage"—meets a syntactical ambiguity, in which "Monsters" may appear to be in apposition to "Criticks." Whether intentionally or not, this ambiguity allows Pope to get his own dart into critics even as he joins them and points out their proper quarry. This point is of some interest to my discussion of "familiar ironies" in critical tradition.

25. Augustine, *City of God*, trans. Marcus Dods (New York: Modern Library, 1950), p. 515.

26. John Lockhart, "Cockney School of Poetry," in *Keats: The Critical Heritage*, ed. G. M. Matthews (New York: Barnes and Noble, 1971), p. 109.

27. Matthew Arnold, "Preface" (1873) to *Literature and Dogma*, in *Complete Prose Works*, 6:154.

28. Matthew Arnold, "On Translating Homer," in *Complete Prose Works*, 1: 169.

29. Ibid., 170–71. Also, for a similar comment with which he replies to the accusation that he has attacked Christianity, see Arnold, "Preface to the Popular Edition" (1883), in *Literature and Dogma*, 6:142.

30. bell hooks, "When I Was a Young Soldier for the Revolution: Coming to Voice," in *Talking Back: Thinking Feminist, Thinking Black* (Boston: South End Press, 1989), p. 15.

31. Adrienne Rich, "The Tensions of Anne Bradstreet," in *On Lies, Secrets, and Silence: Selected Prose, 1966–1978* (New York: W. W. Norton, 1979), p. 22.

32. Gilbert and Gubar, *The Madwoman in the Attic*, p. 77.

33. Julia Lesage, "Women's Rage," in *Marxism and the Interpretation of Culture*, ed. Cary Nelson and Lawrence Grossberg (Urbana: University of Illinois Press, 1988), p. 422. On this subject, see also Jane Marcus, *Art and Anger: Reading Like a Woman* (Columbus: Ohio State University Press, 1988).

34. Compare Stephanie H. Jed's description of how one may find, in the writings of fifteenth-century Florentine humanists, "two diametrically opposed representations of the philologist"—the cool, unemotional scholar and "the enraged castigator of errors"—which cooperate with each other despite their seeming opposition. See her *Chaste Thinking: The Rape of Lucretia and the Birth of Humanism* (Bloomington: Indiana University Press, 1989), p. 21.

35. Virginia Woolf, *A Room of One's Own* (New York: Harcourt, Brace and Company, 1929). All quotations are cited in the text.

36. Of the names Woolf gives here, Mary Beton is identified as an aunt who bequeathed her the five hundred pounds a year that enabled her to be independent, Mary Seton as a science teacher who is a resident of the women's college of which Woolf writes, and Mary Carmichael as a contemporary author whose first novel, though only modestly successful, shows the potential for better things. These names derive from "Mary Hamilton," the traditional English ballad that tells of a woman about to be executed for infanticide—certainly an interesting association in terms of the argument of *A Room of One's Own*.

37. Borges, "The Babylon Lottery," p. 69.

38. Woolf, "Four Figures," 3:194. In this passage Woolf was comparing Austen to Mary Wollstonecraft.

39. Catharine R. Stimpson, "Woolf's Room, Our Project: The Building of Feminist Criticism," in *Virginia Woolf*, ed. Rachel Bowlby (London: Longman, 1992), p. 165.

40. Brenda R. Silver, "The Authority of Anger: *Three Guineas* as Case Study," *Signs* 16 (Winter 1991): 362. Also, on the question of the politics of rhetoric in Woolf's writing, see Pam-

ela L. Caughie, *Virginia Woolf and Postmodernism: Literature in Quest and Question of Itself* (Urbana: University of Illinois Press, 1991), pp. 113–42; and Krista Ratcliffe, "The Troubled Materialism of Virginia Woolf's Feminist Theory of Rhetoric," in Neverow-Turk and Hussey, *Virginia Woolf: Theme and Variations,* pp. 258–67.

41. Virginia Woolf, "Women and Fiction," in *Collected Essays,* 2:145. In this essay Woolf also comments on Charlotte Brontë and other writers in a way relevant to her discussion in *A Room of One's Own.*

42. On this point, see Mary M. Childers, "Virginia Woolf on the Outside Looking Down: Reflections on the Class of Women," *Modern Fiction Studies* 38 (Spring 1992): 61–79.

43. James Baldwin, "Stranger in the Village," in *Notes of a Native Son* (Boston: Beacon Press, 1990), p. 165.

44. Audre Lorde, "The Uses of Anger," *Women's Studies Quarterly* 9 (Fall 1981): 8.

45. Kant, *Critique of Judgment,* p. 159 (1.1.34).

46. Quoted in Jonathon Green, *The Encyclopedia of Censorship* (New York: Facts on File, 1990), p. 201.

47. The quotation from Shakespeare's Sonnet 55 (ll. 4, 5) is taken from *The Riverside Shakespeare,* ed. G. Blakemore Evans (Boston: Houghton Mifflin, 1974).

48. Lorde, "The Uses of Anger," p. 7.

49. Jordan, "On the Occasion of a Clear and Present Danger at Yale," p. 94.

50. Peggy Kamuf, "Penelope at Work; Interruptions in *A Room of One's Own,*" in Bowlby, *Virginia Woolf,* p. 194.

51. David Wojnarowicz, "In the Shadow of the American Dream: Soon All This Will Be Picturesque Ruins," in *Close to the Knives,* p. 33.

52. Nancy Armstrong and Leonard Tennenhouse, "Introduction: Representing Violence, Or 'How the West Was Won,'" in *The Violence of Representation: Literature and the History of Violence,* ed. Nancy Armstrong and Leonard Tennenhouse (London: Routledge, 1989), p. 9.

53. See Karl Marx, *The Eighteenth Brumaire of Louis Bonaparte* (New York: International Publishers, [1935]), p. 26.

54. John Milton, *Eikonoklastes,* in *Complete Poems and Major Prose,* ed. Merritt Y. Hughes (New York: Odyssey Press, 1957), pp. 790, 806.

55. William Blake, "Marginalia," in *William Blake's Writings,* 2:1405. (I omit the editor's interpolated punctuation.)

56. Blake, *Notebook,* in *William Blake's Writings,* 2:938.

In terms of my argument here, it is notable that in spite of all his rage against war, Blake once engraved a prospectus for a war monument designed by John Flaxman. See David V. Erdman, *Blake: Prophet against Empire* (Princeton: Princeton University Press, 1954), p. 320.

57. Adrienne Rich, "When We Dead Awaken: Writing as Re-Vision," in *On Lies, Secrets, and Silence,* pp. 37, 48–49.

58. Adrienne Rich, "Disloyal to Civilization: Feminism, Racism, Gynephobia," in *On Lies, Secrets, and Silence,* pp. 303–4.

59. Virginia Woolf, "Professions for Women," in *Collected Essays*, 2:286, 288.

60. Lesage, "Women's Rage," pp. 420, 428.

61. Lorde, "The Uses of Anger," p. 10.

62. Friedrich Nietzsche, *Human, All Too Human: A Book for Free Spirits*, trans. Marion Faber with Stephen Lehmann (Lincoln: University of Nebraska Press, 1984), p. 93.
See also Nietzsche's argument about the radical differences between Jewish and Christian conceptions of anger in *Daybreak: Thoughts on the Prejudices of Morality*, trans. R. J. Hollingdale (Cambridge: Cambridge University Press, 1982), p. 27.

63. David Hume, *An Enquiry Concerning Human Understanding*, ed. Eric Steinberg (Indianapolis: Hackett Publishing, 1977), p. 10.

64. Virginia Woolf, "Thoughts on Peace in an Air Raid," in *Collected Essays*, 4:175.

65. John Dryden, "The Author's Apology for Heroic Poetry and Poetic Licence," in *Essays of John Dryden*, ed. W. P. Ker, 2 vols. (Oxford: Oxford University Press, 1926), 1:181.

66. John Dryden, "Dedication" to *Examen Poeticum*, in *Essays*, 2:2–3.

67. John Ashbery, "Houseboat Days," in *Houseboat Days* (New York: Viking, 1977), p. 39.

68. Thomas De Quincey, "The Spanish Military Nun," in *De Quincey's Works*, 14 vols. (Edinburgh: Adam and Charles Black, 1862), 3:48.

69. Wojnarowicz, "Post Cards from America," p. 109.

70. James Joyce, *Ulysses* (New York: Random House, 1934), p. 35. The speaker is Stephen Dedalus.

71. David Wojnarowicz, "The Suicide of a Guy Who Once Built an Elaborate Shrine over a Mouse Hole," in *Close to the Knives*, p. 169.

72. Borges, "The Babylon Lottery," p. 72.

73. Kant, *Critique of Judgment*, p. 222 (1.1.54).

74. Arthur Schopenhauer, *The World as Will and Idea*, trans. R. B. Haldane and John Kemp, 3 vols. (London: Routledge and Kegan Paul, 1964), 1:406.

75. Plato, *The Republic*, in *Dialogues*, 1:819 (8:561).

76. Borges, "The Babylon Lottery," p. 65.

CHAPTER SIX   *Getting It*

1. References to John Ashbery's works are given in the text, according to the following abbreviations: T, *Turandot and Other Poems* (New York: Tibor de Nagy, 1953), unpaginated; DD, *The Double Dream of Spring* (New York: Dutton, 1970); TP, *Three Poems* (1972; rpt. New York: Penguin, 1977); SP, *Self-Portrait in a Convex Mirror* (New York: Viking, 1975); HD, *Houseboat Days* (New York: Viking, 1977); AWK, *As We Know: Poems* (New York: Viking, 1979); AG, *April Galleons* (New York: Viking Penguin, 1987); and FC, *Flow Chart* (New York: Knopf, 1991).

2. Donald Davidson, "A Nice Derangement of Epitaphs," in *Truth and*

Interpretation: Perspectives on the Philosophy of Donald Davidson, ed. Ernest LePore (Oxford: Basil Blackwell, 1986), p. 440.

3. In *The Making of the Americans* and other works, Gertrude Stein called attention to the colloquial discourse drawn upon by her writing, including the colloquial "it" that is my concern in this essay. See also, for example, her "Composition as Explanation," in *Selected Writings of Gertrude Stein*, ed. Carl Van Vechten (New York: Vintage Books, 1972), p. 513, where she writes that "it likes it as it is, and this makes what is seen as it is seen."

4. Ian Hacking, "The Parody of Conversation," in LePore, *Truth and Interpretation*, p. 451.

5. Jorge Luis Borges, "A New Refutation of Time," trans. James E. Irby, in *Labyrinths: Selected Stories and Other Writings*, ed. Donald A. Yates and James E. Irby (New York: New Directions, 1964), p. 221.

6. Friedrich Nietzsche, *Beyond Good and Evil*, trans. Walter Kaufmann (New York: Vintage, 1966), p. 24.

7. Kurt Cobain (lyrics) and Nirvana (music), "Smells Like Teen Spirit," copyright © 1991 Virgin Songs, Inc./The End of Music/BMI.

8. Karl Bühler, *Theory of Language: The Representational Function of Language*, trans. Donald Fraser Goodwin (Philadelphia: John Benjamins Publishing Company, 1990), p. 140. The "it" under discussion here also refuses two of the characterizations that Emile Benveniste attributed to third-person pronouns: their "never being reflective of the instance of discourse" and their "not being compatible with the paradigm of referential terms like *here, now*, etc." See his *Problems in General Linguistics*, trans. Mary Elizabeth Meek (Coral Gables, Fla.: University of Miami Press, 1971), p. 222.

9. See Jacques Derrida, *Glas*, trans. John P. Leavey, Jr., and Richard Rand (Lincoln: University of Nebraska Press, 1986). Derrida's "translation" of Hegel's *Savoir Absolu* into *sa* and *ça* (among other things) is especially apposite to my argument here. In respect to "getting it," one might also consider the quasi-Derridean injunction "Get with the program," or perhaps the neo-Lacanian vernacular of the phrase "Get real."

10. Virginia Woolf, *To the Lighthouse* (New York: Harcourt Brace Jovanovich, 1927), p. 217.

11. Maurice Blanchot, "Everyday Speech," trans. Susan Hanson, *Yale French Studies* 73 (1987): 14.

12. James Joyce, *Finnegans Wake* (New York: Viking, 1959). Page references to this work, abbreviated *FW* are given in the text.

13. Anonymous juror quoted in *Newsweek*, May 11, 1992, p. 33; anonymous juror quoted in an Associated Press report by Connie Cass, "Holdout Juror Prayed, Fasted for Conviction," *Gainesville Sun*, May 6, 1992, p. 5A.

14. Quotations from William Shakespeare are taken from *The Riverside Shakespeare*, ed. G. Blakemore Evans (Boston: Houghton Mifflin, 1974). Citations are given in the text.

15. Robert Burns, "Song—For a' that and a' that," in *Poems and Songs*, ed. James Kinsley (London: Oxford University Press, 1969), p. 602.

16. Jorge Luis Borges, "The Library of Babel," trans. Anthony Kerrigan,

in *Ficciones*, ed. Anthony Kerrigan (New York: Grove Weidenfeld, 1962), p. 86.

17. James Boswell, *Life of Johnson* (London: Oxford University Press, 1957), p. 333.

The significance of this anecdote is extended if one notes that Johnson and Boswell were leaving church when this incident occurred. If one recalls the rock of Saint Peter, among other relevant associations, one can see that terms such as *materiality* and *spirituality* turn out to be false oppositions in this context in a way comparable to the opposition between *literal* and *figurative* which I discuss later in this chapter.

18. Wallace Stevens, "The Snow Man," in *The Collected Poems of Wallace Stevens* (New York: Vintage Books, 1990). References to this volume, abbreviated *CP*, are given in the text.

Among other things, Stevens's concluding line in this poem is also a reworking of some wordplay from *Hamlet* (3.4.131–32), in which the Queen responds to Hamlet's question—"Do you see nothing there?"—by saying, "Nothing at all, yet all that is I see."

19. Saul A. Kripke, "Naming and Necessity," in *Semantics of Natural Languages*, ed. Donald Davidson and Gilbert Harman (Dordrecht: D. Reidel, 1972), p. 273.

20. Paul Celan, "Where I," in *Last Poems*, trans. Katharine Washburn and Margret Guillemin (San Francisco: North Point Press, 1986), p. 29.

In respect to this and other points in this chapter about the theoretical implications of vernacular language, see also Houston A. Baker, Jr., *Blues, Ideology, and Afro-American Literature: A Vernacular Theory* (Chicago: University of Chicago Press, 1984); and Henry Louis Gates, Jr., *The Signifying Monkey: A Theory of African-American Literary Criticism* (New York: Oxford University Press, 1988).

21. Naftali Bendavid, "Model Community Hid a Horrible Savagery," *Miami Herald*, December 13, 1992, p. 23A. The story concerns the racially motivated murder—at a party—of Lu Nguyen, a local Coral Springs, Florida youth, by seven other young men. This essay is as much about this incident, and events like it, as it is an extended commentary on one surpassingly beautiful poem by Ashbery, the title poem in *As We Know*, which begins, "All that we see is penetrated by it."

22. John Bunyan, *The Pilgrim's Progress*, in *"Grace Abounding to the Chief of Sinners" and "The Pilgrim's Progress from this World to that which is to come,"* ed. Roger Sharrock (London: Oxford University Press, 1966), p. 246.

See also the similar marginal gloss earlier in the same work (p. 206): "Knowledge and knowledge"; and for a more recent version of this type of idiom, one might instance Derrida, "Afterword" (trans. Samuel Weber), in *Limited Inc*, ed. Gerald Graff (Evanston: Northwestern University Press, 1988), p. 135: "There are police and police."

23. Herman Hupfeld (lyrics and music), "As Time Goes By," copyright © 1931 Warner Brothers/ASCAP.

24. Thomas Hardy, *The Mayor of Casterbridge*, in *The Works of Thomas Hardy*, 18 vols. (1912–14; rpt. New York: AMS Press, 1984), 5:8.

25. Stevens's "glubbal glub" perhaps recalls "old Glubb," the retired sailor in *Dombey and Son*, of whom Miss Blimber (of Dr. Blimber's exclusive school) says, "This is not the place for Glubbs of any sort." See Charles Dickens, *Dombey and Son*, in *The Works of Charles Dickens*, ed. Andrew Lang, 34 vols. (London: Chapman and Hall, 1897–99), 8:198.

26. Quoted in Robert Lewis Taylor, *W. C. Fields: His Follies and Fortunes* (Garden City, N.Y.: Doubleday and Company, 1949), p. 242; emphasis added. See also the comparison John Hollander draws between Ashbery and Fields in " 'Soonest Mended,' " in *John Ashbery*, ed. Harold Bloom (New York: Chelsea House, 1985), p. 209.

27. E. Y. Harburg (words) and Jay Gorney (music), "Brother, Can You Spare a Dime?" copyright © 1932 Warner Brothers/ASCAP.

28. See Kripke, "Naming and Necessity." It is important to note that Kripke (p. 346n) draws a sharp distinction between names and what someone is called. "Sloppy, colloquial speech," he says in a parenthesis, "which often confuses use and mention, may, of course, express the fact that someone might have been called, or not have been called, 'Aristotle' by saying that he might have been, or not have been, Aristotle. Occasionally, I have heard such loose usages adduced as counterexamples to the applicability of the present theory to ordinary language. Colloquialisms like these seem to me to create as little problem for my theses as the success of the 'Impossible Missions Force' creates for the modal law that the impossible does not happen." My argument, of course, is that the "loose usages" of colloquial language so casually dismissed by Kripke get at something that his theory does not (including certain interesting aspects to the presentation of his theory, such as the emphatic "*it*" in the example cited in the text). Not being a philosopher, I cannot speak to the implications of the present argument, if any, for what Kripke was trying to get at.

29. See Adrienne Rich, *The Dream of a Common Language* (New York: W. W. Norton, 1978).

30. See the conversation between the Duck and the Mouse at the beginning of chapter 3 in *Alice's Adventures in Wonderland*; see also Ashbery's excursus on the phrase "It almost seems" in "The Recital," in *Three Poems*, p. 111.

31. Mary Chapin Carpenter (words) and John Jennings (music), "You Never Had It So Good," copyright © 1988 Getarealjob Music/ASCAP and Obie Diner Music/BMI.

32. The question is whether "Let him have it" meant "Hand the gun over to the policeman" or, more idiomatically, "Shoot him." The movie was based on an incident in 1952 involving two youths, Derek Bentley and Christopher Craig, who had been caught breaking into a warehouse; even though both denied that Bentley said this to Craig, as the police alleged, their convictions were based in part on the way this equivocal command was interpreted.

33. Other notable references along these lines might include Shakespeare's *As You Like It*; Clara Bow's title "The 'It' Girl"; *It Happened One Night* (1934), *It Came From Outer Space* (1953), and *She's Gotta Have It* (1985); Pauline Kael's book *I Lost It at the Movies*; and Louise Bourgeois's 1992 installation and performance piece *She Lost It*. See also Ashbery's concluding line to "Letters I Did or Did not Get": "Mystery and death, the way you like it" (*AG*, 41).

34. See Mikhail Bakhtin's account of the *Historia de Nemine* in *Rabelais and His World*, trans. Helene Iswolsky (Bloomington: Indiana University Press, 1984), pp. 413–14.

In this context, of course, one is bound to recall the trick that Odysseus played on Polyphemus in the *Odyssey*—a trick recalled as well in Joyce's term "nomanclatter," to which I have previously referred.

35. See Susan Stewart's remarks on this game and related verbal logics in *Nonsense: Aspects of Intertextuality in Folklore and Literature* (Baltimore: Johns Hopkins University Press, 1980), p. 139.

36. Sigmund Freud, *The Ego and the Id*, in *The Standard Edition of the Complete Psychological Works of Sigmund Freud*, trans. James Strachey et al., 24 vols (London: Hogarth Press and the Institute of Psycho-Analysis, 1953–74), 19:59.

37. See the considerably different analysis of "the 'they' " (*das Man*) in Martin Heidegger, *Being and Time*, trans. John Macquarrie and Edward Robinson (New York: Harper and Row, 1962), esp. pp. 164–68 and 211–14. Even if one refrains from characterizing Heidegger's account in terms of the "moralizing" that he explicitly, if not convincingly, disclaimed, one still can find it to be condescending and obtuse in its grasp of the workings of colloquial discourse, especially in terms of the capacity of that discourse for thoughtfulness and transport. In this respect, if not in others, his attitude toward everyday language resembles Kripke's and recalls the example of Hegel, in his criticism of Kant in the section on "Reason as Lawgiver" in *The Phenomenology of Mind*, trans. J. B. Baillie (New York: Macmillan, 1931), pp. 440–45. Hegel here is as brilliant in his criticism of Kant as he is imperceptive in what he suggests about the role of tautology in "the ethical consciousness." And it is worth noting that Hegel's ruthless condescension in this regard, which discovers a simplistic nature in everyday language because he himself (following his culture) has put it there, is of a kind with his systematic racism.

In contrast to Heidegger's analysis of the "they," I would instance Michel de Certeau's meditation on the ordinary man as "the metaphor and drift of the doubt which haunts writing" in *The Practice of Everyday Life*, trans. Steven F. Rendall (Berkeley: University of California Press, 1984), p. 2. (De Certeau's argument about everyday language throughout this book is relevant to my discussion here.)

38. Charles Dickens [in collaboration with Wilkie Collins], "No Thoroughfare," in *Works*, 32:253.

39. In the "Editor's Introduction" to *The Ego and the Id* (*Standard Edition*, 19:7n), all that is said on this matter is the following: 'There was to begin with a good deal of discussion over the choice of an English equivalent. 'The id' was eventually decided upon in preference to 'the it,' so as to be parallel with the long-established 'ego.' "

40. But see the riff on "it" in David Antin, "is this the right place?," in *talking at the boundaries* (New York: New Directions, 1976), p. 44.

41. "John Ashbery," in *Poets at Work: The "Paris Review" Interviews*, ed. George Plimpton (New York: Viking Penguin, 1989), p. 408.

Following Ashbery's comments on his own work, almost all his critics have adverted to his striking use of pronouns and to the relations between his

writing and colloquial language; but for their comments on his use of "it,"
see especially Marjorie Perloff, " 'Fragments of a Buried Life': John Ashbery's
Dream Songs," in *Beyond Amazement: New Essays on John Ashbery*, ed. David
Lehman (Ithaca: Cornell University Press, 1980), pp. 81, 85; Charles Altieri,
Self and Sensibility in Contemporary American Poetry (Cambridge: Cambridge
University Press, 1984), pp. 142, 152, 159; Andrew Ross, *The Failure of Mod-
ernism: Symptoms of American Poetry* (New York: Columbia University Press,
1986), pp. 188–90; Marjorie Perloff, "Lucent and Inescapable Rhythms: Met-
rical 'Choice' and Historical Formation," in *The Line in Postmodern Poetry*, ed.
Robert Frank and Henry Sayre (Urbana: University of Illinois Press, 1988), pp.
36–37; and Marjorie Perloff, *Poetic License: Essays on Modernist and Postmodern-
ist Lyric* (Evanston: Northwestern University Press, 1990), pp. 277, 281–82. See
also the remarks on tautology and Ashbery's poetry in Jonathan Holden,
The Rhetoric of the Contemporary Lyric (Bloomington: Indiana University Press,
1980), p. 108; and in Anita Sokolsky, " 'A Commission that Never Material-
ized': Narcissism and Lucidity in Ashbery's 'Self-Portrait in a Convex Mirror,' " in Bloom, *John Ashbery*, p. 239. Interesting comments on deixis in Ashbery's work are found in Mary Ann Caws, "Strong-Line Poetry: Ashbery's
Dark Edging and the Lines of Self," in Frank and Sayre, *The Line in Postmodern
Poetry*, p. 51; and in James McCorkle, *The Still Performance: Writing, Self, and
Interconnection in Five Postmodern American Poets* (Charlottesville: University
Press of Virginia, 1989), pp. 77–78.

42. Quoted in John Koethe, "The Metaphysical Subject of John Ashbery's
Poetry," in Lehman, *Beyond Amazement*, p. 276 n.

43. Quoted in Helen Vendler, "Understanding Ashbery," in Bloom, *John
Ashbery*, p. l82.

44. Charles Dickens, *Martin Chuzzlewit*, in *Works*, 6:58.

45. Sigmund Freud, *The Interpretation of Dreams*, in *Standard Edition*, 4:254n.

46. For a very different reading of the figure cut by death in Ashbery's
poetry, see Herman Rapaport, "Forecastings of Apocalypse: Ashbery, Derrida,
Blanchot," in *Literature as Philosophy/Philosophy as Literature*, ed. Donald G.
Marshall (Iowa City: University of Iowa Press, 1987), pp. 317–34.

47. For another example relevant to this point, see Trinh T. Minh-ha's reworking of Julia Kristeva's "Woman Can Never Be Defined," in *Woman,
Native, Other: Writing Postcoloniality and Feminism* (Bloomington: Indiana University Press, 1989), p. 23: "She says to unsay others so that others may unsay
her and say: It's still not it."

Index